Never Too Young to Know

Death in Children's Lives

PHYLLIS ROLFE SILVERMAN

New York • Oxford

OXFORD UNIVERSITY PRESS

2000

Oxford University Press

Oxford   New York
Athens   Auckland   Bangkok   Bogotá   Buenos Aires   Calcutta
Cape Town   Chennai   Dar es Salaam   Delhi   Florence   Hong Kong   Istanbul
Karachi   Kuala Lumpur   Madrid   Melbourne   Mexico City   Mumbai
Nairobi   Paris   São Paulo   Singapore   Taipei   Tokyo   Toronto   Warsaw

and associated companies in
Berlin   Ibadan

Copyright © 2000 by Oxford University Press, Inc.

Published by Oxford University Press, Inc.,
198 Madison Avenue, New York, New York, 10016
http://www.oup-usa.org
1-800-334-4249

Library of Congress Cataloging-in-Publication Data
Silverman, Phyllis R.
    Never too young to know: death in children's lives /
  by Phyllis Rolfe Silverman.
      p.   cm.
    Includes bibliographical references and index.
    ISBN 0-19-510954-6 (alk. paper). —ISBN 0-19-510955-4 (pbk.: alk. paper)
    1. Children and death.   I. Title.
  BF723.D3S58   1999
  155.9'37—dc21   98-50158
                                                                        CIP

ISBN 0-19-510954-6 (cloth)

Printing (last digit): 9 8 7 6 5 4 3 2 1

Printed in the United States of America
on acid-free paper

I noticed people disappeared,
When but a little child,—
Supposed they visited remote,
Or settled regions wild.

Now know I they both visited
And settled regions wild,
But did because they died,—a fact
Withheld the little child!

—Emily Dickinson

Contents

PART III: ON HELPING

Acknowledgments

Many people helped as I wrote this book, from when I first began putting together the proposal to the day I submitted the manuscript to the publisher. I talked with professional colleagues, friends, parents, children, teachers, clergy, and any others who had contact with the bereaved or were themselves bereaved. I talked with people from many parts of the United States, and abroad.

Part of this book draws on data from the MGH/Harvard Child Bereavement Study. I was co-principal investigator of this study, with J. William Worden, as well as project director. A special note of gratitude goes to the interviewers who met with the participating families. In addition to Steven Nickman and me, they were Jane Allen, Susan Creditor, Hadley Fisk, Jane and Paul Lynch, Alyn Robertson, and Marilyn Weller. I want to thank the families, both children and their surviving parents, for agreeing to share their stories.

Elise Bon-Rudin read my early drafts of the proposal for this book and helped me think through what I wanted to say. Sharone Maital, of Haifa University, gladly shared her expertise in child development and was always ready with a new reference. Judith Harding made the National Center for Death Education library readily available; Gretchen Gaines in Maryland generously shared her experience as a pediatric hospice social worker; as did Ruth Danziger, a pediatric oncology nurse at the Sheba Medical Center in Israel. Robert Stevenson shared what he learned developing death education programs in several schools in New Jersey and in Seattle, Geri Haynes talked with me at length about various types of death in children's lives. Jacek Luczek, of Poland, and Danai Papadatou, of Greece, talked at length about their experiences with children and death in their respective countries. Miri Arental, of Jerusalem, talked to me about the day care program she developed in her son's memory, to serve children with cancer. I learned a good deal from my conversations with Julie Stokes of Winston's Wish Child Bereavement Programme; Marilyn Relf, bereavement coordinator at Sobell House in Oxford; and Barbara Monroe, director of social services at St. Christopher's Hospice in London.

Deborah Prothrow-Stith, of the Harvard School of Public Health, gave of her time to describe her program to prevent violence in the community. It was she who introduced me to Joseph and Tina Chery. They shared with me the Louis Brown Peace Curriculum and what their son's tragic murder has taught them. The Cherys, in turn, introduced me to Ulrich Johnson, an academic as well as a community activist, who founded Teens Against Gang Violence. Katherine Manners and Christine Caines-Dodson, of LAMP, talked about their work with families in which a member has been murdered, as did Deborah Cox, of the Boston Department of Public Health. Michelle Papazian, at Children's Hospital in Boston, shared her experience with families in which a child has AIDS.

Pediatrician Ed Gross was open in sharing his experience treating dying children. I want to thank my students who took my course at the MGH Institute of Health Professions—The Place of Death in Children's Lives. The course served as an outline for this book.

I visited a number of bereavement centers for children. I want to thank Gail Cinneli of the Children's Bereavement Center in Portland, Maine; Beverly Hatter, at the Bridges program in Tacoma, Washington; Peggy Smith, of the New Song Center for Grieving Children in Paradise Valley, Arizona; Sharon Losey, patient service coordinator of the Muscular Dystrophy Association's Phoenix, Arizona, office; Linda Hardy and Alan Cunningham, of the Children to Children Program in Tucson, Arizona; Margaret McGovern, of Bereaved Families of Ontario; Myra Clark of the Evergreen Center in Columbus, Ohio; and Hilda Glazer, a volunteer at the Evergreen Center. Finally I want to thank the staff of The Dougy Center—Donna Schuuman, Cynthia White, Joan Schweizer Hoff, and Don Spencer.

A special thank you to Eloise Cole of Scottsdale, Arizona, who is known to many as Rainbow the Clown, through whom she talks about grief and Rainbow's Remedies.

Phyllis Sonnenschein, a parent educator, and Laura Musikant-Weiser, a child psychiatrist, took time from busy schedules to read early versions of this book. They encouraged me to continue and gave me ideas about making the book more reader-friendly. Katrin Boerner, graduate student and research associate, read the manuscript to make sure that all the references were correct and complete. Teddi Marin started reading early versions of the book and continued reading to the end. She read as back-up editor, as someone whose father had died when she was very young, and as a friend. She brought clear thinking and common sense to this work, and she also brought humor that helped me laugh at some of my own editorial mishaps.

My family's role in the writing of this book will be clear as the reader progresses through the book. I feel as if we are always learning together. I thank my children Aaron, Gila, and Nancy, and Nancy's husband Ariel for letting me write about their experiences. My grandchildren Zohar and Maya were superb and willing teachers. Our other children, Ann and Bill, and Bill's wife Martha, as well as their respective children Inbal, Eran, Malia, and now Koby, live at a distance from us. Over the years, they, too, contributed with their interest and support. My husband Sam survived the many months during which I was totally preoccupied with this work. He asked me to acknowledge all the restaurants that were there for us throughout the writing. He listened to my ideas and helped me clarify my thinking. His comments, as always, were very helpful. A special thanks to my son Aaron's dog Sage, who always reminded me that it was important to take time off for walks.

My daughter Gila, from the book's inception to its completion, served as my editor. I do not recommend a mother challenging her relationship with a daughter in this way more than once. That we survived and are still friends is a testimony to her patience, and her willingness to see her mother as a human being with both strengths and weaknesses. She helped me re-think what I wrote, and through our ongoing work, my writing became clearer. Together, this book is what we produced. She is a talented and gifted woman, and I thank her for being herself.

Finally, I want to thank all the parents, children, and young people whose stories are told in the pages of this book. I promised them anonymity. I learned a great deal from them. I also learned that they all enjoyed talking to me or interviewers from the Child Bereavement Study because this was an opportunity to honor and remember the persons who had died. They shared in the hope that others would benefit from their experiences. This book is dedicated to those who have found ways of living with their loss and to their friends, siblings, children, and parents who died. May their memories live on in the lives of those who care about them.

Foreword

ESTER R. SHAPIRO, PH.D.

With this wise and accessible book on children's experiences of death, Phyllis Silverman adds another extraordinary achievement to her distinguished and inspiring career. Only she could have written this thoughtful, useful book, because of her dedicated three decades of research, practice, writing, and reflection with our best bereavement experts: widows, widowers, bereaved children, and their parents. Professionals in the mental health field will find the book offers a meticulously argued conceptual model of childhood grief, based on the newest theoretical approaches and tested through research. At the same time, the book is accessible enough that a general educated readership can appreciate the multiple layers of fateful circumstance, available resources, meaningful relationships, and social attitudes that help a child cope with the challenge of death. She sees grief as a process of change that takes place in a social context. She offers images of growth rather than psychopathology as the best way to understand the struggles of children and parents after a loved one's death. Her work represents one of the few careers in the field dedicated to practice and research with the bereaved outside of a psychotherapy referral. Too much of our so-called understanding of bereavement is based on clinical populations regarded through a psychiatric lens. Phyllis makes it clear that this perspective has at best been unfair—and is all too often cruelly destructive—to children.

The book's value extends beyond its important goal of teaching parents and other helpers how better to support grieving children so as to promote their continuing growth. Phyllis appreciates that it takes a whole community and culture to support, or to silence and stigmatize, the bereaved among us. She has written a book that is first and foremost a call for a national conversation about our failure to teach children about death, and the enormous burden bereaved children and families carry—in addition to their other losses—because of that failure. She teaches us what she has learned from grieving children and families, so that all of us can lend a hand in the many situations where death and grief touch our lives. We learn with Phyllis that children crave opportunities to talk about their dead parents as living persons, but are rarely given that chance. Most adults have accepted the cultural myth that we have to move on to get well. We learn that when children have had some previous opportunity to learn about the realities of death as part of their ordinary lives, they are far better prepared to handle the great burdens of close family deaths. This book can help us initiate a much-needed cultural shift in the national dialogue about death, dying, and bereavement.

Twenty years ago, when I first began my own work with grieving families, Phyllis stood out for her work on the widow-to-widow program. Her model of mutual help was founded on the deep belief that an understanding of what actually happens to people when they are widowed should be the source of any help we offer them. The field was then dominated by facile expert pronouncements insisting that detachment from the deceased offered the only hope for curing the possibly terminal illness of grief. Based on her many interviews with widows, Phyllis argued that grief challenges the bereaved to learn from an intense period of change, as does any crisis in human development. She saw the challenge of grief as requiring both emotional work and the work of rebuilding the self. For any widow, the death of her husband required that she manage the intense emotions of grief while rebuilding intimate routines and recreating social roles. She also saw other widows and widowers as offering the most useful guidance for the newly bereaved. She used a language of change, resources, development, and competence to describe how widows and widowers successfully met the challenge of grief as a life transition.

Her work on the rebuilding of a shared life after a family death brought her quite naturally to her extensive study of how surviving parents best support children's development after the death of a parent. This book shows us the many situations in which children experience grief and offers substantial suggestions on how adults around them can helpfully respond not only to the death of a parent, but also to the death of a sibling and the death of a friend. She speaks from profound respect for the strengths the bereaved themselves bring to their hard-won grieving lessons. She knows what questions we should ask the real experts, in this case grieving children and their families, who have found the resources to grow even while grieving. In describing how we can help strengthen these naturally occurring changes, Phyllis has always turned first to natural sources of support within the person, family, and community. In this book, she focuses as well on how our adult assumptions about grief interfere with a child's actual experience and needs. Children don't grieve all in one sitting. They want to talk about their feelings, but not in the way adults often push them to do, based on expert advice to "talk it all out" so they can "go on with their lives." As children grow and change, they need to tell stories of their lives that still include deceased loved ones.

This book offers beautiful child-to-child mutual help and advice. Children and adults love to teach others what they have learned as a way of restoring a sense of competence. It is valuable and rare to benefit from children's advice offered in the child's own words. Phyllis's poignant conversations with children clarify how images of and conversations with the deceased promote growth in children. She found that children crave opportunities to talk about their parents as living persons, and not about them as dead. Phyllis offers us a unique window into these poignant and life-saving private conversations, and lets these children and their families speak eloquently for themselves.

The book also offers invaluable advice to grieving parents about how to honestly attend to their own needs and effectively support their grieving children. Unlike child experts, who often view parents as inadequate caretakers compared to an abstract ideal, she offers parents clear suggestions that take into account the huge emotional and practical burdens that a death in the family presents. Phyllis finds that most parents, even with the burdens of their own grief, find ways to be effective caretakers for their children. This book helps parents minimize a child's burden of parental grief, so that it does not overly constrict the space for the child's own development. She reassures parents that simply telling children honestly and directly what is happening in their lives and recognizing their own adult feelings of grief buffers their children from feelings of self-blame or rejection.

The final chapter on teachable moments helps us expand our thinking about when and how we can talk to kids about grief. Phyllis describes the elements of true helping in care, continuity, and connection, and reminds us that these resources can be found within our own families and communities. She reminds us of the value of reciprocity in building resourceful individuals and communities. She recognizes that not all families grow with their grief, because the circumstances of a death at a particular point in the family's development can present immense barriers. Yet she offers an understanding of the many pathways for improving how any one of us can learn from painful life experiences.

I would recommend this book for professionals in the mental health and bereavement fields, teachers, pastoral counselors, and any adult interested in helping bereaved children and their families by broadening our own knowledge about death and grief. As a teacher about children's experience of grief, Phyllis has no equal. There isn't anyone else in the field who can be as fully trusted to ferret out the many adult assumptions, psychiatric prescriptions, and cultural biases that all kinds of people, including most professionals, impose on children for their own convenience. Phyllis makes a fierce and dedicated advocate, and I would certainly want her in my court if I was a child, parent, or family struggling with life's adversities. Phyllis is uniquely qualified to offer us a competence-based, developmental, mutual help approach built from sound research with a broad community of the bereaved who share their hard-won lessons with her, and now with us.

Introduction

One July afternoon when my youngest son Aaron was 5 years old, we were riding a bus in Jerusalem. He noticed a woman in a short-sleeved dress with a number tattooed on her arm. I tried to divert his attention to sights on the streets, but he had eyes only for the numbers. Finally he asked me, "Why would someone have a number like that on her arm?" To him, it seemed a simple question—he was asking for concrete information about something he had seen, as he did all the time. Yet for me, his question went much deeper, touching on taboo subjects. Even though I worked with death and dying, I did not know how to answer him. I wanted to protect him from becoming aware of the horrors of our adult world, of the inhuman treatment of others, of death in such numbers that it was hard to imagine. I wanted to guarantee his present sense of safety in the world. Would a lie protect him? I stumbled, I hesitated: "Don't give him too many details, don't frighten him," I told myself. I hoped I could explain in a language that he could understand. And somehow on that long-ago bus ride, I explained about evil people who set out to destroy others, in particular Jews; about his father's extended family whom he would never know; and that the number had been tattooed on this woman's arm by these people who had imprisoned her, but that she had survived. In fact, I did not frighten him. Instead, having the correct information seemed to give him a quiet certainty.

A few years later, when our friend's son was dying, my son wanted to know what happened to people after they died. I had no theology to help me easily answer his question. I did not know what I wanted him to think, but I wanted him to know that it was okay to ask. So I told him that I was not sure what I believed, but that this is something that people think about a good deal. I gave him a short list of options, with the introduction that we really do not know what happens . . . people do not come back to tell us. I told him that some people believe we return to nature; others believe in an afterlife—that we live with God in a spiritual form; others say that life just ends, that there is nothing after; and, finally, some people believe that the spirit lives on in some unknown form. He thought for a few minutes and said, "I think I believe that the spirit lives on." He seemed to make meaning in a way that was comfortable for him. In hindsight, I realized that I was afraid simply to ask what he thought before I gave him choices. I have always wondered why he made the choice he did. My own fears got in the way of a more involved conversation. My brevity and directness were ways of controlling my own anxiety. I recently reminded my son of this conversation. Twenty years later, he says he is still comfortable with his choice, although he is not so clear about what it means.

I am not alone in having difficulty talking about these issues. We in the Western world live with a paradox: Death is all around us, yet we believe that if we do not talk with children about death, it will not touch them. We try to protect and insulate them from this fact of life, which is typically associated with anxiety and pain. By the time they become adolescents, most children have grown up with many illusions about death and dying and much misinformation. Often they feel that they can control when and how people die and whether or not death touches them personally.

In fact, death is always present in children's and adolescents' lives. In their early years, children generally become aware of death when plants, pets, and even people they know die. The death of a grandparent may be the first human death a child experiences. Yet since grandparents are a generation removed and often, in today's urbanized world, geographically distant from their grandchildren, it is easier to distance children from the pain of this loss. For some, like my son, just riding a bus raised his awareness.

From the beginning of their lives, children have the capacity to observe the world around them. They observe many things that they cannot name. Thus, they may sense the cycle of life and death but not yet have words for it. They can also sense that there are forbidden subjects that should not be talked about. As children get older, they begin to realize that they themselves will die. They learn that people grow old and die, but they may not learn how to acknowledge and deal with their sadness and what this loss means to them.

I recently reviewed my own experience with death as a young child. I recalled that my maternal grandfather died when I was a toddler. I found myself crying, more than 50 years later, as I thought about his death. When I asked my mother when it had happened, she said that I was not quite 3 years old at the time and could not possibly remember his death. I was close to my grandfather, and she remembered that they did not talk about his death so that I would not be upset. Only when I described his bedroom to her, what he looked like lying on the bed and that in my memory I knew he was dying, would she acknowledge that I was in the house at the time. However, she had been certain that my aunt took me away before I could see anything. How valuable it would have been for me had she been able to acknowledge with me that his dying and death were important events in my life and to give my grief a name. A name legitimates and demystifies an event. It makes something real, gives a sense of ownership, and verifies for the child his or her ability as an observer and experience as a mourner and that sharing experiences and feelings is valued.

Children often surprise us with their knowledge and the ease with which they can absorb new experiences. The 3-year-old daughter of a friend had been listening for several days to her family's concern about her grandfather's illness and impending death. After he died, her father tried to explain to her that her grandfather had gone to live on a star in the sky. She looked at him with surprise and said, "You mean he is dead?"

Children also face many deaths that occur out of turn in the life cycle and that have an impact on their daily lives. They have to face the fact that friends, siblings, parents, and sometimes they themselves can die. In today's world, they are surrounded by death from violence: in the neighborhood, in the larger community, and in the world. Television brings this violence into everyone's home in a way that allows one to be an observer of life from an impersonal distance. In some of these fictional television programs, death has a fairy-tale quality. The protagonists are not really hurt by the blows inflicted on them and frequently come back to life. Children do not learn about the true consequences of someone dying and that death is part of the real world. They also do not learn how to cope when such a reality occurs.

After a death, young people's grief is frequently not recognized or appreciated. If we do not acknowledge that death exists, we certainly cannot acknowledge the feelings, thoughts, and responses that come after it. Here, too, many adults feel that as long as the experience is not given a name or discussed, children will go on with their lives as if nothing happened. Children need to understand that fear, anger, and sadness are all appropriate feelings when a person we care about is no longer here. They need to know that every death of someone close brings with it sadness, stress, and disruption in our daily lives. Often the people around them, in their families, schools, and communities, do not know how to acknowledge and respond to children's experiences as mourners. In many ways, we are sometimes both deaf and mute to children's thoughts about death. In my earlier work, I referred to our inability to talk about death as a conspiracy of silence. For many it is worse than the silence from the grave. What a great disrespect this is, to ignore the child's reality. We cannot act as if a child does not really know, does not understand, is too young. Children of all ages construct meaning from their experiences. A 7-year-old child who was dying of leukemia said to a researcher: "Jennifer died last night. I have the same thing, don't I?" (Bluebond-Langner, 1978, p. 120). Our hesitancy to discuss these issues with children has consequences not only for them, but for other family members as well. It isolates them from their own experience and from each other (Bearison, 1991). It leads to fear and anxiety as we remain without words for death and the experiences of grief. A graduate student of mine talked about his father's death when he was 6:

> My mother told me that my father had gone away on a trip, and for several years I waited for his return, until one day a cousin told me that when they tell you that someone has gone away on a long trip and they don't come back, that means the person is dead. I got up the nerve to ask my mother; she said yes, my father was dead, but nothing more was said about it. When I pushed her a bit, she added that she didn't know what to say, she didn't want me to be hurt and this seemed to be the best way to do that. No one talked about the sadness, no one legitimated the pain of the loss, the longing and the changes in my family's life as a result. We could not share or help each other.

We need to recognize that how death is introduced into children's lives reflects what we teach children about dealing with the issues of living (Bertman, 1974; Grollman 1967). If we do not teach children ways of coping with death-related stressors in their lives, real or anticipated, if we deny or do not give legitimacy to what they are experiencing, then they will have difficulty with other adversities as well and not appreciate the truth in their own experiences. They need to construct a worldview in which death is recognized and anxiety about the unknown does not drive their behavior. Once it is recognized that our reactions are appropriate and unavoidable, then it is possible to develop strategies for coping that enable us to accept and accommodate to the feelings and changes we are experiencing. Then we focus, not on what is wrong with us, but on what is right and what we can do about it. We all need to be experts in managing grief, and we all need to develop a competence that facilitates our coping from the time when we are young and have our first encounters with this fact of life—people come and go; people are born and die.

To help children in this process, we must confront our own fears and begin to search for the words we do not have. We cannot teach children what we do not know. Frequently, our difficulty in talking with children about death stems from the fact that we have never acknowledged our own anxieties and discomfort with these issues. In some ways, in the Western world at the end of the 20th century, we often experience a certain absurdity when we think about dying. It does not fit with our sense of control over the world. Most of us have difficulty accepting that life, which can be so lovely, so beautiful, and so purposeful, can end so abruptly and with such finality. Thus, when death does arise, the topic often triggers much anxiety, touching on our fears of the unknown and of losing control (Neimeyer, 1994). Learning to accept our helplessness is part of learning to accept that death and the sorrow that accompanies it are part of life.

My experience in writing this book is a good example of how these fears can express themselves and what facing them can mean. For all my experience and years of talking to bereaved people, I had managed to avoid dealing with the death of a child. I could not tolerate the sadness and pain I felt when the subject of a child's death would come up. My fear for my own children would become overwhelming. Now I had signed a book contract and put myself in a place where I had no choice. The pages of this book became wet with my tears as I began to do what I had successfully avoided all these years. Only when I accepted this pain and cried my way through it was I able to continue. Only then could I really hear what bereaved parents were telling me about their losses. We can be available to our children and help them to learn only when we can allow ourselves to recognize our fears and let ourselves feel some of this pain.

One set of parents described their experience with neighbors prior to their 5-year-old son's death from cancer:

Josh was bloated from his medication, and the neighborhood children would not come to play. Their parents said that his appearance frightened their children, and they would not force them to visit. When a neighbor offered to prepare meals for us, I told her what I really needed was just someone to come by once a week and visit with me. Nobody ever came. It was as if his illness was contagious.

Whose fear was this? Was the pain of facing a dying child too much? For whom? These parents' anxiety stood in the way of their children learning about death and learning how important it is to help a friend. Given support from their families, children at this age are very accepting of differences in each other. They probably would have come to play if their parents had allowed it. But they could not do so without their parents' guidance. They needed permission to discuss with their parents what was happening to this sick child and later, they would need support to help them cope with his death.

Living and dying are the components of life, the deck of cards *all* people are given and over which we have little or no control. This book is about how we sort out these components and learn how to make the best out of what we are dealt. In particular, this book is about children and their reactions to death. The focus is not so much on what happens to people when a death occurs but on what they do about it. It is also a book about how to help children and adolescents see death as part of life.

In part, the book is a reaction to an attitude in our society that pain and suffering can be avoided at all costs and that if they occur, something must be wrong with us. We live in a world that is focused on being happy and looking at life through rose-colored glasses. The extreme feelings and emotional pain that may be associated with death and grieving are often identified as deviant or something to be feared and avoided. We use drugs and tranquilizers to hide this pain, shorten it, and mask it. Responses to death are often seen as indications of emotional illness, and attempts are made to diagnose them according to established psychiatric criteria. I would not want to live in a world in which pain and sorrow following a death were not seen as appropriate and expected. How else should I feel if someone I care about dies? The focus on pathology is reinforced by research that has focused on identifying factors in the bereaved that put them at risk of developing severe emotional problems after the death of a parent or a sibling. The research tries to isolate factors that lead to a "good" outcome or a "bad" outcome, and it is often suggested that by going through certain stages or completing certain tasks, people will recover from their grief. Instead of teaching coping skills, interventions are often more concerned with easing the pain and getting over the loss.

In some ways the focus on outcome only adds to the tension that mourners experience. They read about these findings and then they worry about their responses, about whether they are mourning correctly to avoid subsequent problems. A young man whose best friend died of muscular dystrophy told me:

> I always have the feeling I haven't grieved Corey's death. I read Kübler-Ross, and I am not following her stages. They don't match my experience, and I keep thinking I must be doing something wrong. Yet when I think about it, what I am doing feels right to me. I'll never get over it. It's really changed me in so many ways.

The focus of this book, then, is to help shift our thinking away from a medical model of pathology. Instead, I look at how children and their families respond to the death of a child, a parent, a sibling, or a friend, how they mobilize resources and learn to adapt in ways that are appropriate for them. I focus on a certain openness and flexibility that has been identified in many children and adults (Wampler, Halverson & Deal, 1996). Often if this openness did not exist before, it develops afterward. I look at how this openness works, how people learn, and how they develop adaptive strategies and find new direction in their lives.

This book is designed for people who are helping children learn about the place of death in life, and/or who are bereaved. They include parents, friends, and other members of their community, as well as clergy, teachers, health professionals, and those who specifically work in the field of bereavement.

Knowledge in its way is power. We are all potential mourners. We all need to understand what influences children's and adolescents' behavior, as well as our own, when a death occurs. The more we do so, the easier it is to be creative and comfortable in moving into the previously uncharted territory around death. This book attempts to chart that territory and provide a picture of how people cope in adaptive ways with death. Adaptation involves growing and dealing with change. One mother learned to be open in a new way only through pressure from her family and community. This recent widow recalled:

> My 14-year-old's Sunday school class was going to visit a funeral home. I didn't want him to go. I thought he was too young to be exposed to this kind of information. Only at the insistence of the rabbi did my husband and I agree to let my son participate. One month later, my husband died suddenly from a heart attack. My son was able to explain to his brothers and to me what would happen at the funeral. He was upset, but his knowledge gave him a command of the situation. This eased some of his own stress, as well as some of ours.

This mother has become a strong advocate for educating children about death. She recognized that children who know about death can mourn, can be consoled, and can console others.

The book is divided into three parts. The first part presents a historical and theoretical framework for understanding the place of grief in our lives, including the relationship between developmental stages, family dynamics, and grieving. In the second part, the bereaved themselves talk about their experiences. This part includes chapters on the deaths of parents, children, siblings, and friends. Discussion of the dying process is included when a long illness is involved. The third part provides a picture of what helps the bereaved to cope and empowers them to take charge of their lives. The final chapter focuses on how to introduce death into children's worldviews.

This is not a book that tells individual stories from beginning to end. Rather, I have woven together theoretical discussions with the stories I was told. All the names have been changed to protect the privacy of those who agreed to share their stories, but I have remained faithful to the details of each story. In a few cases, I combined similar stories to present a composite family picture. Most of the material on families in which a parent died is from the Massachusetts General Hospital Child Bereavement Study. I was co-principal investigator and project director of this study, which looked at the consequences of parental death on children aged 6 to 17. All the other material comes from interviews I did specifically for this book. I talked with bereaved children and parents and other young people who experienced a death. The families I chose to include are, for the most part, those who learned, over time, to live with their loss. They have much to teach us about coping and adapting to their new situations. I interviewed people from different racial and ethnic backgrounds, from different parts of the United States, and from other countries. The people I spoke with have different faiths and different mourning customs. Although the outer structure of their mourning may be different, most of the inner processes are similar. Therefore, I do not mention the family backgrounds as I tell the stories. In the words of Harry Stack Sullivan (1972, p. ix): "We are all much more simply human than otherwise."

PART 1

Making Meaning
of Death and Grief

INTRODUCTION

My father told me: "Mother was sick, she went to the hospital and she died. That's it—there is nothing more to say." I was 13. He did not take me to the funeral, and I was not included as a mourner in any of the family's rituals. As a teenager and as a young woman, I always experienced a sense of malaise for which I had no name. As I got older, I learned I was grieving for my mother. I found words for all the things I was feeling. When I finally asked my father about his behavior—he said that was the advice he was given, to simply carry on and not dwell on the loss.

—35-year-old woman, looking back

To understand the place of death in children's lives we need to look at the beliefs and behavior of the adults around them, as well as those of the larger society. None of us lives in a vacuum. The attitudes and values of our particular society influence what we believe and how we think; they provide a framework for ordering the things that happen to us, for defining our purpose and place in the world, for relating to ourselves and others, and for making sense of our experiences. Although death is a biological fact, what it *means* to us and what we teach our children about it are the result of socially shaped ideas and assumptions (Charmaz, 1994). These values, attitudes, and beliefs are not fixed in stone, but are responsive to and modified by dynamic historic, economic, and social forces as well as by our changing understanding of human behavior (Fulton & Owen, 1994). Theories of grief are, therefore, always in flux. There is often little constancy in what is expected of mourners and what help is considered appropriate. While we often search for clear guidelines about what to do during this difficult period in our lives, in my mind there are, in fact, no easy formulas for dealing with this aspect of the human experience.

The basic themes that hold this book together are set out in Part 1. As will become clear to the reader, the main focus of the book is on how people cope, accommodate, and go on with life, in the face of a death and in a world that is often radically changed as a result. My goal, in Part 1, is to identify the forces that influence how we feel and behave when faced with a death in a child's life. I see this part as a tool to inform readers about the complexity of the picture, guide them to develop a vocabulary for connecting to these issues and making sense out of what is happening, and finally expand their coping repertoires to identify ways of adapting that work for them. I explore the historic forces that influence our thinking and ways of making sense of our experience, as well as the various theories of grief and the current understanding of human behavior that influences the way death and grief are viewed in contemporary Western society. Death and grief are not viewed as conditions from which we recover—rather, they are expected life-cycle events that we will all experience.

Although the experience of a death perturbs a mourner's life in a variety of ways, I emphasize two aspects: the experiencing of strong and often strange feelings, and the experiencing of a changed world. It becomes apparent that when a person dies a good deal more is lost than a life. Also lost are a relationship, the self that existed in that relationship, and a way of life. In this book, loss, therefore, is seen in a relational context. The way both adults and children understand what was lost affects how they cope and accommodate, negotiate and renegotiate their roles and place in their world, over their life cycle.

The chapters in this part of the book provide a language for following how the bereaved find ways to live in this changed world. After a death, both children and parents are in a new situation, on a new road. In such situations, all of us flounder, not necessarily because of personality defects or deficiencies or the use of inappropriate psychological defenses but because we may be overwhelmed by events and lack knowledge and perspective on what is happening. The interface between mourners' need to learn, their learning styles, and contemporary models of grief that influence how they understand their experiences will make a difference in how they cope and the kinds of accommodations they continue to make over their life cycle. I emphasize that to protect children, they need to be involved in the family drama and taught, in age-appropriate ways, age-appropriate coping skills that help them understand what is happening and accommodate to their new situation. These ideas are developed in the four chapters in this part of the book and frame and focus the remaining chapters.

Chapter 1 begins with a brief review of the social and historical forces that influence our thinking about death. I look at how death and our understanding of grief are affected by the changing attitudes and values of society. The second part of Chapter 1 reviews how theories of bereavement have evolved during this century. I question the common view of grief as a psychiatric condition which, with the proper treatment, can be cured. I also examine the consequences for the bereaved of the idea that there is a right way to die and a right way to grieve.

In Chapter 2, concepts of stress, coping, and adaptation are described as ways of understanding how grieving people respond. The mourning process is approached as a time of transition that leads to change. This process also leads to both bereaved children and adults finding ways of constructing new relationships to the deceased, creating places for the deceased in their current lives, without living in the past.

In Chapter 3, various concepts of development are presented, providing a framework to understand how children of various ages think about the world and understand the nature of death, and therefore what they experience as lost when a parent, sibling, or friend dies. At various ages and stages in their lives, children and adolescents relate to and experience others in their lives differently; this affects how they will experience the loss over time. Development does not end with childhood or adolescence. How parents react is related to where they are developmentally as well.

The primary context in which children grow is that of the family. Chapter 4, the final chapter of this section, looks at the family as it has changed over the century, including changes in the roles and expectations of parents. Children are not passive recipients who simply absorb what the family and the world around them have to offer. There is a mutuality in every family as it deals with the expected and unexpected events in its life cycle. This chapter also describes how parents respond differently to death and the grief that follows depending on their parenting styles, and how families can change and grow as they deal with the stresses and strains they experience at such times in their lives.

CHAPTER ONE

Historical and Theoretical Perspectives

Ours are the loss and agonizing grief,
The slow, dead hours, the sighs without relief,
The lingering nights, the thoughts of pleasure past
Memory, that wounds, and darkens to the last.
When death strikes down, with sudden crush and power,
Parental hope, and blasts its open flower.
Most vain to tell, how deep that long despair,
Which time ne'er heals, and time can scarce impair.

(Story, 1851, pp. 57–59)

Every society and faith system has developed some way of integrating the fact of death into life and into children's lives. Without exception, all have rituals for disposing of the body and beliefs about what happens after death (Neuberger, 1987). These beliefs and rituals are designed to help mourners deal with the loss of a member of the family and the changes in themselves, their family, and the community that the absence creates (Van Gennep, 1960). Every society also has a way of dealing with the influence of the dead on the lives of the living. Some societies fear that the dead will come back as ghosts, or do not mention the deceased so as not to disturb their journey to the next world (DeSpelder & Strickland; Rosenblatt, Walsh, & Jackson, 1976). In other societies ancestors are worshipped in family rituals and therefore remain part of the family (Klass, 1996). In this century, traditional customs and rituals have fallen into disuse. There is a space that leaves people without guidance; death is seen as a failure of medical science, and expressions of grief as a weakness in the mourners' psyches.

DEATH IN A SOCIAL AND HISTORICAL CONTEXT

An Expected Part of Life

Throughout history, death was an everyday occurrence in most communities, and children experienced it as an expected part of their lives. Such killers as the plague and infectious diseases were constant companions. Children were often not named during the first year of their lives until it was clear that they would survive. A large number of children did not reach adulthood and were rarely memorialized with their own graves and individual stones (Aries, 1981). People usually died at home and were buried from their homes, their bodies prepared by members of their families. Children both witnessed and participated in these activities. They were accepted as part of the family drama and provided with some education by example that prepared them for the inevitability of death. Basic religious faith prepared children to be ready to "meet their maker" and to accept their fate or destiny, following the model of adult death to which they were witness. For example, a family diary from the 1850s reported a conversation between a minister and a dying young woman (Mary Elizabeth Edmonds; see Edmonds, 1847–99). The minister asked if the woman was ready to meet God. She answered that she was and quietly awaited her end. In fact, given the limitations of medicine at the time, there was little else that could be done.

The Growth of Technology: Death as a Failure of Science

Since the late 19th century, philosophical and theological perspectives have been informed by the growing influence of science and medicine. Science has provided us with unimaginable means of mass destruction, as well as treatments, cures, and technologies that have extended life. We have more control over sickness and health, over disease and prevention than ever before in recorded history. Life expectancy has been extended to a point that could not have been imagined a century ago. Most of the infectious diseases of childhood have been eliminated. Families no longer have many children with the expectation that several of them will not survive childhood. The death rate from cancer in children is declining, and we read about lung transplants, gene therapy, and the ability to prolong life with some good quality. Although we do not have a cure for genetic diseases, such as cystic fibrosis and muscular dystrophy, or for diseases like AIDS, there is some ability to lessen their immediate debilitating consequences.

In this technological world, where logic and reason prevail, it is possible for death to be neither seen nor heard. Aries (1981) called it the Invisible Death, and Fulton (1965) referred to the Denying of Dying (1965). Gorer (1965) characterized the treatment of death in the mid-20th century as a new pornography in that the subject is taboo, as sex once was. Gorer noted that even the rituals that once identified a person as a mourner, such as flowers on the door or a black armband, are no longer in use. The fact that death in this century has moved out of the home and into the hospital has made it even more invisible (Glaser & Strauss, 1965; Krulick, Holaday, & Martinson, 1987). Children are, for the first time, excluded from death scenes, from funerals and other services, and often from the mourning rituals as well (Aries, 1981).

Acknowledging Death

By the late 1950s, researchers had begun to note the negative consequences for the dying of trying to avoid the fact that death happens (Feifel, 1959,

1977; Fulton, 1965; Quint Benoliel & Degner, 1995). This was a period of social change. The growing consumer movement challenged authority in diverse areas, such as the war in Vietnam and the authority of the medical professional to control birth and death (Corless, 1985). The discussion of death in the larger society was popularized by the work of Kübler-Ross (1969), who identified stages of dying that many treated as applicable to all. There seemed to be a readiness in the larger society for this kind of information. Ill people were encouraged to talk about their impending deaths, and it became unacceptable not to face death openly. This openness did not always apply to dying children, who still were not told what was happening to them.

At the same time, the hospice movement was taking form in England. Dame Cicely Saunders (1994) developed hospice, a program that enabled people to die with dignity, in a relatively pain-free condition and often in their own homes (Kastenbaum & Kastenbaum, 1989; Lattanzi-Licht, Mahoney, & Miller, 1998; Wald, 1995). The main energy for the development of hospice programs in the United States came from volunteers, many of whom were dissatisfied with the care a dying family member or friend had received (Corless, 1985). They were influenced by the English experience. During the past 20 years, hospice has grown into an international movement. In the United States, it is now governed by federal guidelines and funded by various insurance programs, both public and private. Only more recently, however, have hospice programs developed frameworks for caring for dying children (Davies, 1996; Martinson, 1976; 1987). Children are sometimes served as part of a larger hospice program. Now we are witnessing the growth of special child-centered hospices.

Is There a Right Way to Die?

Weisman (1972) observed that we cannot live constantly with the fact that we will ultimately die, even if we are suffering from an illness from which we will not recover. This would make living in the present almost intolerable. We need to live in the moment as well. We live with what Weisman called "middle knowledge"—we are aware of death but it stays in the background. Accepting the concept of middle knowledge does not mean fostering denial. It means that we live with contradicting philosophies and with the flexibility to move among many ways and kinds of knowing. The adequacy of how we cope must be tested against the world as it really is, not how we would like it to be. Weisman did not believe that dying always follows an orderly progression. Rather, he described the goal as providing options for people to achieve an appropriate death, that is, a death that they can live with. People, and children in particular, need the opportunity to create a reality suitable for themselves until the very end.

Lofland (1978) and Aries (1981) pointed to the dangers of focusing only on the final act of dying. This focus was the primary concern of what Lofland referred to as "the death movement." Lofland called this focus a "romance

3333

with death." She described what she observed as the "Happy Death Movement," in which most of the energy was invested in helping people die. According to Lofland, modern technological advances allow us to assign people, long before their actual deaths occur, to the role of "dying persons," a role in which they have no legitimate function in society. She wrote that this approach left people living as nonpersons for long periods. For example, 5-year-old Josh, mentioned in the Introduction, lived for five months in this role. He still wanted to play, and he was still involved in family life and in the birth of his younger brother. Yet the larger society beyond his family could not respond to his needs and for them, he was a nonperson.

Lofland suggested that those who work with the dying need to shift their focus. Like Weisman, she advocated both the acceptance of the fact that people's lives may end soon, and the importance of helping people remain involved in living in spite of the constraints of their illnesses or disabilities. In this view, the focus moves from the quality of dying to the quality of living until the actual time of death.

How We Die: The Limits of Science

The experience of the hospice movement, which led to the expectations that the dying would receive more humane treatment and that there would be a place for death in how we view life, did not permeate the daily lives of most Americans. Even today, referrals to hospice are often made in the last days of life, especially when children are involved, largely because health care professionals find it difficult to talk with patients about death (Bartholome, 1995).

Death in the late 20th century is seen as a failure of modern medicine, an obstacle to be overcome (Feifel, 1986). The health care system and many other institutions in our society continue to support the delusion that death can be avoided. One woman told me that when the doctor came to tell her that her child had died, he was upset and kept repeating, "It shouldn't have happened, it shouldn't have happened." She understood that there had been little hope for her child, and now she had to reassure the doctor, who could not accept the fact that he could not sustain this life. The science and reason that guided his practice gave him a false sense of control. Hers was not an unusual experience. Many bereaved parents have had the same experience with health care providers. Worse still is the family who is sent away from the deathbed so that health care professionals can do their "work." In reality we can defer death and make it possible for some people to live longer, healthier lives, but we cannot remove death from human experience.

The prolongation of life as a result of modern technology can make the process of dying more terrifying than death itself. Ethical issues about artificial life supports have raised the question about the right to choose how and when to die. Often people are hooked up to machines that will keep them alive physically but not living in any meaningful way. In such instances, for the individual to die, the family needs to decide to end treatment. We tend to think that end-of-life decisions apply primarily to the elderly who can be hooked to respirators and maintained with artificial life supports. But the right to die without the aggressive intrusion of medicine applies to children as well. This is one of the most difficult decisions physicians and families have to make. One mother had to tell the doctor what they all knew: Medicine could not cure her teenage daughter's cancer, which had spread throughout her body to the brain. Her parents wanted their daughter to die at home with as little pain as possible. The doctor admonished the mother, saying, "I do not understand you; when a house is on fire, you do everything to put out the fire. How could you suggest that we no longer treat this young woman? There are still drugs to try." The mother reminded him that these were intrusive, debilitating, and experimental drugs, although they gave the doctor a sense that he was doing something. By this time, the mother had finally come to accept that there was nothing medicine could offer her daughter. The family could not avoid the pain of the loss; all they could realistically hope for was that death could bring their daughter peace and an end to pain. Science, in the form of the doctor's inability to accept his helplessness, did not help; it significantly hindered the natural process of this death. In fact, it further added to the parents' stress, since they felt that they were going against medical advice. Science can offer no answer to the sorrow and pain of the caregivers and families. The rush of activity, of trying to do something, leaves no room for coming to a time when quiet acceptance of the inevitable may be the only option.

We need to keep in mind that not all deaths occur in the hospital or after an illness (Nuland, 1995). There are also accidental deaths, sudden deaths, and deaths for which the pain cannot be controlled. There are deaths that we often think should not have happened—suicide, accidents, murder, medical error. Nothing is more distressing than the death of a child or young person, whether anticipated or sudden. We cannot prevent the death of some children for whom there are no cures. We cannot prevent all accidents and all natural disasters, and we surely do not know how to prevent violence and war.

Recent Developments in Thinking about Death

At the end of the 20th century, we are witnessing a period of transition in how death is dealt with in our society. There is a growing awareness of the limits of science and that patterns of treatment and care of the dying are inadequate. There is a new focus on the whole person, with physical, emotional, and spiritual needs. This process of change is leading to even greater openness and more humane care for the dying (Byock, 1997; Lattanzi-Licht et al., 1998). In this context, people with terminal illnesses are not referred to as dying but as people in the end stage of their lives. The nature of our "death system" is slowly changing, and consumers are becoming more and more engaged in the discourse (Morgan, 1995). There seems to be an increasing readiness to hear. The press, television, and radio have provided extensive coverage about dying and mourning. There has been an active debate about euthanasia and assisted suicide that has led to legislation in several states and an appeal to the U.S. Supreme Court. On admission to the hospital, all patients are required to designate surrogates who can act on their behalf if they are incapacitated. Whether it is a parent who assumes this role for a child or an adult serving another adult, this need to designate a surrogate brings the subject of how and when to die to the forefront. It often stimulates discussions about the choices and options people have as they approach the end stage of their lives.

Nonetheless changes have not permeated every level of society. For example, in November 1995, the Robert Wood Johnson Foundation issued a report documenting the gap between what is known and what is done in the health care system when someone is dying. The report noted that not only could physicians and other members of the health care system not deal well with end-of-life issues, families were equally uncomfortable bringing up questions of when treatment is no longer helpful and how to manage pain. Neither the health care system nor those who use it are comfortable with the inevitable fact that people die. Nor do they easily accept that medicine cannot fix everything. One conclusion of this report was that if people want control over their own end-of-life care, at this time, they must leave the hospital. This is no different from the situation that Bartholome (1995) described when children are dying. The Robert Wood Johnson study, reported widely in the press, raised readers' consciousness about the issues and the options that may be available at this time in their lives. However, although there is something new in the air, in many ways we are still at the frontier in dealing with end-of-life decisions, whether for a child or an adult who is dying. Perhaps this tension between what some consider an ideal way to die and what actually happens is as it should be. Dying and grieving are part of living, and, to some extent, we need to accept that not everything can or will be controlled. We are striving to be sure that the people who are dealing with these issues at this time in their lives are in charge, to the extent that this is possible.

WHAT HAPPENS AFTER A DEATH: VIEWS OF GRIEVING

Our understanding of the grieving process, like our view of death itself, has changed over time and reflects the thinking that is dominant in the historical and social periods in which we live. The ways in which a society views death inform and influence its expectations of appropriate behaviors for mourners.

Public Mourning

In the 19th century, in part as a result of the individual finding a new sense of personal value, emphasis was placed on the loss, and elaborate expressions of survivors' grief developed. Aries (1981) called this the Age of the Beautiful Death, which was reflected in funerary statues and public rituals acknowledging the loss. Visiting graves was common, and people wore dark clothes for an extended period to identify themselves as mourners (De-Spelder & Strickland, 1996). The deceased were memorialized in a variety of ways, such as embroidered pieces done by children that hung in homes.

Religious faith played an important part in people's coping with loss. In the early 19th century, Supreme Court Justice Joseph Story, whose poem begins this chapter, experienced the premature deaths of five of his seven children. Even in a period when children's deaths were common, this was a large number. He wrote poetry in memory of one of his daughters and described in his papers how his faith sustained him (Silverman, 1997). Story was able to continue because of the way he gave the events of his life meaning. His religious faith supported his psychological needs. He believed that he would meet his children again in the afterlife, and this belief gave him solace.

Mourning as a Psychological Issue

In contemporary Western society, science has had an important impact on religious philosophy, pushing the belief in an afterlife to the background and minimizing the value of ritual (Parsons, 1994). Seeing death as a medical failure affects our understanding of survivors' reactions after the death. By the middle of this century, Gorer (1965) observed that mourning traditions had disappeared and the focus was on restraint, making the pain and sadness associated with loss a personal matter. In a way, mourning has been sanitized.

Explaining human behavior is no longer the reserve of philosophers and clergymen, and, for the most part, contemporary views of grief are framed by modern psychological theories. During this century, we have witnessed what Meyer (1988) called the creation of the modern psychological individual. Meyer suggested that the qualities that define this individual are related to the complex social changes taking place in the Western economic, cultural, and political systems that foster the ideology of individualism. Psychological theories following this view of reality focus on individuals' responsibility for their own inner psyches, as well as those of their children, ignoring the influence of the social context. Attitudes toward grief that developed in this context emphasize restraint and individuals' inner ability to cope. Bereavement is not seen as a communal issue, but as an individual one. Time limited and contained within the emotional life of mourners, grief is characterized as something that mourners will get over, as if they have an illness from which they will recover. We talk about the resolution of grief; we are told unresolved grief could lead to emotional problems or psychiatric illness, although it is not clear what "unresolved" means in this context. The image created is that grief is a germ that has infected the body and can be expunged with proper treatment, rather than something that changes the ways in which people live their lives.

Most theories of grieving rarely mention the meaning of the relationship that is lost and the larger disruption in living that mourners experience. Their goal is to explain how an individual mourner can arrive at a place where grief ends. This end is reached by passing through a series of tasks or steps. By following these steps, grief will end, and the mourner can return to normal functioning as quickly as possible. Mourning is made simple.

Letting Go and Getting on with Life

Many contemporary psychological theories of grief are based on the work of Freud (1961). Freud's early characterization of grief pointed to the necessity of detaching one's memories and expectations from the deceased. Freud believed that the work of grieving was to let go of the deceased; once emotional investment was removed from the relationship to the deceased, the mourner's emotional energy would be freed for new relationships. With the investment in a new relationship, grief would be over.

This view and the accompanying psychologization of grief were compatible with the value placed on individual independence and autonomy in Western society. Dependence on others was seen as a negative quality. Relationships with others were viewed instrumentally—in terms of having one's needs met—and the focus of development in children was on separation and individuation. Thus, when a relationship ended, as with a death, it was appropriate to consider how to sever these ties. In this view, by implication, people were seen as having sequential relationships, as if it was possible to have only one close relationship at a time. Different kinds of relationships were not accounted for. In reading Freud's thoughts about personal deaths in his family, one clearly sees that he was aware that this detachment was not possible (Silverman & Klass, 1996). Yet this construct remained the backbone of most subsequent psychological theories of grief.

In 1944, Lindemann identified three tasks that composed the "grief work" of the mourner: emancipation from the bond to the deceased, readjustment to the environment in which the deceased is missing, and the formation of new relationships. He also observed intense guilt in the people he studied and treated, who were all survivors of a tragic fire at a Boston nightclub, the Coconut Grove, in which hundreds were killed (Lindemann, 1944). We cannot discount that some of the feelings of guilt and anger he observed in the survivors were connected to survivors' guilt. These feelings are not unlike those described by Holocaust survivors, who often have difficulty reconciling their own survival with the death that surrounded them (Frankl, 1972, 1978). Nonetheless, even today, guilt is invariably looked for in mourners. Often when it is not there, the observer reports that the mourner is repressing or avoiding these feelings. Lindemann saw grief as ending when the mourner severed the relationship to the deceased. He recognized that the bereaved had to adjust to an environment without the deceased, but focused on the need to "let go" in order to do so.

Children Do Mourn

The work of Bowlby (1961) had an important impact on subsequent research on bereavement in this century. Before then, mental health professionals did not believe that children were capable of grieving. Bowlby's research (1961, 1981) established that children do grieve. Bowlby studied young children who were separated from their mothers during the bombing of London in World War II and the problems these separations caused. Although his early work was not concerned with death, he recognized that these children were grieving the loss of a key relationship that was critical to their sense of well-being. He described this relationship as attachment behavior—emphasizing the importance of a mother figure in children's growth and ability to thrive. The source of this attachment behavior emanated, he hypothesized, from an instinctual need to be close to a mother figure.

Bowlby saw the grief in these children as a form of separation anxiety, which, unlike when a death occurred, could be rectified by a reunion with their mothers or prevented in the first place by limiting the separation. He identified a period when the children were in shock, numb, and full of disbelief that the loss had occurred, and then their gradual acceptance of the impossibility of a reunion. He also described a phase of yearning and searching that was typical of young children, when they tried to find the lost person and be reunited with her. He thought that there was a strong tendency to keep a clear visual memory of the deceased, but that the intensity of this memory diminished. Following a phase of disorganization and despair, which occurs as the mourner realizes that the deceased will not return, there is a phase of reorganization in which the bereaved lets go of ties to the deceased and establishes new relationships.

Contemporary child psychology largely ignores research on inevitable aspects of human experience such as death and grief, and their impact on childhood. Bowlby's work has been reframed to emphasize the importance of the child's attachment to critical caregivers and the impact this attachment has on subsequent development and adult behavior. We learn about different types of attachment behavior in children, but little is said about the relationship between this behavior and children's evolving reactions to death and mourning. For example, Bowlby's work has led to changes in hospital practices, so that parents are now allowed to stay with children of all ages during hospitalization. We also need to recognize that experiences where children learn to cope with lesser losses are, in some ways, practice for children to deal with more permanent losses through death.

Furman (1974) suggested, from her work with preschool children who had lost parents, that three tasks confront mourners: to understand and come to terms with the reality and circumstances of the death, to mourn, and to resume and continue their lives. She observed that these young children accepted the deaths of their parents only after a struggle between disbelief that the deaths had occurred and confusion about why the deceased were not coming back. Mourning, she wrote, involved mastery of this process as the child mourners she studied loosened their ties to the deceased. Mourning ended when the children identified with a part of the deceased, thus allowing them to keep aspects of their lost parents with them forever. The key to all this, Furman noted, is the process of detachment that occurs when the deceased do not come back and children withdraw their emotional investment in what is no longer there. This theoretical emphasis on detachment as a critical aspect of grief will be revisited throughout this book to point to the fact that this concept does not account for what most people experience.

Other researchers have also found that children experience and react to loss, even when they cannot articulate what they are experiencing. Shapiro (1994) wrote about infants who experienced grief over disruptions in caretaking or parental depression. Grief is represented and remembered in infants' body images. Sullivan (1965) also described the imprint on the body of preverbal experiences.

Is Grief an Illness?

The main focus in most bereavement research was on outcome, that is, did the death affect the bereaved in a negative way emotionally? Most of the early research was conducted by practitioners who were working primarily with mourners who came for psychiatric help and subsequently became their research subjects (Furman, 1974; Volkan, 1981). The problems these people presented were then generalized to the larger population of bereaved people. Their problematic behavior became the model for normative bereavement behavior. It was thought that if the "correct" form of mourning was followed, these behaviors could be prevented. The pain and tumult following a death were labeled pathological and signs of illness. Grieving was separated from the normal life cycle and became something to be feared.

This view of grief as an illness permeated many layers of society. It seems to be a continuation of the invisible death that Aries (1981) described. Grief is taken to the "doctor's office," where it can be contained and controlled and will not intrude on the life of the community. Like an illness that can be treated with a little penicillin, grief is seen as something that can be tied into a neat package and finished. The community does not deal with the fullness of the way people's dying changes the world for those who mourn. Although we are seeing more and more programs designed to help people find an appropriate death, we have not come far in how we deal with bereavement. Lifton (1983) reminded us that we cannot accept death without dealing with mourning, which, in its way, is a constant reminder that people die. We see heroic stories in the media about how people die. When the subsequent pain of grief is discussed, the emphasis is on how to limit and control it and, ideally, make it go away. Even as we witness the growing effort to expand our perspective beyond the medical model, which is described in the next chapter (Attig, 1996; Klass, Silverman, & Nickman, 1996; Parkes, 1996; Shapiro, 1994; Worden, 1991), there still seems to be a trend toward models that focus on deviance, recovery, and cure (Figley, Bride, & Mazza, 1997; Rando, 1993).

Adult mourners sometimes express concerns about whether they and their children are grieving correctly, so as to avoid any subsequent problems. When pathology is invariably associated with bereavement, it reinforces parents' fear of facing death with their children. They worry that exposure to a death and the experience associated with grief will lead to problem behavior in their children. The message they have received emphasizes that feelings that are not expressed will lead to negative sequelae. On the other hand, in a society that cannot accept extremes of behavior, even when appropriate, parents worry that if the children express too much feeling they could lose control (temporarily or over the long run), and such loss of control is equally dangerous. This view only inhibits and handicaps parents who want to involve their children in what is happening.

OTHER INFLUENCES AND NEW IDEAS

Our difficulty with grief comes, in part, from the way human behavior has been described by the dominant psychological sciences of this century. We characterize behavior in linear terms, as if one experience can lead to one outcome. However, people can rarely be put into a simple cause-and-effect model (Bruner, 1990). We are beginning to recognize the complexity of the human condition and human relationships. In recent decades, we have witnessed a shift to a more realistic view of how we live, appreciating that we are interdependent, that "no man is an island." This shift was propelled in some ways by the women's movement. Women observed the importance of relationships in people's lives, that the goal of development was not independence but interdependence (Gilligan, 1993; Miller, 1986). We now acknowledge that relationships with others frame our sense of self and how we live our lives.

These relationships frame how we organize and think about death, that is, how we make meaning of this aspect of our lives. Relationships with the deceased need to be included as we try to understand the relational world of mourners, especially children. We are moving toward what I call a relational view of grief. Stroebe, Gergen, Gergen, and Stroebe (1996) noted the influence of the historical and contemporary social context on how we grieve and understand death. In their review of recent research on bereavement, their own and others', Silverman and Klass (1996) concluded that the relationship to the deceased does not end at death. The bereaved do not detach from the deceased, nor does bereavement end. The fact that most bereaved people report that letting go of the deceased was not consistent with their experience seemed to be overlooked in a model of grief that focused on the inner emotional reactions of the mourners, rather than including the relational and contextual part of their lives and who they are (Silverman & Klass, 1996).

We are participating in a changing system that is increasingly looking at the complex human relationships that make invisible deaths impossible. We are moving toward a view of the world that understands that there are things that science can do for us, but that reason can only take us so far on this life journey (Levine, 1984). We are at a place where former ways of doing things are no longer sufficient, but new ones have not yet developed. We have to recognize that we cannot control death, but that we do have choices about how we react to it. This is not an event that will happen to others—all of us need to be expert in coping, in making meaning out of death and our subsequent grief.

CHAPTER TWO

Bereavement
A Time of Changing Relationships and Transition

> The worst thing that happened when my son died was that I felt that the world had fallen apart. I felt as if every part of my body was stressed and stretched out. How could I take this news in? It simply could not be true. Even worse was that I had no clue what to do, what to say. I know my husband and other children were also upset, but all I remember was that we just clung to each other. I know that people reached out, but I can't remember a thing!
>
> —Mother of a 15-year-old killed in a car accident

When we think of bereaved people, we think of tears, immense sadness, a sense of heaviness in the body, despair, and great stress. In fact, feelings after a death are dynamic and changing all the time. In spite of our wishes to the contrary, the world does not stop when we receive bad news. The news may cause great disruption and change the course of our lives, but life does go on. As adults we have the capacity to know that life will continue. For children and even teenagers, this may not be so apparent. Children do not have a sense of history or enough experience to be certain that life will go on. In the words of a 10-year-old: "When my mom died, I couldn't imagine how anything would continue."

How do we reconcile the fact that one minute there is life and then there is none? How do we accept the fact that life will go on but without this person? Reconciling this dissonance does not happen with one action or one activity. It happens a bit at a time as the bereaved also deal with the myriad other issues facing them (Altschul, 1988; Silverman, 1986; Silverman & Nickman, 1996).

It is not easy to describe the dynamic, interactive process that is set in motion after a loved one dies. In this chapter, I develop a view of bereavement that reflects the complexity of this process. This description creates a framework for understanding how people cope with death, providing a perspective that can help people find a comfortable place for death in their lives. I begin by looking at bereavement as a time of stress and focus on how mourners cope with this stress. I include a brief overview of theories related to stress and subsequent coping, which provide the background for looking at grief as a period of transition that leads to change in the mourner's life, rather than to recovery.

THE LANGUAGE OF GRIEF: A RELATIONAL PARADIGM

A Time of Change or a Time of Illness?

Death is a normal life-cycle event. Sometimes it is anticipated, as in old age or after an illness; other times, as with the death of a child (whether sudden or anticipated), it appears to be out of turn in the contemporary life cycle. After a death, the mourners face a period of change or transition.

Bereavement was described for a while as a time of crisis in people's lives. Crisis is defined by the Webster's Third International Dictionary (1967, p. 537) as a "turning point, a decisive moment . . . either endangering or felt to endanger the continuity of the individual or his group." The period around a death is certainly a time of crisis for the immediate family involved, but it extends well beyond this moment (Silverman, 1966). The widowed report that they experience a series of crises or critical periods, each requiring different responses over an extended period. I suggest that grief could best be characterized as a time of transition (Silverman, 1966), what Marris (1974) called a time of loss and change.

In the English language, several words are used to describe people's reactions after a death: *grief, mourning,* and *bereavement.* Grief typically refers to the ways in which people express the feelings that arise after a death: sadness, crying, and despair. Mourning has been described as the mental work following the loss of a loved one. Altschul (1988) defined mourning as the psychological process by which an individual adapts to the loss of a loved one. Mourning also includes the cultural traditions and rituals that guide behavior after a death (Bowlby, 1980). Bereavement refers to the state of having experienced a loss. *Grief, mourning,* and *bereavement* are words that are often used interchangeably. In this book I use them as nouns, verbs, and adjectives as appropriate, to describe the process people go through as they cope with death.

None of these words reflects the fullness of what a death introduces into the life of an individual, family, or community. Our dilemma is to find a language of bereavement that moves us away from the view of death and grief as an illness and toward an acceptance of death as part of life. In fact, it may not be possible to find the "right" words for the complex series of changes that occur after a death.

When grief is characterized in the language of medicine, it is described in terms of symptoms people manifest, as if they suffer from a "condition." A good deal of attention is focused on the profound sense of emptiness and sadness, the sense of unreality, and the associated physical or emotional manifestations of these feelings (body tensions, sleeplessness, sadness, and tears). The implication is that there is something wrong.

Mourners are often told that if they can get their feelings out, the symptoms will go away. However, if mourners become too vocal in expressing their pain, help may be offered to quiet it, to relieve the symptoms with sedatives or other means that really only mask the pain. Mourners receive a mixed message: Too noisy is a problem, but too quiet is an equal problem. Thus, mourners themselves are not clear about what is expected or acceptable behavior, especially in a society in which many mourning traditions and customs have fallen into disuse. We sometimes wonder whose responses we are reacting to—those of the mourners or those of the observers in their social network who are uncomfortable with the expression of extreme feelings. This is especially true with regard to grieving children and our reactions to them.

Often parents do not have a realistic understanding of how children see their world and their capacities to deal with it. Parents may worry that their children are not more expressive. Yet children see themselves as quite expressive, given their age and stage of development. When they are not able to be more articulate, it may well be that they do not have the vocabulary or the concepts to give words to what they are experiencing. Thus, it is not easy for parents to connect to their children's grief.

The implication here is that once the feelings are out, all will be well. This view of grief does not consider that the process is much more complicated and that the impact of the loss is pervasive, involving much more than the need to deal with feelings.

Characterizing the Process

Mourners are reacting to many aspects of the loss, beyond just their emotions. On multiple levels—individual, family, and community—they are dealing with changes: in how they see themselves, in the way they live their lives, in their connections to important others, in their patterns of relating to others, and in the relationships of others to them. They are dealing with shifting relationships. Changes occur in the social system of which the mourners are a part and with which they interact and in the space that was filled by the mourners' relationships to the deceased. This is a circular process. Community reactions to the death may change friendship patterns, and the role of the extended family may shift as well.

If grief is viewed as an expected life-cycle stressor, as a time of transition and change, even if it comes out of turn in the life cycle, our attitudes toward our reactions will be different. Our reactions do not stigmatize us as defective or deviant; rather, they point to the struggle common to all of us— to find ways of coping and adapting to this loss and changed situation. This is not a static situation, whether the mourner is a child, an adolescent, or an adult. The way we react today will not be the same tomorrow. By then the situation will have changed, simply because we are alive and living. There is no straight line between being bereaved and recovering. In fact, the very idea of recovery, of returning to a sense of self, to a way of life as before, is impossible. We must move away from the era of invisible dying and invisible grief and toward a recognition that everyone can and must develop expertise for coping with dying and with grief. We do not and cannot take away the pain, but we can learn how to deal with it.

By talking about transition, we recognize that this is a period of disruption, stress, and change for both adults and children of all ages (Baker & Sedney, 1996). In fact, the overall process of grieving may not be that different in children, adolescents, and adults. Age is only one of many factors that influence how a mourner responds. Some of the intensity and nature of the responses will differ, depending on who died, the mourner's relationship to that person, and what is considered appropriate behavior in the mourner's culture. Individual differences, which partly relate to age, reflect differences in the capacity to articulate and experience what is happening, ways of making meaning, and family roles. Grief is seen in a relational context.

A Time of Stress

The mourners' efforts to identify and respond to all the changes they are living through lead to their experiencing a good deal of stress. Stress also comes from their lack of prior awareness that grief is so pervasive and is accompanied by so many changes. Stress for a child may come from adults not recognizing them as mourners and failing to include them in the family drama. Strong and extreme feelings and reactions after a loss should be recognized as appropriate under the circumstances, rather than judged and labeled as problematic or symptomatic of an illness, as often happens today. Although we need support and assistance from others, we need to learn that we will not be "cured" of this malady. Instead, we need to acknowledge the bumps, the derailments, the disappointments, the stressors, the bad moments of life that cannot always be avoided or prevented. Things happen that are not our fault and over which we have little or no control. Our energy needs to be devoted to learning that adversity is also part of the life cycle and to learning how to manage this adversity.

This time of transition consists of many crises and stressful periods. The Institute of Medicine (IOM), an agency of the U.S. government, identifies types of stressors in terms of their intensity and the duration of the impact of the events on people (Elliot & Eisdorfer, 1982). One type of stressor is acute and time-limited. For example, going to a new school, awaiting minor surgery, or feeling rejected by a peer are momentary and probably have the least long-term implications. In children this type of stress may lead to disruptive behavior that is short-lived and responsive to assurance and some direction. Intermittent stressors in the IOM classification are the result of interpersonal conflict in a given situation: abuse by an alcoholic parent whose drinking is erratic, parents whose fighting puts the child in the middle, street violence, or the monthly visit to the hospital to determine the status of the child's disease. If the respite periods between these stressful encounters are not used to develop new ways of dealing with the situation, these can soon become chronic stressors. Chronic stressors are those associated with permanent disabilities (as for a child born with a degenerative disease that increasingly incapacitates) for which there are few, if any, respite periods and for which relief may only come with death.

There can be no doubt that the death of a loved one is an event that leads to all three types of stressors—acute, intermittent, and chronic. In fact, bereavement may not lend itself to such classification. Stress in this context is a dynamic, changing phenomenon that is an integral part of losing a loved one.

Antonovsky (1979) identified universal stressors—war, murder, hunger, and death—that affect everyone. The death of a loved one is always stressful, but some deaths may be more distressing or traumatic for the survivors than others: sudden deaths, deaths that mutilate the body, and deaths that are self-induced. Freud (quoted in Altschul, 1988) stated that trauma is any experience that calls up distressing effects, such as fright, anxiety, shame, or physical pain, and that challenges the resources of the victim's ego. Van der Kolk, McFarlane, and Weisaeth (1996) defined a traumatic event as one that disrupts and creates great stress in the individual whose resources are inadequate to respond effectively. Almost any death, expected or unexpected, can be for the moment traumatic, even more so in a society in which death is not accepted as a normal part of the life cycle and few resources are available to help the mourners cope.

Challenging How We Make Meaning

Bereavement, then, is not simply something that happens to us. In my thinking, the way people view this event, which is clearly stressful, relates to how they assess what is going on. Death is something that we must make sense out of and respond to accordingly. Neimeyer (1997) described a constructivist point of view, in which human beings are seen as meaning makers, striving to punctuate, organize, and anticipate their engagement with the world by arranging it in themes that express their particular cultures, families, and personalities. How people construct meaning also relates to where they are developmentally, from both the cognitive and emotional perspectives. Children also make meaning, and where they are developmentally will very much color how they understand and react to the death. The concepts of development are discussed in greater detail in Chapters 3 and 4.

In their studies of stress and coping, Lazarus and Folkman (1984) used the concept of meaning making to understand how people define and respond to stress. They defined stress as the relationship between individuals and their environment, which is *appraised* as taxing or exceeding their resources. An event becomes stressful when those who experience it do not know how to define what is happening and what to do about it or feel that their well-being is in danger. Antonovsky (1979) understood that in many stressful situations, what is overwhelming for some can be transient and fleeting for others. If individuals do not feel threatened, their resources are not taxed, and if their coping strategies are appropriate to deal with the problem, then they will be able to find ways of coping with the situation.

Applying this concept to bereavement, we see that when someone we care about dies, we are naturally distraught and upset and experience our world, at some level, as crumbling. The sense of disarray may come because our way of mapping or coding the world is challenged or not sufficient for the situation (Neimeyer, 1997; M. White & Epston, 1990). There may be aspects that the bereaved know how to handle, such as organizing a funeral or calling people to let them know that the death has occurred. If they have accessible mourning rituals and practices, these can provide some comfort and direction for how to act. The stress may be greater if these traditions are not in place or have no meaning. The lack of funeral and mourning rituals in the community in which the mourners live may mean that people have little comfort, support, or direction as they initially try to deal with the death. There can be a vacuum—even in finding an appropriate way to dispose of the body.

For many individuals, their resources may be taxed not only by their own ignorance or developmental limitations, but by the inadequacy of societal resources. A society with an unrealistic understanding of the course of grief can stigmatize mourners by being afraid of their grief and pulling away from them (Silverman, 1969, 1994). The extreme feelings that the mourners experience and cannot control may completely unnerve both them and those around them. The mourners experience greater stress as they face not only their ongoing emotional responses long after they think they should be finished, but their inability to reconstitute their sense of self and their world as before. Few mourners can put their lives back in a tidy package in a short period, as they are often asked to do (Altschul, 1988; Silverman, 1977, 1986; Stroebe et al., 1996). Their expectation that they should get over this event in short order only adds to the sense of disorder. They feel stigmatized, and their grief is further delegitimated (Silverman, 1969, 1994), or to put it another way, they feel disenfranchised (Doka, 1989). It is important to look at how the mourners make meaning, as well as at how the society in which they live informs and frames their sense of order and meaning. With time, most mourners' ways of making meaning change. The process of grieving opens new doors and can be seen as the impetus for developmental change. Stress can also emanate from the fact that this process of change is not recognized as a part of the bereavement process, either by the bereaved or by the larger community around them.

Additional Stressors

Stressors lead to other stressors whose impact extends over time. For example, a parent's death can lead to a decline in family income, a shift in the family's routine, the loss of the family nurturer, the need to change schools, and so forth. Stress for dying adolescents may result from their increasing inability to take care of themselves, particularly since independence is so important at this stage. For the parents, the stress may result from the need to provide constant care and from watching their children become debilitated, knowing that the only end will be death. Each stressor differs in the ways in which it unfolds, leading to other stresses in the individual and in the social system. Each may require different repertoires of coping strategies. The death of a child is an acute stressor; over time, it may be experienced as an intermittent stressor or a chronic stressor as the parents struggle to find ways to deal with the many changes it has introduced into their lives (Bluebond-Langner, 1996).

It is not only the immediate impact of any given stressor that is important. We cannot separate the event from the long-term perturbations it has in the system and how it is reacted to over time. These reactions can change how the stress unfolds and is experienced. There are different degrees of intensity at different times, so the nature of the stress changes. This intensity relates to the success of the strategies the mourners use to cope with what they are experiencing and to their ability to identify the vicissitudes of what is happening.

Coping

The concepts of stress and coping go together. The way people cope, that is, respond to the stress they are experiencing, may be more important to their overall morale, social functioning, and health than are the frequency and severity of the episodes of stress (Rutter, 1983). There are many definitions of coping (Hauser & Bowlds, 1993). Lazarus and Folkman (1984), who have influenced a good deal of the thinking in this area, defined coping as a *process* of managing the demands of a situation that has been assessed as stressful. Managing may not be the best word. Coping implies actively grappling with the event and trying to do something about it. Each action sets into motion a process of adaptation that extends over time, one effort leading to another. Coping involves how people manage, master, tolerate, reduce, and minimize the internal and environmental demands and conflicts. It also involves people developing new interpretations of what is happening so that a new story begins to evolve out of their experience (M. White & Epston, 1990). Hauser and Bowlds (1993) emphasized the importance of the *process,* rather than individual acts. People respond with a set of responses, not an enduring trait or style, and the focus is on the process of managing stress, rather than on mastery. Coping with the death of someone close to us may be an ongoing process that continues in different ways for the remainder of our lives.

Grief behavior (crying and sadness) can be understood as coping efforts, that is, giving voice to the emotions stimulated by the loss. Planning the funeral is another part of the coping process. How people cope at each point in the process helps create the scenario that will follow. At every point in the bereavement process, mourners are acting and reacting, trying out new ways of responding and of giving some order to the world and then revisiting and remaking a new order. The bereaved use a range of coping strategies, some familiar to them, others that they are constantly discovering. They try out solutions and find new ones, some adaptive and some, for the moment, maladaptive.

We need to consider the consequences of different coping strategies. It is important to look at what is happening to people, but also at the effectiveness of what they *do* with it: Does it solve or resolve a particular problem, does it help redefine the situation to make it possible to do something about it, or simply create new unsolvable problems? People who seem to cope more effectively have confidence in their ability, in the short or long run, to continue to find ways of redefining the situation, mitigating the stress, and making things better as they move on to the next issue. Antonovsky (1979, 1987) called this ability "a sense of coherence." This sense of coherence affects how people assess the stress and examine it. It is tied to the family's openness, to their ability to define and redefine the problem and not be defined by it. Aspects of these qualities are described in Chapter 4. This ability is also related to the family members' cognitive and emotional development, referred to earlier and discussed more fully in Chapters 3 and 4.

Effective coping involves giving this stress expression and voice and seeing it as acceptable and expected. It is not always profound actions that make a difference. For example, a 15-year-old reported what his father said to him and his teenage siblings after his mother's death:

> Each of us has to take on a job, washing dishes, taking out garbage, doing laundry, shopping, and cooking. If we all pitch in, we will manage. Dad did the shopping, my sisters helped with cooking and laundry, and I did all the little chores that no one else wanted—like taking out garbage and folding laundry, and we did get through that awful first year.

His father's inclusion of the children helped this child to feel less stress despite the changes they had to make.

Coping that does not seem to remediate or relieve the situation may result from needs that tax and exceed available resources or that tax the individual's or the family's ability to learn. Thus, ineffective coping can be another source of stress. It may be impossible to tease these two concepts—stress and coping—completely apart. It is difficult to imagine a stressful situation in which the participants do not do something in response to what is happening. We are always coping; even being frozen in the moment is a reaction.

Baker and Sedney (1996) noted that children have different ways of coping than do adults. Young children are more likely to distract themselves, cling to familiar activities or routines for comfort, deny the loss for periods, and use fantasy to cope. Yet the use of distraction, familiar routines, and even denial or fantasy also come into play from time to time in all of us.

Roles associated with gender have a clear influence on coping styles. Cook (1988), in describing bereaved fathers, stated that men use distraction as a coping mechanism more than do women. Studies have found that, beginning in childhood, boys seem to develop a way of coping and adapting that leads them to take pride in their ability to "stand alone," whereas girls seem more committed to maintaining their relationships with others. Piaget (1954) first observed this difference when he watched young girls and boys at play. The boys would easily argue with each other about the rules until they came to an agreement, but the girls would stop playing, rather than jeopardize their relationships with each other (see also, Gilligan, 1993). Wertlieb, Weigel, and Feldstein (1987) also found gender differences in the preadolescents they studied. The boys seemed to focus more on their own responses, seeing the solutions in themselves, whereas the girls turned to others for information and support. The boys were already incorporating the societal expectations of greater self-sufficiency into their behavior. The girls seemed to be more aware of their need for others and the importance of relationships for their well-being.

Hauser and Bowlds (1993), building on the work of Lazarus and Folkman (1984), identified two main modalities of coping strategies in adolescents. The first consists of problem-solving strategies, such as reframing the problems, that are directed primarily at addressing the issues in the environment or in the individual that pose a threat. This modality is similar to what M. White and Epston (1990) called externalizing the problem. Externalizing involves stepping back from the troubling situation to examine it and its meaning. The second strategy is to regulate emotions, especially the distress that comes as a result of the threat. Hauser and Bowlds suggested that denial and distraction are good examples of behaviors that can help young people achieve a sense of balance, even for the moment. Wertlieb and his colleagues (1987) identified similar coping styles in children aged 7–10. They described how children of this age can direct their coping behavior at something in themselves or in the environment, whether they are trying to manage an external problem or one relating to their own feelings.

Stroebe and Schut (1999) reframed these coping modalities that involve regulation of feelings and managing external forces to reflect the experience of people who are dealing with death. Although they describe coping behavior in adults, these behaviors can apply to children as well. Two types of behavior are identified: loss-oriented behavior and restoration-oriented behavior. Loss-oriented behavior helps mourners face their grief and the sense of loss that follows a death. It focuses on the nature and closeness of the mourners' attachment to the deceased, and their ways of keeping this attachment alive. Restorative behavior involves dealing with the new reality, the need to change, and the need to find new roles and identities. Stroebe and Schut (1999) proposed that as the bereaved cope, they alternate between these modalities. This is probably true of most people, especially children.

Most people, whether they are adults or children, use more than one way of coping. These ways of coping may include information gathering, allowing oneself to be supported by others, taking direct action, retreating or cognitively trying to control one's feelings, and finding ways of constructing a relationship to the deceased. People use different responses at different moments in time, in response to different aspects of what they are experiencing. They need to integrate and move between problem-solving strategies and strategies for dealing with their feelings so that it is not an either-or situation. These behaviors are responses not only to what they are experiencing internally, but to the external factors that result from the social context in which they are involved.

Transition

The concept of transition provides a way of mapping the stress that the bereaved experience and the coping strategies they use to deal with the stress over time (Bowlby, 1961; Silverman, 1966). When does the time of transition begin? We can say it begins with the death. As you shall see in later chapters, when a death is anticipated, there may be a brief rehearsal for what life may be like afterward. In reality, however, we cannot really deal with the death until it happens. This is especially true for younger children, whose sense of time is anchored in the here and now.

The transition takes place on several levels. As mourners, young and old, discover that they need to find a new way of living in the world, they realize that they may have to shift the way they relate to themselves and others. In addition, since the bereaved's relationship to the deceased does not end, mourners develop a continuing bond, keeping the deceased in their lives in a variety of ways. Thus, the work of this transition period requires that individual mourners and grieving families develop resources and capacities for dealing with changes in their feelings, in the ways they live in the world, and in their relationship to the deceased. The transition does not have an ending date because the bereaved will continue to renegotiate the meaning of the loss for the rest of their lives. In this process, they develop new perspectives on their feelings and experiences and find a place for loss in their lives, which leads them to live differently in the world. In the following sections, each part of the transition is examined in more detail.

A New Sense of Self. A period of transition (or transformation, as Parkes (1996) called it) always involves a turning point for those involved, a change in status, a shift in roles, and a new sense of self to live in a changed world (Silverman, 1966, 1986, 1988). The changes with which the mourners must deal may call into question the way they relate to themselves as well as others. The bereaved have lost not only the persons they mourn, but the relationship to these persons and their sense of self in that relationship (Silverman, 1981). They find new direction, new ways of living in the world, a new sense of who they are. While a changing sense of self is normally a part of every child's life, for bereaved children this process is sometimes accelerated. The identity shift can be developmental, as is described in Chapter 3. It is important to recognize that the loss will have different meanings for each member of the family and that these differences will affect their interactions with others, as well as the family dynamics that were contingent on the presence of the deceased. Roles assigned in the family may shift, and new roles may evolve as the family members realize that the self that interacted with the deceased is lost, that, for example, they are no longer parents or siblings to that child. Family issues related to these shifts are discussed in more detail in Chapter 4.

Rutter (1983) wrote that although stress can be seen as leading to a deficit situation, it can lead to a positive outcome as well. If you view stress not so much as what happens to you, but as what you do about it, then you can also look at stress as opening the possibility of growth. Bereaved children often talk about feeling older than their peers, about not being as concerned with what dress to wear to a prom or worrying about whether they will be accepted for the soccer team. One of the stresses they experience at this time is the lack of understanding by their peers that something has changed in them. They begin to value the more intimate aspects of relationships and take themselves and their lives more seriously (Silverman, 1988).

Connecting to the Deceased. In Chapter 1, I noted that letting go of the deceased was often recommended as the preferred way to resolve grief in order to be able to invest in new relationships. In fact, this is a paradoxical situation. We cannot live in the past, and we cannot live as before, as if the deceased are still part of our lives. However, as we listen to the bereaved, we realize that although death takes away the possibility of a living relationship with the deceased, both children and adults seem to find a way of constructing a connection that is both comforting and sustaining (Klass, 1988; Klass et al., 1996; Normand, Silverman, & Nickman, 1996; Pincus, 1974; S. S. Rubin, 1992; Silverman & Silverman, 1979; Silverman & Worden, 1992). Attig (1996) said that mourning is what we do within ourselves to transform our relationship to the deceased. Although the process involves much more than this, this transformation is an important aspect. Transformation is different from detachment.

Rubin (1996) suggested that there are really two intertwined parts to mourning. The first part deals with our psychological responses, how we function in our world, and the changes the death brings. The second part deals with changes in our relationships to ourselves, to others, and, most important, to the deceased. Ongoing links with the deceased are normative parts of the process of adaptation and accommodation. In children, this connection and construction may have an impact on their identity formation; in adults, it affects identity transformation (Conant, 1996; Silverman & Nickman, 1996).

Constructing a relationship to the deceased is part of an interactive process with the other mourners, both in the family and in the larger community (Silverman & Klass, 1996). The support and shared memories of others help give the construction shape and direction (Nickman, Silverman, & Normand, 1998). One father described how the extended family and community played an integral role in this process after his son was murdered:

> Every Christmas we go to a shelter where we give presents to the children in our son's memory. Instead of shopping with the list he collected from all the relatives, we have a list from the shelter children. We feel close to him, and we talk about him with these children. Everyone tells their favorite story. He was quite a character, and keeping his memory alive this way is very important to us.

Silverman and Nickman (1996) identified the elements from which children construct a relationship to the deceased. The children identified a place where the deceased could be found, such as in heaven; they experienced the deceased in dreams and as watching over them; they sensed the presence of the deceased; they reached out to the deceased by visiting the grave and initiating conversations; they thought about the deceased; and they kept things that belonged to the deceased. In fact, both parents and children use these same ways of staying connected. To some extent, these ways form patterns from which the relationship is constructed. Although these patterns change over time, there is never a time in which there is no relationship to the deceased.

Normand (1994) identified four clusters that reflect ways children construct a relationship to their deceased parents: seeing the parents as visiting ghosts, holding on to memories from the past, maintaining an interactive relationship, and seeing themselves as their parents' living legacy. I think that although children move from one pattern to another over a period of several years, these clusters are not exclusive. At any one time, children may exhibit behaviors that fit more than one cluster. Experiencing the deceased as a visiting ghost generally occurs within the first months after the death. In Normand's sample, the ghost's presence was frightening, unpredictable, and out of the children's control. The children saw themselves as passive and felt that this connection was largely at the ghost's discretion. This feeling may also have been influenced by the children's relationships with their parents when the parents were alive. As is discussed in Chapter 6, other children experienced the ghost as friendly and welcomed the visits. In preserving memories of the deceased, the children maintained a connection based on reminiscences of the past when their parents were alive. Those who maintained an interactive relationship to the deceased actively reached out to their parents' spirits. Becoming a living legacy can include aspects of the other clusters. The children showed signs of internalizing aspects of the deceased's values, goals, personality, or behaviors. Doing so helped them remain connected to their parents' legacy. Thus they saw themselves as immortalizing their parents.

CHANGE OVER TIME

People respond to any loss over time, for it is with time that they mobilize and use their inner resources and the resources in the world around them. Therefore, it is important for both adults and children to appreciate that this stress will not go away in a short time. Duration is irrelevant if we see grief as a process of negotiation and renegotiation over the life cycle. Grieving is an ongoing process. Children clearly negotiate and renegotiate the meaning of the loss. As they mature, their understanding and perspective on what was lost changes. For example, retrospective studies of people who lost their parents in their early years have pointed out that the deaths continue to be an issue throughout their lives, not as unresolved grief, but as part of the way "things are" (Edelman, 1994; Harris, 1995; Silverman, 1988). The grief is no longer intense and all-consuming, but it is still there. Children have a longer life ahead of them, so they carry the meaning of this experience with them for a longer time than do adults.

Since change occurs over time, it can be divided into phases during which people do the "work" of the transition. The concept of tasks associated with grief has received a good deal of attention and is often talked about as the work of grief. Worden (1991) described four tasks, similar to those described by Furman (1974) and Lindemann (1944), that are widely accepted not only as things the bereaved need to do, but as a way of understanding grief. However, tasks do not stand by themselves; they are things that people need to do to get from one place to another. They are relevant only when they are anchored in time and place in a process. Attig (1996) questioned whether the term *task* is really appropriate. He noted that the dictionary defines a task as circumscribable, modest in scale, and completable. Thus, the very word is inappropriate, since it implies something that is well defined and that can be finished.

For example, one of the tasks frequently listed is accepting the fact of the death. When a mourner is initially numb and in shock, it may be inappropriate for him or her to deal with accepting the reality of the death. Immediately after her husband's death, a widow must get through the funeral; notify people of the death; understand the family's finances; deal with work, social security, pensions, and health and life insurance; explain the death to the children and deal with their issues; and just get through each day. The children may be busy learning about funerals, appropriate behavior, mourning, and what to do with these strong and strange feelings. They know at one level that the death occurred. Is this acceptance? Or does acceptance come later when they experience the new reality in a more intense and clearer fashion? The concept of acceptance of the fact of the death is implicit in all these actions and feelings, but it is revisited again and again in new ways. We cannot therefore ask, When is the task completed? Accepting the fact that someone has died is something that is done repeatedly during a lifetime, as you shall see in later chapters.

It may perhaps be best to abandon the word *task* and talk instead about *issues* and *processes*. These words better reflect the negotiation and renegotiation we do all our lives as we deal with what is happening to us and what has happened to us. People are constantly in motion, and it is therefore impossible to delineate when one activity ends and another begins. It may be more helpful to divide the process into periods that reflect differences in how people experience the loss as they move in time away from the actual death. They are also dealing with different issues at different times. While these phases or stages of transition help articulate the process of grief, the line is not straight or clear. We move back and forth and can simultaneously be in more than one place at a time. Usually, we follow a helixlike movement toward a place where life is good again and we can look ahead with some excitement. Yet even then, a part of us will remain connected to the deceased and will be sad that this person is not with us.

We are using words to define a process that is a living phenomenon. These words simply help to highlight some of our experiences along the way. When, where, and if we find ourselves in any of these places is part of each individual narrative. In the next sections, I look more closely at each of these phases, which are further illustrated by the stories in later chapters.

Initial Responses

The initial period after a death brings with it numbness, disbelief, and a sense of moving on automatic pilot—in short, a clouding or veiling of the mind that allows the bereaved to get through the rituals of burial and the early period of mourning. It is almost as if the body has a way of protecting mourners from the full impact of the death, which may overwhelm them. Sadness, crying, despair, and feeling forlorn seem to come in bits and pieces. Outsiders are often not aware that mourners are not doing well. As a result of their numbness and almost reflexive behavior, the mourners are able to maintain control and not put too many demands on those around them. In hindsight, most people report that they were not really in charge at this point. They were "on automatic pilot."

In time the numbness becomes more permeable. For parents this process may be hastened by the need to care for children who are also grieving. As the numbness lifts it is often accompanied by a sense of being afloat—of losing direction. Slowly the mourners let themselves acknowledge that their typical ways of coping, of making meaning, no longer work in the same way. Whether they are parents, children, widows, siblings, or friends they gradually face a growing awareness of the impossibility of life continuing as before. The stress associated with this growing awareness may be expressed in a sense of disorientation, tension, and anxiety.

How do they define and understand what they are experiencing? Their sense of order in the world is challenged. Even when their faith system provides an understanding of the place of death in life and they believe that the deceased have gone to a better place, this faith may not suffice to comfort them at this time. In the long run, this faith may help, but they must also continue to live their lives on a day-to-day basis without the deceased in a way that requires new skills and new ways of organizing their lives.

Baker and Sedney (1996) noted that in this early phase, children need to make the experience of the death real and to be told the story of what happened. Children need to understand, in specific and concrete terms, not only what happens to people when they die, but how, where, and when the death occurred. They need to feel protected and safe. They can really confront the depth of their feelings only when they are supported and know that life will continue. This will not all happen in this initial period.

Children, regardless of their age, whose parents died report a feeling of numbness and a sense of disbelief. Looking back to how he felt when he received the news of his father's death two years before, a 10-year-old recalled:

> It hurt much more then, than now. I was in shock. I wasn't sure what to do. My mother said it was okay to cry and I sure did a lot of that.

Some children, as we shall see in subsequent chapters, went to friends, neighbors, or other relatives so as not to have to deal with the news. Parents sometimes misunderstood this move, thinking that the children weren't upset (Silverman & Englander, 1975). They did not always recognize their children's need to find something that was constant and familiar given that their world had just fallen apart.

Children, as illustrated in Part 2 of this book, also talk of protecting their parents by trying to be helpful. They hope that this behavior will provide a bit more stability in the environment and not burden their parents more than is necessary (Silverman, Weiner, & El Ad, 1995). Bereaved siblings have similar feelings (Hause, 1989). Some children also describe how they kept their feelings in so as not to upset their parents (Silverman & Silverman, 1979; Silverman et al., 1995). In this early period, both children and adults move away from and come close to what has happened as they let the pain in bit by bit (Fry, 1995; Silverman & Silverman, 1979).

Facing the New Reality

The period sometimes called "recoil" refers to a time when the numbing lifts, sometimes in a dramatic way, as if a spring had snapped. It now seems possible for the new reality to come into the full consciousness of the bereaved. These feelings may have emerged from time to time earlier, but were pushed aside. People find their own ways of visiting the fullness of the loss. For some there is a dramatic confrontation that brings it to the foreground; for example, they may forget and set an extra place at the table or buy a toy that would have been suitable for their deceased child. The bereaved are struggling with many forces that are pulling on them. They are pulled by the unfamiliar and painful feelings they are experiencing, the empty space in their lives, and by their growing awareness of the need to change. This may be the period when people feel the most depressed, as if they have hit bottom.

It becomes clear during this period that life is going to be different from the way it was before. Since the profundity of the changes is rarely talked about as part of the bereavement process, mourners are not prepared to deal with the new reality. They may feel totally inadequate and be sure that they are going crazy because six months to one year later, people are asking why they are not over the loss already. Most of their friends and relatives will have returned to their own lives, and the bereaved may feel very alone. Neither those who offer them support nor the mourners themselves are aware that the process has only just begun. In addition, bereaved parents have to consider not only their own needs for continuing support, comfort, and new information, but, at a time when they themselves are the most fragile, the needs of their remaining children.

Baker and Sedney (1996) suggested that if children have received appropriate support to this point, they can now visit the emotional pain associated with the loss, achieve some acceptance of the loss, and reevaluate their relationship to the deceased. Children's experiences parallel those of the adults in the children's world: Dealing with the reality of the death and facing its finality can occur only when the family and the individuals are ready—when they are present enough for each other that it becomes safe and when they recognize that their pain is only a small part of the bereavement process. To suggest, as was noted earlier, that these are tasks that are completed is a disservice to the bereaved. Issues change and are changed as the accomplishment of attending to one issue becomes part of the ongoing life of the family from which other issues and activities follow. Even as their parents become more available to them and they put together the story and all the details of the death, the impact of the death for children will take on different meaning, as described in Chapter 3, as they grow and change over their lifetimes (Silverman, 1987).

One of the most difficult things that all mourners need to do is to bear the pain—the strong, upsetting, and strange feelings that they are experiencing. For bereaved children, the strangeness may be even more stressful. Learning to cope with these feelings will take time, education, and the ability of those around them to acknowledge their feelings. As was noted earlier, these feelings are similar to what adults experience when their earlier numbness no longer serves them well. One of the dilemmas parents face is how to synchronize the needs and responses of the various family members, who may depend on each other to have their needs met while being at different points in the process. Because the process is reactive and interactive, how a child moves or reacts always depends on the interface between the child and other mourners, including other children. The reactions of adults may set the stage for the children's sense of reassurance or vulnerability. In Chapter 4, some of these family issues are described.

Accommodation

Over time, people make accommodations to the death. This is not an end to grieving but a time when people have a sense of their ability to prevail, to deal with the pain, and to find new ways of living in the world. It is a continuing process.

Most people seem to reach a point at which grief no longer runs them; rather, they run it. Although they still feel some of the pain associated with the loss, it is no longer the driving force in their lives. There is always a place in their hearts and minds that still feels the pain of the loss and is connected to the deceased. This is not an atrophied spot, but a place where a relationship with the deceased is constructed, nourished, and sustained, changing with time. Faith and religion often provide meaning and comfort that may have eluded the mourners earlier (Cook & Wimberly, 1983; Kushner, 1989).

The identity shift described earlier is consolidated at this time. The detours become part of what is now "normal" for people, influencing how they move on with their lives. For bereaved children who are entering puberty, for example, bereavement and adolescence become intertwined. The road these children would have followed through adolescence is changed permanently. Baker and Sedney (1996) noted that it may be difficult to determine when grieving ends and normal development resumes. In fact, their adolescence will never become what it might have been before the death. It is now colored and informed by their grief. We cannot divide their behavior to ask what is a result of adolescence and what is the result of the death. In the words of a teenager whose mother died several years before:

> I feel older than my classmates. I have lived through something they do not understand yet. I am different, and it is okay.

For children, accommodation brings them to a new developmental place. The bereavement may change or enhance the developmental trajectory in ways that we are just beginning to understand. In the words of one young woman:

> My life is different because my father died, not necessarily good or bad.

As part of the identity shift, the bereaved can look in on themselves in different ways and relate to others from different places. They find voices they did not have before and are involved in relationships that give them a different sense of mutuality and exchange. A new self has evolved (Silverman, 1988). They can recognize that this is an ongoing process that has altered the fabric of their lives in many ways in the present and will continue to do so in the future.

As one widow said:

> My friends find it hard to believe how I have changed since my husband died. I expect different things from people. I say things I never said before. I decide what is best for the family. If I was going to survive, that's what I had to do.

And a bereaved mother noted:

> I have a different sense of strength and a clearer idea of where I want to go in my life. We all seem to be in a different place.

My 11-year-old grandson, reflecting on the death of his dog, wrote:

> What happened after Teepee died would bring me a new, fuller, bigger perspective on life—one that would take a long time to accept, that death is part of life. Eventually this new view was totally incorporated, but in the early stages of this turning point, it wildly tumulted my young mind.

Attig (1996) looked at this process and asked: How do we relearn the world? Relearning or learning is very much a part of the bereavement process (Silverman, 1969). People need to learn that making an accommodation is an active process that is directed at what can be seen as a new beginning. A good deal of learning may be necessary to live in a manner appropriate to the mourners' new situation.

In summary, mourners deal with their extreme feelings, see a shift in their sense of self, construct a relationship with the deceased, and deal with a changed social context. These processes have to be seen in an interactive, ongoing context, each influencing the other and thus changing what the mourners are dealing with as they go along. We no longer talk about an end to mourning; rather, we talk about an ongoing process of living that is evolving and changing. People of all ages do not "recover"; they adapt, they accommodate, they change.

CHAPTER THREE

Grieving and Psychological Development

> After our 10-year-old died, our 4-year-old son kept asking if God
> would take care of his brother, and our 15-year-old daughter kept
> asking if there is a God how could he let this happen to her brother.
> She kept yelling at her brother to stop asking such stupid questions.
> We had no easy answers.

How do we make sense out of the different expectations of these children
and their different responses to the death of someone close to them? These
differences are, in large part, related to where children are developmentally
in their life cycle. Their responses and the accommodations they make depend on how they appraise, understand, and make meaning of what is happening. Children's developmental stages not only influence how they understand death, but what they experience as lost—that is, how they
understand the relationship that they lost and the coping mechanisms that
are available to them.

Meaning making is an active process, but not always a conscious one.
No matter how young they are, children struggle to make sense out of what
is happening (Rogoff, 1994). Parents need to understand that children's reality may have a logic, consistency, and integrity of its own. The meaning
that children make may seem strange to adults, if we do not consider that
it reflects their age, stage of development, and experience in life. For example, my 6-year-old granddaughter cried while talking about the funeral of
her dog. Without a pause, she then said that she had found a frog. She could
not explain the connection and talked about how the frog was green and
was jumping around and that she could hold it in her hand for just a minute.
At first, this statement seemed like a non sequitur. As I thought about it, I
realized she may have been trying to explain that life is ongoing. In spite of
her great sadness, here was life that she could relate to and that she was excited about. A year later she could stay with her sadness a bit longer and
tell me how much she still missed her dog. An 8-year-old, whose mother
was sure that he did not know that his father was dying, told the inter-
viewer:

> I knew my father had cancer. I am not blind. He was so thin and tired all the
> time. He kept getting sicker. Just like someone I saw on TV.

Television and his own growing ability to generalize from one situation to another helped him make meaning out of what he saw.

The goal of helping children of all ages to cope with death is to promote their competence, facilitate their ability to cope, and recognize that children are active participants in their lives. Their ways of reacting are not static; they both stimulate and respond to what is happening around them. Piaget (1954) observed that children are initiators of activity from the time they are born. They change and evolve as they mature and develop, especially in terms of how they see themselves. Their growing sense of self is intimately related to their growing ability to reflect on their own behavior and the role of others in their lives. As their sense of self emerges and changes, it leads to different ways of organizing and making sense of their experiences at different points in the life cycle.

MEANING MAKING AS A DEVELOPMENTAL PROCESS

Life in Motion

The process of change over the life cycle can be viewed from a developmental perspective. It is beyond the scope of this book to provide a full review of what is known about both adult and child development. However, it is impossible to understand how people, especially children, cope with death without examining some aspects of this developmental process.

What do we mean by development? *Development,* as it is used in this book, is an evolutionary process, an unfolding not only of the physical child, but of the child emotionally and cognitively. In contrast, the term *maturation* is associated with physical growth from infancy on. Scarr (1982, pp. 852–835) thought of development as being

> genetically guided but variable and probabilistic because of influential events in the life of every person that can be neither predicted nor explained by general laws.

Scarr was describing a complex phenomenon, suggesting that in some ways each person has his or her own developmental trajectory. This view of development was supported by other research (Lerner, 1989), which demonstrated that the content and order of stages of development in any given child's life are be altered by the child's experiences and the context in which the child lives. These factors lead to the child's individuality.

As Bruner (1989) noted, development is not something that people do by themselves. The interaction of genetic dispositions and experience and of the individual with significant others and with the culture all contribute to how a person experiences and understands what is happening to him or her.

Is development always a growth process? Some say that in every developmental experience, there may be a gain-loss relationship (Rutter, 1983). At a simple level, when children learn that death applies to them as well as to others, they begin to lose a naive, sheltered sense of self and their faith in their parents' ability to protect them from all adversity. Some say that dealing with small losses like leaving home to go to school prepares children for larger losses from death and other separations. It may be more accurate to recognize that the importance of meaning making lies in the interaction between the child's developmental stage, the events in which the child is a participant, and the behavior of those around him or her, as exemplified later in this chapter.

Development implies movement. People are always in motion for one reason or another. Yet they do not grow physically, emotionally, intellectually, spiritually, and socially in an even manner or necessarily always follow the same patterns. The social context and the significant others in their lives influence the direction and nature of this movement. Fowler (1996) found that children's faith systems evolve and change just as do other aspects of their relationships. While developmental motion is often divided into stages or phases, Kegan (1982) reminded us that individuals are not their stages of development. If we want to understand a given child, we need to capture the direction of his or her movement, the meaning the child is making of this movement at this time, and the nature of the interaction between the child and his or her world.

Piaget (1954), whose research influenced most subsequent research in this century about children's lives (Basch, 1983), recognized that children are both observers and actors in their environment. He saw the human mind as acting upon its environment to *compose* it, find it, make meaning of it, and give it order. Children do not see and order the world in the same way as do adults, but their order makes sense to them. The meaning they make results from the interaction between how they learn, what they are learning, what and how they feel, and the interaction with their teachers. According to Piaget, there is an ongoing conversation between individuals and their world. The back and forth movement between the inner self and the world in which this self interacts leads to a process of adaptation that can go several ways. For learning to occur, there has to be a fit between the child's ability to grasp what is going on and the adults' ability to explain it in a language that is understandable to the child.

Piaget (1954) identified a series of learning stages, each based on its own organizing principles: sensorimotor (infant), preoperational (preschool), operational (school age), and formal operational (adolescence). These stages reflect the changing perspectives from which children view the world and know others. Children's command of language and how they integrate what they have learned into behavior and judgment are also essential components of the differentiation of children's behavior from one age or stage to another. Young children who feel sad or frustrated may cry, be demanding, and be unable to see the situation beyond its immediate impact on them. Adolescents may feel the same sadness and frustration, but they can give words to their feelings and see the context that stimulated their feelings. Their impulse control may not appear to be much better than that of young children if they lash out in a disorganized, demanding manner. Yet, unlike younger children, older children may be able to see what they are doing and recognize their own part in it.

As children mature, their capacity to be aware of the environment that exists beyond their immediate view increases. At each stage, children's understanding reflects the ability to observe not just the external properties of the world itself or their experience with it, but also the properties of their mind that help them compose order and make sense of their experience. With this ability to compose order comes a growing self-awareness or consciousness. All this leads to children's greater ability to visit their own experiences, that is, to look inward and reflect on what is happening to them. M. White and Epston (1990) described this phenomenon as the ability to be both the performer and the audience to their own performance. Infants, children, adolescents, and adults have different abilities to understand and to look in on what is happening. As some see it, they may literally live in different worlds (Basch, 1983).

Kegan (1994) suggested that the stages or phases that have been identified are merely moments of dynamic stability. Following Piaget's lead, he saw development as a move toward greater complexity and coherence in the way children structure relationships between themselves and others. R. W. White (1959) wrote that the concern of children is not, as Freud suggested, to tame their impulses but to learn to interact with the world in more and more complex ways. This movement is not hierarchical or even sequential in nature; it is a spiraling process (Kegan, 1982). The process moves in the direction of the child's increasing ability to grasp the complexity in his or her immediate world and in the world beyond. Gilligan (1993) considered developmental progression an interplay of "voices," creating a central theme that is then woven into the cycle of life. Children, adolescents, and adults develop a richer perspective on themselves and others that allows them to move toward greater mutuality and become more capable of negotiating and renegotiating their relationships.

Sometimes a new experience is assimilated into what Kegan (1982) called the old "grammar," leading to one kind of accommodation. However, when it is impossible to assimilate the new experience into the old, then the accommodation leads to a new "grammar," or what Piaget called a "new schema." This inner "conversation" is marked by periods of stability and periods of dynamic instability. The time after a death is clearly a time of marked instability. The processes of assimilation and accommodation are essential to this movement and in many ways constitute the process of development as well as the process of grief. In assimilation, the child perceives information and fits it with an already existing schema; the information is matched to and made to fit an already explored and familiar category of thought or action. In accommodation, the child encounters new information that does not fit any existing category of thought; thus, an existing way of thinking about an issue must be modified to create a new schema. Learning may result from trial and error, imitation, or the guidance of a teacher.

The need for a new schema may be stimulated by the acquisition of a new skill, such as learning to walk or achieving sphincter control, or by external events like a death in the family. In any accommodation, aspects of the past are always present and still apply (Marris, 1974; Silverman, 1982). There is rarely a distinction between the past and the present; we do not start fresh with each new schema. Social context influences the goals and direction of development. Children are encouraged to behave in one way or another to meet the social expectations of those around them. In this context, the experiences of boys and girls may be different because of the different definitions of gender-appropriate behavior. For example, Brown and Gilligan (1992) observed that adolescent girls often appear to move backwards in some aspects of development. They can be inhibited or redirected by the "glass ceiling" that society places over their behavior as they begin to learn to be what Debold, Tolamn, and Brown (1996) referred to as "good" women: compliant and passive.

Development in children moves at a pace that is obvious to the observer and seems closely aligned with physiological processes and changes in the body. However, it is not a phenomenon reserved only for children. Hetherington and Baltes (1988) suggested that development is a lifelong process. Although not always so apparent in physical terms, it is a process that extends from birth to death. Therefore, it is important to look at the motion in adults' lives as well. Parents' ability to reflect on their own behavior and to understand the behavior of others, especially that of their children, makes a huge difference in how they cope with a death, their subsequent grief, and the way they parent. These qualities are associated with an individual's sense of self and how that self is constructed. This, too, is a process in motion.

Emerging Sense of Self

There are many definitions of the concept of self. Basch (1983) described the self as the uniqueness that separates the experiences of an individual from those of all others, at the same time conferring a sense of cohesion and continuity on the disparate experiences of that individual throughout his or her life. The self is the ability to process and connect experiences, to direct behavior, to know who one is and what one is doing.

Our sense of self changes as a result of how we differentiate ourselves from others and how we include others in our lives, connected to a changing capacity as children mature. When death occurs, the self that was formed by and in the relationship to the deceased is lost. Mead (1930) said that we can only know ourselves as we know others. For Sullivan, development of the self is the result of relationships with "others," rather than a study of the self-contained person (Youniss & Smallor, 1985). Piaget (quoted in Youniss, 1980, p. 4) wrote:

> There are no . . . such things as isolated individuals. There are only relations. There is no self outside relations because the self can only know itself in reference to other selves. From the start, meaning is social rather than private.

Clinchy (1996) reminded us that the self is not something finished that one carts about from one relationship to the next. Selves-in-process are always being coconstructed and reconstructed in the context of relationships and a changing capacity to know others. Both the lost relationship and the self as reflected in that relationship are mourned when someone dies. For example, a year after her husband died, one mother said:

> I am John's mother, but I feel like I don't know who I am anymore now that Jim is dead. If I am not his wife, then who am I?

Her very sense of self was embedded in this relationship. She continued to know herself as a mother, but she lost the self she knew in her relationship with her husband.

In talking about a relationship, I am focusing not simply on the bonding or attachment between a parent and a child that occurs in infancy, but on the interaction between the parents and the child. Bowlby's (1980) theory of attachment emphasizes the importance of an early bond with the primary caretaker of a child. In this book, I look at attachment in the context of relationships that involve exchange and mutuality, as referred to by Sullivan (1972) or Piaget (1954) and elaborated on by Kegan (1982) and others.

Kegan's work provides a way of understanding how children see the role of others in their lives, how relationships change, and how the varying nature of these exchanges affects their growing sense of self and the quality of their relationships. This view of a growing sense of self can help us understand what a child experiences as lost when a death occurs in the family. Kegan (1982) observed that children initially do not have the ability to differentiate themselves from others. Preschool children generally cannot reflect on their behavior. They have only a limited ability to look in on their own behavior, to reflect on their feelings and thoughts, and to understand others as people in their own right. The roles of others in children's lives change as they move forward in this evolving process. Over time, children develop an increasing ability to know that others have a point of view separate from their own and, finally, that these two points of view can coexist. By the time children reach late adolescence, they can hold two points of view at the same time, and their relationships with themselves and others change completely.

This perspective challenges the emphasis in some theories on individuation and separation. For Sullivan (1972) and Piaget (1954), the goal is not to achieve the ability to stand alone, but to be able to focus on relationships. Selman and Schultz (1990) defined the capacity for autonomy as the ability to understand, coordinate, and negotiate one's needs with the needs of another person. This view recognizes the importance of relationships in children's growth, not separation. Autonomy is not defined as independence from others. Rather, it is the ability to recognize the need for others and to participate in interdependent relationships that reflect newfound abilities to understand others as well as oneself.

Using this conceptualization, we can ask what a particular death or loss means to any given child, that is, how are children's relational worlds disrupted? What is it that children experience *as lost?* What they experience relates to their ability to know another person, and this ability affects how they perceive their relationship to the deceased. Thus, the ways both children and adults experience and make meaning out of the death and cope with it over time are related to where they are developmentally.

As children mature, the ways in which they experience and construct the persons they lost change, as does their relationship to themselves. Hence, over time, they mourn a different loss and have a different capacity to do so. For example, a 4-year-old girl who loses an older sibling may feel the loss of a playmate, of someone who did things with her that her parents would not do. She may even feel a bit of pleasure that she no longer has to share her parents' attention. By the time she is an adolescent, she will experience the loss anew. She will then understand that she lost someone with whom to share her life story: a companion, a buddy, and a role model. She may also appreciate how much her sibling lost by dying so young. The child's ability to hold an image of the deceased will also change as the child changes. Dealing with death is not a static process. There is a constant interaction and change over time as the mourners deal with this experience, as they mature, and as this developmental process itself is affected by the death.

CHILDREN'S UNDERSTANDING OF DEATH IN A DEVELOPMENTAL CONTEXT

Studies of children and death have focused primarily on children's ability to understand the nature of death. Researchers have looked at how children understand the finality and universality of death and how this understanding changes as they change developmentally. Most of this research has been with nonbereaved children and needs to be understood in this context. Nagy's (1948) study of children in Hungary found that they did not understand that death is final until they are at least of school age. Subsequent research used similar questions to assess when children develop a mature view of death. A mature view of death was defined as involving an understanding of the universality, irreversibility, nonfunctionality, and causality of death (Wass, 1984; Speece, 1984; Speece & Brent, 1996). Universality refers to the understanding that all living things must eventually die and the recognition that death is inevitable, inclusive, and unpredictable. Irreversibility refers to the fact that a dead person cannot return to life. Nonfunctionality refers to the fact that all life functions end at death. Causality refers to the understanding of why people die. It implies more than that the person had cancer or was in an accident; rather, it encompasses the understanding that we all die, that is, with life, comes death. These concepts clearly interact with each other in an almost circular way.

In his review of the literature, Orbach (1988) found that by the time they are seven, most children today have a fairly mature understanding of the concept of death. Speece and Brent (1996) made the same observation. By the time they enter first grade, most children understand the finality of death and are beginning to see that even they may die. Causality seems to give them the most difficulty. By the time they are in their early teens, children are able to recognize in an abstract way that death results from both internal and external processes and is an inevitable outcome of the fact that we are alive.

Children's understanding of death is presented in an orderly manner, as if children move in a linear way from one level of understanding to another. These stages of understanding of death have been associated primarily with children's ages but they also have to be understood in the context of children's life experiences. Thus, in real life, a child's view of death may not move in a simple straight trajectory that follows a clear line of logic. Thoughts about death, in both children and adults, are never clear-cut or rational. Often we see traces of early thinking about death even in adults. Many of us expect the deceased to appear many months or even years after the death has occurred. The silence from the grave may be one of the most difficult facts for any of us to accept. Belief in magical thinking does not end with childhood, although most of us are unwilling to admit this (Silverman & Silverman, 1979). For example, a man told me that his brother died when he was 14 years old. Each night, when he was asked to lock the door before going to bed, he thought that he was locking his brother out and worried where his brother would sleep. He understood that this was in his mind, but these feelings persisted nonetheless. He did not tell anyone about these worries for years. He was sure they would think him crazy, since it was clear to him that it was not generally accepted, in his family or among his peers, that the needs of the deceased should be considered as if the deceased were still alive. He admitted it only when he found that other adults had similar experiences of thinking about the dead as still alive, or still having the same needs as the living. These adults felt as if they were still thinking magically, and observing these thoughts in themselves was embarrassing.

Bereaved Children's Understanding of Death

Children's experiences influence their understanding and construction of death. The understanding of death does not break down into clear and distinct age-specific categories in bereaved children. This understanding is not simply a cognitive exercise in what they think about death (Bluebond-Langner, 1996). Rather, children are dealing with the impact of death at the personal, social, and emotional levels; thus their cognitive understanding of death may not be consistent with their level of maturity and may be different from the understanding of children who have not experienced death. For example, children of any age who lose their parents are more likely to attribute living qualities to the deceased's spirits than are nonbereaved children (Silverman & Worden, 1993). Bereaved teenagers describe the spirits in heaven as being able to move, see, and hear. They also recognize that this is a response to their own need to believe that their deceased parents are still involved in their lives (Silverman & Nickman, 1996). They have the ability to distinguish between the body and the spirit or the soul as would be expected of children their age. Their understanding of death is, in many ways, quite mature, yet they display qualities that are usually associated with younger children. Whether children have what is considered a mature cognitive understanding of death is not sufficient to explain their reactions when faced with a real death.

Earlier I noted that when a death occurs, we lose not only the person who died, but a relationship and the sense of self that existed in that relationship. This is true, regardless of our age, and applies to the death of a child, parent, sibling, friend, grandparent, or other significant member of our social network. To understand any one person's grief, we need to acknowledge and legitimate all aspects of what was lost, recognizing that the experience of a lost relationship or lost self varies according to the mourner's developmental place. Taking the perspective thus far proposed, we can begin to look at how children of various ages experience the loss of someone close to them. Although the discussion in the following sections is divided into age groups, these age groups should not be understood as clearly delineated states of being, but as parts of an ongoing process.

Toddlerhood. Children aged 18 months to 3 years are in the preoperational stage, according to Piaget (1954), and the impulsive phase, according to Kegan's (1982) categories. At this point, their impulses propel their behavior in an almost reflexive, automatic fashion. Toddlers have language and mobility and a secure sense that people and things continue to exist outside their view. They are concrete; they cannot think abstractly, logically, or in an orderly fashion. Their sense of what they want guides the limited order they see in their world and is their primary tool for meaning making. Toddlers develop their own view of the world, giving both animate and inanimate objects speech and motivation that can include a story line that outsiders may not comprehend. They think that people can read their minds and that wishing for something will make it so. They go from one particular event to the next with no sense of connection between them. They cannot yet look in on their own behavior to reflect on what they are doing and to see its consequences. They act impulsively or reflexively.

Although children at this age are beginning to be able to hold a physical representation in their mind of another person, they cannot yet hold such an image of themselves. They certainly have no ability to be empathetic to the needs of others. Their attention span for any activity involving accommodations to others is short, although they can be responsive to requests from important others to get their approval. For example, a 2-year-old refused his mother's request to make his cousin, whose mother was ill in the hospital, welcome by sharing his toys with her. He could not consider this other child's perspective or feelings or see the connection between her feeling welcome and his behavior. When she touched something, he grabbed it back stating "mine." When his mother simply said that she would like him to let his guest play with his toys, he gladly acquiesced. This was a request he could understand. His mother's immediate approval was enough motivation for him to share.

Toddlers have little real understanding of how death differs from going away. The line between themselves and others is still hazy, and their sense of self still depends on the presence of or feedback from others to feel safe and whole. Pattison (1977) stated that young preschoolers need concrete persons to love them and maintain their sense of well-being. Children who lose a parent at this young age lose someone who holds them together; directs them in the world; gives them treats; buys them nice things; and meets their needs for nourishment, approval, and gratification. Since their inner core has no way of holding itself together without the parent, they need a surrogate to fill in as quickly as possible. Because they see the world as revolving around themselves and have a sense of their own omnipotence, they often assume that death, their own or that of someone near them, is a result of something they did: "I had a fight with my sister last night and then she died"; "God is punishing me by making me so sick because I went outside when my mother told me not to."

Death as such does not have any meaning to a young child. However, although young children may have no words for death, they understand when something is lost and can show their concern and distress in nonverbal ways—in dreams; body language; and agitated, searching behaviors (Bowlby, 1961). Children often use language and play to visit and revisit the deceased. This kind of interaction helps them locate the deceased (in heaven or in a grave) and find a way of recognizing that the dead person is not coming back. For example, a 2-year-old, told that his mother had died in an accident and was not coming back, only gradually began to realize that she was not there. He continued to ask for her for months afterward; the way he looked at her picture gave the impression that he appreciated that something was missing and that it was unclear to him where she was. He also needed to hear from his father that his mother's sudden disappearance had nothing to do with anything he did, so that his sense of self was not jeopardized and he continued to feel well cared for in a secure environment. At some point, he stopped asking for his mother, apparently accommodating himself to her absence and accepting the new caretaking arrangements as normal and appropriate.

Preschool–Kindergarten Age. From about age 3 to age 6, children are still in Piaget's (1954) preoperational stage and in Kegan's (1982) impulsive phase. At this age, children have more patience and begin to recognize and acknowledge their own behavior, impulses, and perceptions. They are not yet able to see fully that they can control these feelings and impulses. They cannot distinguish their own perceptions of an object from the actual properties of the object or construct a logical relationship between cause and effect. Although preschool–kindergarten children can recognize that people exist separate from themselves, they cannot yet recognize that other people have their own independent purposes, take another person's point of view, or understand that this view could be distinct from their own (Kegan, 1982). They can build an imaginary world around real objects without seeing any contradiction. Children in this age group do not have any inner conflicts about what is real or not or whether their perceptions are correct or not. They do not try to rationalize two contradictory thoughts. For example, a boy may understand that most crickets are happier living in a tree but insist that "my cricket really is telling me he wants to live in this jar and stay with me in my house." He may know that he has a brother, but he cannot step outside of himself to take his brother's perspective and realize that his brother has a brother, and it is *him* (personal communication with R. Kegan, Harvard Graduate School of Education, 1990). At this age, children can hold only one feeling at a time. They may experience different emotions sequentially, but have no sense of how they are related. They begin to distinguish between inner feelings and stimulation from the outside.

By about age 4, children have a limited and unclear understanding of the word *death*. Although they are capable of expressing the idea that death is related to sorrow and sadness, the word *death* does not arouse an emotional reaction per se. Death as a concept is unclear. Children at this age, who still believe in the magical power of their own thinking, may believe that death was caused by their bad behavior or something they said or did not say. They may think that the dead can come back to life and that the dead cannot get out of their graves because the gravestones are holding them down.

Children in this age group are much clearer about who died and about the sense of loss in their lives. They still have little sense of the world as an orderly place without their parent, but are not quite as fragile as younger children. They can accept the concept that the dead are living with God, but are usually quite literal about it. In a world where children are taught that the dead go to heaven, younger children think of the dead as literally going to heaven. For example, a 4-year-old asked: "Can Jody [his sister] have a peanut butter and jelly sandwich for lunch when she gets hungry in heaven?" God is understood as a parent surrogate who will take care of them or the deceased, as the case may be (Fowler, 1996).

Younger children are more likely to think that death is something that will not touch them and that is avoidable. Whether it is they who are dying or a parent or sibling who died, the focus is on the need to be cared for, not to be left alone. Older preschool children focus on death as separation (Pattison, 1977). They still depend on others to care for them, frame their world, and provide feedback about who they are. They are therefore aware of the danger of being alone and being uncared for. If they are dying, their greatest concern may be for someone to be with them, to keep them company.

A moving example of how 4-year-olds and younger children try to make sense out of what they are seeing occurred at a young mother's funeral (Campbell & Silverman, 1996). The children had said good-bye to their mother at home immediately after she died. The youngest, aged 18 months, seemed to understand at some level and had said "Bye-bye—mommy all gone." Yet at the funeral, the children repeatedly ran up to the coffin and kissed her, looking back as they ran away. Each time they did so, they seemed very disappointed. It finally became clear that they were trying to see if, like Snow White, their mother would wake up with a kiss. After an adult tried to explain that their mother's death was not the same as what had happened to Snow White, they were forlorn and retreated quietly as they tried to understand this new information.

This is also an example of how the interaction between children and the environment can change the developmental process. These children began to deal with the fact that their magical thinking was not working because the adults around them responded to them in a manner and language appropriate to their stage of development. Vigotsky (1978) described such behavior as a "zone of proximal development." He observed that adults can lead children toward the next phase of development by providing new information and a new perspective in a language the children can understand. This concept is essential when we use the developmental context to try to help children and adolescents understand what is happening after a death.

To gain a better understanding of how children progress through these stages, we can return to the 2-year-old mentioned earlier, who is now 4 years old. We see that he now has a sense of what is missing in his life. He can identify his mother's picture, but is aware that he does not have a mother in the same way that other children do. He needs to know that she loved him and would be pleased that he is being taken care of. He wants to know where she is now and if she can see him. Consistent with his family's philosophy, he places her in heaven. He wants to visit her grave. Since his father has remarried, he begins to understand that he has two mothers, one who is with him now and one who is dead. Most important is the fact that he feels cared for. He feels no deprivation and takes this new reality for granted as part of the way things are.

Elementary School Age. As children move on in the continuum of development, they make a transition to the next period, in which concrete operational thinking, as Piaget (1954) called it, dominates. Kegan (1982) labeled this period imperial—a term that acknowledges that at this age, children can recognize their own needs and then organize their relationships and their world to meet these needs. This stage is a period of rapid changes, so that a first grader and a fifth grader are in different places on this continuum. First graders are just beginning to see the world differently, whereas by the

fifth grade, they are quite comfortable in who they have become. Relationships with peers and teachers are important. The children are learning to
read and have additional resources to help them learn about their world.
They have begun to think symbolically and can maintain inner mental rep-
resentations of objects and people, differentiating between what is internal
and external to themselves and thus identifying enduring qualities in their
behavior. In addition, they can use language to control their behavior and
are beginning to organize and classify things and people in their environment.

However, elementary school-age children do not yet have a sense of
themselves that comes from being able to reflect on their inner motivation,
attributes, individual biography, or ability to control their feelings. It may
be difficult for them to hold more than one feeling at a time. They can reflect on what they feel and begin to see connections between these feelings.
They articulate these attributes and feelings in concrete terms that describe
themselves: "nice with brown hair"; "I have lots of friends"; "I like this friend
[and] she likes to play dolls like I do"; and "I was sad, but now I'm happy."
They become more self-contained, developing a private world that they can
keep to themselves. They can also recognize that others have a distinct point
of view.

A child of this age sees no contradiction in expressing the good things
she sees as a result of her sister's death: "I am sad my sister died; now my
parents are home more to take me places." While adults may have difficulty
with her feeling that she has benefited from the death, this is not a problem
for her.

Elementary school-age children can distinguish between their point of
view and that of others. However, they cannot step outside themselves to
hold both views at the same time and consider reconciling them. For example, a second grader may comment: "I'm not friends with John anymore;
he didn't want to play ball when I did." Learning to cooperate comes over
time during this period, as the children participate in making deals to have
their needs met and, in turn, to meet those of their peers. To some extent,
they live in the moment. Peer recognition and acceptance are essential. By
the time they are in the fifth or sixth grade, they do not want to stand out
as different, which could happen if a parent or sibling dies. For example, an
11-year-old said that at all costs she would not talk about her father's death
at school. It was most important to her that she be seen like everyone else.

The idea that there is a connection between events—that one event can
cause another—is now part of the children's repertoire, so they can reason
sequentially and understand cause-and-effect relationships. However, thinking abstractly to make generalizations and to form hypotheses may be just
beyond their reach.

At this stage, the understanding of death becomes more specific, factual,
and precise; children's reactions appear to be more matter-of-fact than emotional. There is a noticeable increase in their concern about the possible death
of relatives. The children become curious about the causes of death, such as

murder, illness, old age, and accidents, and become interested in death rituals, funerals, and burials. For example, an 8-year-old boy was present when his grandmother died at home. After he was told what to expect at her funeral, he took out a tape measure to see what size coffin she would need.

Elementary school-age children may be able to describe concretely how someone stopped breathing and could not move. A 6-year-old explained to her class that her cat had died. She shared with them all the details she had observed about the death and the funeral. She was matter-of-fact about how sad she was and, in her own matter-of-fact way, was sure that this was an event to share. If others around them are not anxious and uncomfortable, children at this age have less fear of death, and their reaction to it is appropriately emotional following what they see around them. Often the death of a grandparent or other close relative of that generation may stir children to consider their own vulnerability. They may say, with some amazement: "Then I can die, too." Toward the end of this period, as they move into adolescence, they are aware of the inevitability of their own death, although it may seem to be a distant possibility.

At this age, children can accept the inevitability of death and rituals related to it and show a deeper understanding of the biological processes of death and its finality. A 10-year-old was clear that his dog should be buried after the dog was run over by a car. He carefully dug a grave and afterward made a headstone. He felt that in this way he was accompanying the dog as far as he could on the dog's journey to heaven.

When a parent dies, a child of this age loses someone who acted in the service of his or her needs: Who will play ball with me? Who will help me with my homework? Who will get me to school in the morning? For that self to remain intact, the child needs to believe that the world can continue in the face of this death. A sense of continuity becomes critical. Since these children have an expanding vocabulary, they may seem more grown up than they are. In fact, they may not be able to say what is really going on inside them and do not yet know that when a critical death occurs, the world, indeed, does go on. They may show their stress in behavior that can be out of control. They do not have a sense of the future; rather, they live in the present, and sometimes see death as an inconvenience (Pattison, 1977). They may not know how to ask for reassurance. In some ways, this is a difficult age for parents to "read"; they are not sure how to make sense of their children's ways of thinking.

Some of the dilemmas of this age are exemplified in the experience of 8-year-old Billy, whose father had died four months earlier. Billy's mother described how Billy refused to go to school one day and could not tell his mother why. A month later, while talking to his mother about his deceased father, he said that he hated his friend, who had told him that if his father had died, he would be crying all the time and asked why Billy was not crying. Billy could not take his friend's perspective to ask what he meant or how he came to this conclusion. He felt hurt, criticized, and betrayed by his friend, but did not connect his reluctance to go to school with his friend's comments. He could not explain himself to his mother or his teacher until he poured out his story during this later conversation about his father. Even then, he did not see the connection until his mother put it together for him and tried to help him see that his friend was just trying to understand what it was like. While Billy had a sense of the world operating in an orderly fashion outside himself, he expected that his friends would see things as he did. Yet his friend expected that Billy would behave as he imagined he might. For this 8-year-old, his friend's misunderstanding meant that he was losing his connection, his continuity with a world in which his friend was a stable component. He was also losing someone whose feedback he could count on. He was confused by his friend's expectation that he should be constantly crying. With the help of his mother's explanation, he was able to resume his friendship.

Again, we can revisit the 2-year-old whose mother died. At age 8, his life is full with new friends and what he is learning in school. He may now ask more questions about what his mother looked like and what she liked to do. He may want to visit her grave and know more about the details of her death. He begins to be curious about the person who gave birth to him, asking such questions as "Whose tummy did I grow in?" and if he is like her in any way. He begins to express more directly some of the sadness he feels that she died. He may also sense other people's sadness in talking about her and is ready to learn how to deal with these feelings. He knows too that his interest in his biological mother does not jeopardize his relationship with the mother who raised him.

Adolescence. Adolescence is clearly identified with obvious biological changes. These growing children must deal with maturing bodies that are subject to sudden bursts of growth and hormonal changes that affect their moods and the range of feelings they experience. Adolescence can be an uneven and choppy time, since there is not always a synchronicity among cognitive, emotional, and physical development. This is a period that spans many years as adolescents emerge from the egocentric view of the world associated with the concrete operational period in their lives. They are now entering what Piaget (1954) called the formal operational stage and Kegan (1982) labeled the interpersonal phase. They have a growing ability to act more independently, which makes it easier to shift the locus of their activity outside the family.

The greatest shift in the way they see themselves and others comes with their emerging ability to think abstractly, to look in on their own feelings and behavior, and to take another person's point of view. Not only can they now think hypothetically and deductively, but they can understand the perspectives of others at the same time that they consider their own views, wishes, and needs. They can now construct personal histories, looking back and ahead in their lives. With this ability to hold several views at once, they begin to see that relationships are reversible, circular, and reciprocal. Adolescents can appreciate differences and are learning to coordinate independent points of view—their own and their friends' and their own and their parents'. This ability will lead to a capacity for mutuality, empathy, and reciprocal obligations, a coconstruction of personal experiences that involves sharing their inner thoughts and feelings with others to develop a common sense of the world.

Adolescents can also see that they may have more than one point of view about something and that they can coordinate these views as well. They begin to recognize that the emotions they experience are coming both from within themselves, and from their interactions with others. Furthermore, they give up the concept of God that they held when they were younger—someone who is fair and literally rewards good behavior. Adolescents develop beliefs and values, with attachments to a God that is loving, caring, understanding, and provides support. The focus is more interactive (Fowler, 1996).

Adolescents begin to recognize their needs as something that they can observe and satisfy in a conscious fashion. They can be said to *have* their needs or *hold* their needs, in contrast to younger children who can be said to *be* their needs, which, in an almost reflexive way, guide their behavior. The change comes with the ability to step back and look in on what is motivating their behavior at any given time. Younger children see differences between themselves and others as a conflict between their needs and those of others. Adolescents, however, often express differences in terms of their own wishes to do one thing or another and how to reconcile these wishes with the wishes or expectations of others.

The self that develops at this stage is embedded in attempts to coordinate their various views with those of their friends or family members. The fear of rejection is no longer the result of worry about being misunderstood, as it was for 8-year-old Billy. Rather, adolescents fear that they will fail to reconcile their wishes and needs with those of others. Maintaining relationships and obtaining approval from peers are central to their sense of well-being. Adolescents can no longer experience themselves as separate from this interpersonal context. It is as if their sense of self exists in the in-between, that is, in the relationship between themselves and others, and thus they are not clear who they are outside these relationships. If these relationships end, they are likely to feel not only sad or wounded, but incomplete.

By adolescence, we begin to see clear differences in the way boys and girls frame their relationships to others. Boys' behavior reflects the movement toward self-reliance, autonomy, and independence. In contrast, girls seem to take a more connected stance. The language they use to describe their relationships involves taking other people's perspectives and acknowledging their dependence on each other for their sense of well-being (Lyons, 1990). This connection to peers is often seen as a way-station to finding a sense of self that moves beyond dependence and toward the independence and objectivity prized in our society (Erikson, 1950).

In the long run, both boys and girls need to learn that it is possible to care for themselves *and* to care for others, to maintain a relationship while resolving differences. Both sexes may be handicapped by societal pressures that push them in opposite directions. This does a great disservice to both sexes. In reality, connections to others remain essential for all people—children and adults, boys and girls—although the way people act on these connections may be different. For Kegan (1994), as for Selman and Schultz (1990), learning to negotiate between one's needs and those of others is the next stage of development for adolescents. Who they are and who they become are very much a result of their relationships and interactions with others. We must recognize this fact to understand the fullness of the loss when someone dies. Adolescents begin to ask theoretical and philosophical questions about what happens after death and become involved in discussions about those who have died. They do not believe literally that the dead go to heaven. They distinguish between the soul and the body. They are often preoccupied with questions about life after death, but sometimes are skeptical about its existence. Their interest in life after death is often speculative and philosophical. The death of someone close to them adds a real dimension to these explorations. For example, a 16-year-old reflected on his belief system shortly after his father's death:

> I know some people believe that there is nothing after death. I prefer to believe that there is a soul and that we go to heaven.

Adolescents can be clear that they, too, will die and seem stoic about this fact. At the same time, they seem to fear death. In the words of a high school senior:

> As I have gotten older my thinking about death and what I might lose became more real. I have had that fear since I first realized I could die. Now I know that what I fear most is that I will die young. Maybe I was influenced by my father's early death. I didn't think of that until recently. I want to live a long time. There is a lot to do. I see kids my age being reckless, driving drunk, not taking care, not looking at the fact that they could die from the way they were behaving. It doesn't always do much good to talk about it; they don't want to hear.

This is the age when children take chances, thinking that nothing will happen to them. In today's world, adolescents often have to cope with the death of friends from illness, accidents, homicide, and suicide. Their emerging understanding can be severely tested, although the capacity of some to ignore the implications of their behavior is remarkable.

Death in the family creates a vacuum in the lives of these young people. They can talk about their emptiness, their pain, and their hurt. They may have just begun to appreciate their parent as a person in her or his own right, who served as a role model and helped them develop new perspectives and new identities. They have lost someone to talk with, someone who they enjoyed being with. They can also recognize all that the deceased lost by dying so young. For example, a 17-year-old reported:

> My mother would be so proud of me; I wish she had lived to see me graduate. It gave her great pleasure to see me do well.

If a sibling dies, adolescents can recognize that they lost someone with whom they could construct a shared reality, a peer in their parents' world. The realization of the disruption the death can bring to their lives is clear to them. They can articulate their need for continuity. A 13-year-old said very clearly:

> I went outside to see if the sun was still shining. After my brother's death, I needed to be sure that the world was still there. I wondered how that was possible when something so awful happened.

She is aware at this point that her very sense of self has been challenged. Her world is no longer orderly and predictable, but she is able to consciously seek ways of ordering it and to find the continuity and stability she needs. She also told me what she had lost: a friend and a role model. Her older brother had been helping her reach out to new friends and mediating between her parents and herself to let her explore the world a bit more on her own. She recognizes that this situation is changing, since her mother is now becoming overprotective. She can understand her mother's behavior, although she is unhappy with the constraints it imposes on her.

This is an age when we see more clearly the consequences of the different ways that boys and girls are socialized (Gilligan, 1990). Boys begin to contain their feelings and are less likely to talk about them, feeling that "real boys don't cry" (Silverman, 1981; Silverman & Worden, 1992). Girls often become surrogate caregivers or their parents' allies. They are more aware of their feelings and their distress and often can say so explicitly. A death in the family can cause great changes in the ways adolescents interact with the world. The death of someone close may bring to the fore the importance of connection and care for everyone who is affected.

The boy who lost his mother at age 2, now 16, looked back at her death:

> The most important thing for me was that I always knew my father was there and that nothing changed on a day-to-day basis. It was the natural thing for my father to take care of us, and he did. I was sad, but I can't remember more than that . . . everything continued as before. What I liked was that he was always helping us remember my mother. We have pictures in the house, and we talk a lot about her. Now I realize what I lost. Don't misunderstand. My life has been good. I think I am like my mother in some ways. For sure I look like her. I don't know what my life would have been like if she had lived. I think it was harder for my sister. I can hear what she says now. She remembered my mother and talked a lot about what it was like before. When I was younger, I didn't understand what it meant to her.

Beyond Childhood

This view of development can also serve as a guide for looking at adult development. Many adults still have difficulty taking the point of view of others. They organize the world primarily to meet their needs or live on the other side of making deals. These observations reinforce the idea that relational development is not tied to age. Kegan's (1982) view of development takes us past adolescence. Kegan suggested that none of these stages can be clearly associated with age once people move into concrete operational functioning. He postulated the existence of at least two other stages: the institutional stage and the interindividual position. In the institutional stage, the capacity of individuals to think about how they will author their own identities and psychically administer their ideologies guides their behavior and how they organize their sense of self. With this new sense of self, they can develop what Kegan called interpersonal mutuality.

As was noted earlier, the studies of women have awakened us to areas of differences in development that may be connected to gender. Traditionally, men are seen as more task oriented and women as more likely to want to process feelings and maintain connections. Does this mean that Kegan's theory is designed to support a male view of autonomy and independence as the most desirable end of development? This possibility has always bothered me. I found that widowed women often develop a new sense of self that they boastfully see as more independent and self-reliant. In contrast, after the death of their wives, widowers seem to move to a position in which they value relationships more (Silverman, 1987). The widows did not suddenly become less relational, less involved in their relationships to others. Nor did the widowers become less independent. Kegan considered these later periods times for the development of individual consciousness. A new, empowered view of self evolves. People are no longer embedded in their relationships but can construct relationships from a position of personal authority. Although they can decide *for* themselves, they do not have to decide *by* themselves. We do not take leave of our connections; rather, we look at them and nourish them in different ways.

This dichotomization of human development, in terms of being relational or being independent, does not hold up under scrutiny. There seems to be a universal pull on us as humans. On one hand, we yearn to be included, to be part of, close to, joined with, to be held, admitted, and accompanied; on the other hand, we yearn to be independent, autonomous, to experience our distinctness (Kegan, 1994). This may be a struggle we have all our lives, from the time we first said no at age 2. However, all this is in the context of our relationships with those around us. Thus, when we consider the meaning of a loss and how we cope with it, we must understand the importance of relationships and what is lost with the death in both how we grow and who we become.

CHAPTER 4

Children in the Family Context

> Since my brother died, nothing is the same; my parents don't seem to
> talk to each other, we don't act as a family like we used to. I try to
> think about what I can do to bring people together. I have a good
> sense of humor, and sometimes I can get everyone to laugh and that
> feels good, even if it is only for a few minutes.

It is impossible to talk about children without looking at the family. Just as children's understanding of death is framed by the historical and social context in which they live and how they grow and develop, the way they cope is influenced by the family of which they are a part. In the family, children receive the nurturance and support, love and care without which they will not thrive. After a death, we often talk of the individual mourner. Shapiro (1994) reminded us that we should actually talk about mourners in the plural. She described grief as a family developmental crisis, interwoven with the family's history and its current developmental moment. The family members' grief radically redirects the future course of their life together. In the context of the larger society and the community in which they live, each family constructs for itself a coherent system that guides, explains, and accompanies its members as they deal with the vicissitudes of life. The ways in which children, of all ages, experience and respond to stressors reflect, in large part, what they have learned and experienced in their home environment. It is only in this family context that we can begin to understand how individual members cope with death.

How do we define a family? What does it look like? Who should be included? The family is more than a group of individuals living together. It is a social system composed of people who are joined together by a common history and future, usually united by bonds of blood, marriage, mutual consent, or adoption. The members believe that their relationships are sanctioned by moral, religious, legal, or social rights and obligations. The family provides us with ways of organizing our experiences. It frames the way we make meaning and define our place in the inner world of the family, as well as in the larger social networks with which we interact. It is in the family that children learn to deal with others, to form relationships, and to develop a sense of who they are.

In this book, I am concerned with families in which childbearing and child rearing are the primary activities around which families are organized. In this context, the family constitutes parents and their dependent children. The term *parents* does not necessarily mean a mother and a father, married to each other, raising children born to them. Child rearing may take place in single-parent families, families composed of same-sex parents, and multi-generational families in which the primary caregivers may be grandparents. In any of these constellations, children may join the family through adoption or birth. My primary concern here is with the patterned network of interaction that determines how the family does its work and how bereaved parents parent their grieving children.

CHILDHOOD AND CHILD-REARING PRACTICES IN A HISTORICAL PERSPECTIVE

Childhood and the very nature of the family can be viewed with a historical lens similar to that used to look at death. We can see that views of children and the role of parents in raising their children have changed radically over time—the values and beliefs about the definition of childhood, definitions of appropriate child-rearing practices, and the roles and contributions of children in the family and society (Youniss, 1994). The very essence of a family's responsibility and obligation to their children has changed. The function of the family has shifted from a unit of production, to which all members contributed, to a unit organized around child rearing, designed to provide emotional and social support to its members.

The concept of childhood as a separate period in the life cycle is a relatively recent phenomenon that has taken shape only in the past 100 years. At one time, children were thought to be "tabulae rasae," passive recipients or objects of the adults' and community's efforts to rear and educate them. Behavior was judged in terms of the morality of the dominant religion, not in terms of the child's developmental or emotional stage. Children were whipped at home and in school to make them behave or to drive the "devil" from them. Children were sent to work at a young age, and by the time they were 7 or 8 years old, they were considered small replicas of adults, with the responsibility to contribute economically to the family. They were raised with the expectation that they would follow in their family's footsteps and conform to the norms of the larger society.

In most parts of the world today, children's expectations for their future do not extend beyond the confines of their families and villages. There are still places where children are considered property that parents can and do dispose of at will. In contrast, in the United States, each generation expects their children will be better educated and have better lives than they did. Courts protect children from parental abuse, and children can no longer be treated as their parents' property (Krause, 1977). In recent years, the courts have increasingly taken a more active role in children's lives, resolving custody battles, acting in loco parentis, and determining what is in a child's "best interests." This becomes very important when a child is orphaned and there are questions about who will raise him or her.

During this century, the age at which childhood ends has been extended in the Western world; with the extension of education, children's dependence on and connection to their parents extends beyond adolescence. Stillion and McDowell (1996) included young adults up to age 24 in their definition of childhood. Bakan (1966) noted that the term *adolescence* came into usage to describe children who, because of compulsory education through high school, were still at home and in dependent roles. At one time, children in this age group would have been out in the workforce accepting the responsibility of adulthood and contributing to family support. Bakan described adolescents as marginal people in today's society, with no acceptable constructive outlets for their growing energies and abilities.

With the advent of modern psychology and psychiatry, which conducted systematic studies of human behavior, another dimension was introduced into our thinking about childhood. Freud's work changed the way we think about the responsibility of parents for what happens to their children. Parents were made aware that their early relationships with their children would largely influence the kind of adults the children would become. They were told that with appropriate guidance and education, children could control their own destinies, that is, all was not preordained. This was a marked shift from views in which behavior was considered to be the result of divine will or possession by the devil. This, together with other societal changes of this century, led to a shift in child-rearing goals.

The basic goal of socializing children to conform to society's norms did not change. However, the emphasis in the socialization process, that is, what was considered desirable and appropriate behavior for children and the roles of the parenting figures in this process, changed considerably (Hetherington & Parke, 1993). The role models for raising children provided by the grandparent generation were not necessarily applicable to current conditions. Emphasis shifted from conformity to self-expression to self-actualization. Over the past 50 years, with each addition to our understanding of what motivates and guides children, new approaches to child rearing and living with adolescents have been proposed, sometimes with the power and certainty of a legislative act. Parents and teachers have been bombarded with advice about how to raise and teach children to ensure their happiness and success in life. They often feel pressured that if something is "wrong" with their parenting or if their children undergo any kind of traumatic or difficult experience, then the children will become emotionally damaged. These attitudes and values have important implications for the bereaved family.

We can see the impact of these shifts in child rearing in the story one recent widow told me. Following her husband's death, she had little energy to attend all the programs the PTA sponsors on how to give children the best start in life. Her husband was supportive of trying to give their children a relaxed childhood. Now she is panicked because she is told that if she continues this practice and does not follow the guidance of the latest "expert," her children will suffer. Her daughter is already excluded from the softball team because she did not go to softball camp and participate in preparatory after-school programs. With her husband's support, they were able to withstand this pressure. Now she has to rethink her child-rearing practices and her ability to withstand the pressure alone.

As child-rearing practices shift and change, as parents rely more and more on the advice of experts, bereaved parents are less clear about how to parent their grieving children. We can trace some of the changes that have occurred in the last part of this century that have had a great impact on parenting practices. Elkind (1994) described a shift from the nuclear family, which was the dominant model before and after World War II, to what he called the permeable family. In the nuclear family, or family of procreation, the father worked to support his family while the mother stayed home to care for the children. The mother's role as homemaker was considered essential to the child's well-being. Elkind noted that there was an imbalance in these families because parents sacrificed their own interests and values to meet their children's needs. These families also had more clear-cut, sometimes rigid, boundaries between public and private space, home and work, children and adults, and the work of men and women. Children and adolescents were often overprotected and socialized to take on, as adults, the traditional roles of men and women, husband and wife.

The period of the nuclear family overlaps with the period of the Invisible Death described in Chapter 1. Children were sheltered from knowledge of death and from the dying. People died in hospitals and were buried from them, out of sight of the children. As part of their traditional role as the family protector, men took care of the public aspects of dealing with a death, such as arranging the funeral. It was not considered appropriate for them to talk about emotions or to show their true reactions to a death. These behaviors were reinforced by the view of grief as something that could be contained and recovered from. The more private consequences of the death were not legitimated or acknowledged, and it usually fell to women, who were at home, to deal with the emotional and social implications of these difficult issues. Women were involved in meeting the daily needs of family members, which could include being in the hospital with an ill child, since men were expected to continue to work. Over time, this division of roles led to a contradiction, in that later models of "healthy" grieving were closer to women's experience, focusing on feelings and the need to acknowledge and talk about them. As differences between the grieving styles of men and women were noted, men were criticized for the way they dealt with their grief. The coping techniques they used, such as distraction, keeping busy, and working things out by themselves, suited their traditional societal role (Cook, 1988). Yet these techniques were now seen as the antithesis of how one was supposed to grieve.

In the late 1960s, as the feminist movement emerged, women demanded relief from the constraints of the nuclear family. They raised questions about their role as full-time homemakers and caregivers and sought to have their role in the family recognized as legitimate work (Friedan, 1963; Martin, 1985). Research on women's experience put new value on women's ways of knowing and relating to the world (Belenky, Clinchy, Goldberger, & Tarule, 1996). Women moved into the workforce outside the home, and the balance shifted to what Elkind (1994) called the permeable family. In the permeable family, parents' needs were considered more. Hetherington and Parke (1993) observed that families are more parent-centered. Parents put greater emphasis on sharing the responsibilities of child rearing.

During this period, people saw themselves with many more options, including the choice of whether to even have children. Children were often in child care so that both parents could work. Two incomes were needed to support families as well. The number of single-parent families grew as divorce became an acceptable option for unsatisfying marriages and as single women increasingly felt comfortable having children on their own, either through adoption or birth. The education of children focused on developing their competences and skills from an early age. According to Hetherington and Parke (1993), more emphasis was placed on children being self-sufficient and autonomous. Teachers and the schools were assigned some responsibility for teaching children about such matters as sex, problem solving, and coping in personal relationships.

During this time, there was a sense that parents could create an idyllic world for their children. Childhood illnesses were less prevalent, and children were protected from an awareness of death, which was still a taboo subject. Although Kübler-Ross (1969) and the death-and-dying movement were beginning to gain momentum during this time, their approach was not applied to children.

In the past two decades, we have begun to hear about the loss of childhood. Elkind (1994) noted that as we expected more and more of our children, childhood began to shrink. Children were prematurely encouraged to be independent and self-sufficient. Elkind and Kegan (1994) both thought that what we expect of children is unrealistic, since it ignores children's ongoing, albeit changing, needs for care and involvement in the life cycle. Kegan wrote that we are deceived by aspects of adolescent behavior. We have rushed children through childhood with all types of enriching and "maturing" experiences. In part, adolescents can look and talk like adults, but in many ways we have not been consistent in what we expect of them. Somehow we are impatient or label parents as failures when their children do not live up to the expectation that they should be more grown up than they really are. Both Elkind and Kegan saw the lack of attention to the appropriate needs of children as a cause of many of the pathologies afflicting children and the society as a whole, including drug abuse, teenage suicide, and adolescent pregnancy. This lack of attention compounds the lack of preparation to deal with loss in a realistic way. When children are grieving, their grief is often not honored. There is little room, in today's world, for pain or an unhappy young person.

Seligman, Reivich, Jaycox, and Gillham (1995) noted that some of the difficulty in parenting in the late 20th century emanates from the focus on enhancing a child's self-esteem as an end in itself. Parents have been instructed to teach their children to feel good about themselves, rather than how to cope with problems and deal with difficult situations. Seligman et al. stated that it is not enough *not* to let our children be devastated by a mistake they make; children need to learn from their experiences, so they do not repeat their mistakes. These observations have important implications for defining parents' roles in helping children understand the place of death in their lives and how to cope after a death has occurred. These are occasions when children depend on their parents to teach them. Yet, parents cannot teach their children what they themselves do not know. The chaotic period after a death may not be the best time for either parents or children to begin to learn. This learning needs to begin when children first become aware that people die.

Typically we are concerned with how the family influences children's growth and the need for parents to recognize the individual characteristics of their offspring and understand the differences as they grow. The importance of parents in framing their children's behavior cannot be underestimated. However, it is critical that we recognize that growth is often a two-way process; children can also stimulate responses in the adults around them. Parents need to acknowledge that they are influenced by their children and that their children make contributions to the family (Bell & Harper, 1977; French, 1977).

Scarr and Ricciuti (1991) found that children's personal characteristics affect the responses the children elicit from others. Individuals in the same environment have different memories of the same event; for example, there can be a wide variation between the experience of different children in the same family (Boer & Dunn, 1992; Dunn & Plomin, 1990). As discussed earlier, children are not passive participants in life's drama but actively make meaning out of their experience. They do so in different ways at different times and phases of their childhood and in so doing, elicit different responses from their parents or caretakers. Parents' sensitivity to these differences can be important when dealing with death.

One way to look at these differences is to focus on parents' need to "read" their children. Children often do not have the skills and understanding to explain themselves and their view of the world to us. It is up to us to find ways to listen to them with an awareness of their developmental and cognitive understanding. The key listeners here are their parents. Often men and women parent and listen differently. When a death occurs, mothers seem to assume the caretaking role more easily, whereas fathers may be less able or have more to learn to respond to the changing emotional and relational needs of their children. As you will see in the stories presented later in this book, these differences can cause difficulties. The surviving parent or parents may have different capacities to understand the losses as their children or the other parent experience them.

ORGANIZING TO DO THE FAMILY'S WORK

The functions of a family evolve and change from the time of marriage to when children are born, as children grow to independence and leave home, and finally to the time when a couple reaches old age (Rhodes, 1981). Various crises or shifts in the couple's relationship need to be negotiated during each of these evolving periods. For example, when children are born, the parents must develop and implement an approach to child care. As the children grow and mature, the parents need to make new accommodations in the way they parent and respond to their children's changing needs. These parent-child relationships can extend over many years, depending on the number and years between their children. After children grow through childhood and adolescence, they eventually leave home and begin a new family cycle of their own. Parents also continue to mature and change over their lifetimes.

Shapiro (1994) described five dimensions of a family's movement over time: the movement of each individual, adult or child, through a unique life cycle; the interaction of these individual life cycles at this moment in the family's history; the developmental motion of this interacting family organization over the course of the family's life cycle; the interweaving of intergenerational family life cycles, as the young parent with his or her own children is simultaneously an offspring in a maturing family of origin; and the movement of the family through the course of historical time in its given sociocultural location. Shapiro's and Rhodes's (1981) conceptualizations complement each other. Any stage in the life cycle needs to be examined according to the five dimensions Shapiro identified, thus providing a way of looking at individual development in the family unit.

My primary concern here is with the patterned network of interaction that determines how the family does its work beyond the social and historical forces that I have already identified. Which aspects of this work are relevant to understanding how death is dealt with in the family? We need to attend to how the family system is organized, how various roles are assigned, how gender differences are reconciled, and how various members react and interact to provide a nourishing environment, not only for the children but for all family members.

Family Boundaries

The family's flexibility and openness to new ideas are important factors in how the members behave (Olson, McCubbin, Barnes, Larsen, & Wilson, 1989; Reiss, 1981). An open family has a greater ability to accept or invite the social support that can facilitate their accommodation to inevitable changes in the life cycle, such as coping with a death.

The notion of boundaries around the family is important. We need to know if these boundaries are open or closed. How easy is it to permeate the boundaries, that is, can family members or others come in and out with ease?

Are neighborhood children welcome to drop by, or is it always necessary to make an appointment? Does the family let others, from their church, for example, know their business or help them cope when someone has died in the family? This notion involves distance control. Control can go in either direction—to keep others out or to let them in. It can also be a measure of how affection and support, as well as anger, are expressed in the family (Kantor & Lehr, 1975). Do family members value their autonomy so much that they are essentially isolated from others around them? Can they acknowledge and share their dependence or interdependence on others in an atmosphere of mutuality?

Family Sense of Coherence

We need to ask if the family has a coherent image or a way of making meaning that reflects who its members are. Some theorists have called this shared meaning making the family narrative, that is, the story the family maintains about itself (Reiss, 1981). This narrative serves to guide the way family members care for each other and how the family functions in the world. It is no different from the meaning making discussed in earlier chapters, except that this is a group process.

Patterns of Communication

Communication patterns in the family—how and what information is exchanged and between whom—are essential to understand the family. Communication patterns affect how people make order in their lives. Do family members coordinate their needs and activities? Do they have a shared sense of meaning in their actions, feelings, and activities? This information is critical in understanding what transpires between grieving parents when a child dies. Do orders come down in a hierarchical manner, or do discussion and exchange take place? The concepts of control and power are key here. Women who are widowed may be uncomfortable assuming the authoritative role in the family. Power struggles may become evident as we recognize how much control is exercised by whom in the family, not only among the family members, but between them and the outside world (Kantor & Lehr, 1975). In a closed family system, people need order and predictability. They may not be able to tolerate chaos and have little flexibility when a death requires that they reorganize the way they function and maintain relationships with each other.

Grief, according to Shapiro (1994), disrupts family stability. The disruption is evident in the way feelings are expressed in the family and the way the family members interact with each other, how they fill their social roles, and how they make meaning together. Family roles and communication patterns may shift as mourners adjust to living without the deceased. We see identity crises in younger and older mourners. If a key member of the family is dying or has died, we deal not only with this loss and the end of a relationship, but with a shift in all the other relationships in the immediate social network.

The Family as a Problem-Solving Unit

As was previously noted, mourners deal with much more than their own inner feelings. Dealing with news of a serious illness or of a death is a gradual process as the family responds to different aspects of the loss and its meaning for each of the members individually and as a group. If a "breadwinner" dies, the family's economic situation changes because the family now becomes a single-parent household. If an only child dies, the parents lose the immediate demands of the role of parents; the way they organize their day changes and how they see themselves must change as well. With any death, as noted in previous chapters, there is a social as well as an emotional disruption.

Grief mobilizes a family's resources for managing intense emotions and reorganizing daily interactions (Shapiro, 1994). Even in the most stressful situations, there are people who prevail and others whose lives seem to be driven by the stress, whose actions do not seem to lead to effective problem solving.

A good deal of research has been and is being conducted to try to identify factors that would place bereaved children and adolescents at risk of developing emotional problems. This approach stems directly from the model of grieving that focuses on death as a cause of pathology. Yet a direct cause-and-effect relationship cannot be found. A serious illness or death in the family does not, by itself, lead to emotional problems in those affected by the events. Inevitably the research turns to the larger social context to explain the pathologies that do develop (Sandlar, Miller, Short, & Wolchik, 1989; Silverman & Worden, 1992, 1993).

We can hypothesize that children or adults whose coping styles are ineffective did not live in a social context that enhanced this process of growth. A dynamic developmental process leads to an individual's or a family's growing ability to change how they make meaning and how they respond. Reiss (1981) noted that each family is a problem-solving unit that shares a common meaning-making system with which its members approach problems. Like Antonovsky (1987), Reiss observed that for many people, this meaning making is associated with an inner sense of coherence. Antonovsky saw this sense of coherence as a critical resource in the individual and Reiss identified it as a resource in families. This meaning-making system provides the individual and the family with an orderly approach for stepping back from the situation, learning what it is, and then organizing and giving it meaning. This approach, in turn, helps the family members identify and utilize resources that can lead to adaptive coping strategies. In any particular family, it is this meaning-making system that will guide the family's behavior when the family faces unexpected changes, illness, and death.

When a parent dies, if the surviving parent can find a way to create an affirming meaning-making system, then the number of subsequent stressors for the children, such as difficulty in school, sleeplessness, and fear for the surviving parent's well-being, may be limited. If the surviving parent does not manage to recognize the ineffectiveness of trying the old methods and cannot see the need for new directions, then the family may indeed be in trouble. For example, a newly widowed mother of three described how her husband's sudden death led to initial chaos:

> At our age, we never thought that one of us might die. My husband talked about preparing wills, but I would hear none of this. I didn't want the children to go to their grandmother's funeral. They got together with their father and insisted. I was not comfortable with this. When my husband died, I just went along with whatever the children wanted to do. I was helpless. I keep worrying about how I can keep them in line. My son needs his father. He was a great role model and he did keep things in order. I don't know if I can do it. Sometimes I think we have to learn a whole new way of living together as a family.

In this example, the family's meaning-making system was totally disrupted by the father's death. The father was a key person in setting family agendas and in resolving crises. He was the family member who recognized that the children needed to be included in all aspects of the family drama and that death was a part of this drama. It is difficult for the mother to involve her children in problem solving and to see that her children are grieving as well. Her view of them reflects her own need for order by focusing on the children's need for discipline. This family had no language for discussing death. They had to move to a whole new problem-solving system and a new meaning-making system without the father to mediate the mother's fears and guide her in meeting the changing needs of the growing children.

Styles of Coping

Reiss (1981) conceptualized several styles of family coping. Some families brought premature closure to the task, drawing only on their inner resources. They functioned almost as a closed system. This was the initial tendency of the widow just described. Reiss also identified families who were more open in the way they coped. They looked for new ways of coping and gave every member a chance to make suggestions and to participate. More open families have a flexibility and openness in the way they respond; they can work together to solve problems. In this way they limit subsequent stressors and create a new family narrative. An affirming sense of coherence does not insulate the family and its members from the pain of the loss. Rather, it may support a family in accepting the pain and recognizing their distress as appropriate. It means that people have a sense of their own ability to learn about what is happening, a faith in their ability to prevail, and an openness to all available support and needed assistance.

When a child dies, there are two parents whose meaning-making systems need to be coordinated. It is not unusual for the parents not to be in the same place at the same time. In the words of one mother, three months after her oldest son died of cancer:

> My husband was ready to have a night out, and I thought that was a good idea. We got as far as the driveway before I changed my mind. At the door and looking at the babysitter, I would say, "Let's go!" We tried three times. I finally pushed myself because he needed to just go out to dinner with me. We had a 5-year-old who needed a lot of attention, and I still wasn't sure what the time of day was. We needed a lot of patience with each other. We sort of took turns being out of it. We were always good at pacing ourselves so we could continue to talk and be there for each other.

When their son died, the open coping style of this couple served them well. They could respect their differences and support each other as they tried to deal with the death.

Focusing on Children or Parents

Another way of describing this process is whether the parents are parent-centered or child-centered (Silverman et al., 1995). In a child-centered family, the parents are aware that the needs of their children are somewhat different from their own. They understand that children may express their grief in age-specific ways and that they (the parents) may need to learn more about these ways. Children are included as mourners in the family drama. These families have many of the attributes Reiss (1981) identified in open families.

In contrast, in parent-centered families, the parents relate to the new situation from their own point of view. From widowed parents, we hear about their fears and concerns about their ability to parent alone. We hear not what the children are feeling or doing, but what the children's behavior stimulates in their parents. These parents do not seem to have a grasp of the impact of the death on their children or that age makes a difference in how children react. In many ways, their lack of flexibility and efforts to maintain control make these families closest to what Reiss (1981) called the closed family. The key question is whether the family is able to change some of the organizing values and attitudes that sustain it to meet the new conditions it is facing and to write a new story. The way they do so will relate to the time and place in the family's history and to the larger social context in which the family's history is embedded.

Parents' personal construction of the world, that is, where they are developmentally, affects their parenting and how they deal with a death. It also influences family dynamics. The goal of any intervention to help the bereaved should be to help them move developmentally to a place where they can gain a fuller understanding of what is happening and thus be able to cope more effectively. Kegan's (1982) phases point to a meaningful direction for this growth. The work of Newberger and White (1989) and that of Belenky and her colleagues (1996) provides another dimension to this movement. All these researchers used a cognitive developmental approach and were influenced by the work of Piaget (1954) and Kohlberg (1984).

Newberger and White (1989) studied mothers' awareness of their children's behavior and sensitivity to their needs, identifying three perspectives that reflected mothers' behavior. Their focus helps us understand aspects of parenting that can be relevant in a bereaved family with children. Belenky et al. (1996) investigated how women learn and acquire knowledge. If learning is a critical aspect of the process of accommodation, then variations in how people acquire knowledge are important in helping families move in this direction. There is consistent overlapping in the findings from these different studies on how people make meaning, although researchers label their observations differently.

Newberger and White (1989) described mothers who understand their children as extensions of themselves and organize their role as parents with the assumption that they and their children have the same needs. This is called an egotistical orientation, in which children become extensions of their parents. Belenky and her colleagues (1996) talked about women who were at a similar developmental place, who were silent and almost without a voice. These women had no ability to look outside themselves and could not separate their needs from those of their children. Following Kegan's (1982) reasoning, these parents were behaving like school-age children in the imperial phase of development; they often looked to authority figures for guidance and instruction. In what Newberger and White called a conventional orientation, the mothers understood their children by drawing on tradition, culture, and models in their environment to provide them with definitions and explanations of their children's behavior. These mothers relied on socially defined notions of correct practice and responsibility to define their parental role.

Belenky et al. described women who were received knowers. These women saw the world in dualistic terms, that is, that there are good and bad, right and wrong, ways of doing things. They learned from others who legitimated their ideas and worried about what people wanted from them and thought of them. This position approximates teenage behavior in what Kegan called the interpersonal phase. The role of others was critical, in that it provided these mothers with recognition, approbation, and guidance in what they did. The women's sense of themselves as parents did not exist outside of this context. They did not yet have a sense of an inner authority that might guide them in understanding their children.

In the third construct, what Newberger and White (1989) called the subjective-individualistic orientation, these mothers easily understood that their children were unique individuals and organized their interaction with their children around meeting and identifying the children's needs, rather than fulfilling what other people defined as their obligations. These mothers could recognize the value of their own experience and could use it to build knowledge. Belenky and her colleagues (1996) found several steps in this process that described the direction in which these women were moving. Women find an inner authority that allows them to hear themselves think, in what is called procedural knowing. In this way of knowing, the voice of reason dominates. People learn to understand others' points of view, the value of stepping back and developing some objectivity. These women were moving in the direction of the institutional or interindividual phase, described by Kegan (1982). They were more likely to see their children in terms of the children's own needs; the interaction between them was characterized by exchange and mutuality, thus respecting both the parents' and the children's needs.

This view approximates women's development as described by Gilligan (1993). Gilligan observed that women need to learn that they can simultaneously take care of themselves and others, that there is no conflict in doing so, and that it is possible to hold two or more points of view at once and deal effectively with all of them. This way of thinking is reflected in what Clinchy (1996) called connected knowing. In this way of seeing the world and learning, people can connect their voices with those of others and accommodate to several points of view.

These conceptualizations can help us understand any given parent's ability to see his or her children as mourners and to provide the care they need. This developmental approach has important implications for helping bereaved people, as you shall see in Chapters 11 and 12. It provides a framework for understanding what kind of change is needed. Parents who have not yet reached a place where they can look in on their behavior and see their children's needs as separate and different from theirs will not be as responsive to the needs of their grieving children. In the face of a death and the changes that follow, parents have to learn to consider how their children are making meaning out of the world, whether it is an 8-year-old's inability to go to school or an adolescent's decision to use a ventilator or to stop treatment. Parents need to find a way to hear and include their children and to accept that they themselves may need to change to do so.

Adult mourners have the additional stress of being responsible for and responsive to their children when they (the parents) may be least able to react. Given that children are responsive to their parents as well as parents are responsive to them, this is always a complicated interaction. In considering how a family is responding and the interactions between its members, one needs to recognize the fit between the ways various family members respond. Developmentally, do the parents' and children's needs complement each other, or are they in conflict? Is there flexibility to move in a direction that is mutually empowering, thus facilitating their adaptation and accommodation? How we label this process is not important. What is important is that we keep in mind that this is a changing process and that just as any given individual is in motion, so, too, are families. The death and the accompanying struggle to deal with all it means may lead to marked changes in the way family members relate to each other and to the larger society. We should keep in mind that society also has to change.

CONCLUDING THOUGHTS TO PART 1

It is almost impossible to write a fixed scenario for how children will respond to a specific event, given all the variables that interact with that event in the course of living. When we move away from the focus on pathology or on clear cause-and-effect relationships, we can identify a certain openness and flexibility that benefits many children. Most people have a quality of resilience that can lead to adaptive behavior and to developmental leaps in the face of adversity. Scarr (1982, pp. 852–853) proposed that

> human beings are made neither of glass that breaks in the slightest ill wind nor of steel that stands defiantly in the face of devastating hurricanes. Rather, in this view, humans are made of new plastics—they bend with environmental pressures, resume their shapes when the pressures are relieved and are unlikely to be permanently misshapen by transient experiences. When bad environments improve, people's adaptations improve. Human beings are resilient and responsive to the advantages their environment provides. Even adults are capable of improved adaptations through learning, although any individual's improvement depends on that person's responsiveness to learning opportunities.

Although we may not be permanently misshapen by a death, our shapes may change from what they might have been without this experience. The death of someone close to a child will cause a dramatic shift in the child's life. The nature of the shift and the child's response to it will depend on the social context, family dynamics, and the relationship to the deceased, as well as the resources in the environment that make learning easier or harder. The new shape is not malformed—just different, going in an altered direction.

Paradoxically, during periods when we had less understanding of individual differences in children and paid less attention to children's developmental and psychological needs, children were also more aware of death as a part of life and had a more accepting view of life's exigencies. We need to learn how to take the best from both worlds: to help children relate to the rhythm of the human life cycle and to appreciate the qualities they bring to the relationship.

We cannot protect children from the pain or disruption of a loss—bereaved children will always experience the fullness of the loss. However, we can help them feel less overwhelmed. If children have been taught to deal with the other changes they have experienced, they will have the tools to deal with this one. Rutter (1983) pointed out that protecting children from experiencing major life events would leave them ill equipped to deal with life. Death is certainly one of these major life events. If we exclude children or protect them from death and bereavement, what we are really doing is not preparing them to deal with life. We are not teaching them anything. We are not helping them to grow and develop. Children who are seen as participants in the family drama and who are actively involved in it are much more equipped for living. Whether a stressful event leads to growth, temporary difficulty, or long-term trauma is not simply a function of the pervasiveness and persistence of the stresses. Rather, it reflects the personal and social resources available to the mourners and their ability to give meaning to the experience in a way that facilitates their utilization of these resources.

Children need attention and support so they can learn to cope and deal with the changes that a death will bring to their lives. They need to feel legitimated and have a place to turn to for sharing, support, and guidance. Even adolescents who are trying out more independent roles and may protest their parents' interest as intrusion, need the support and attention of their families. If they are part of a working family system that has the flexibility to grow and change, children and young people will learn how to respond effectively to the stress caused by a death and to cope competently as they go through the experience of being alive.

2
The Stories
People Tell

INTRODUCTION

*Tell me a story. A story of where we are and how we got here and the
characters and roles we play. Tell me a story, a story that will be my
story as well as the story of everyone and everything about me, a story
that brings us together in a . . . community.*

—Berry (1990), quoted in Kelly (1995)

In this section I tell the stories that children and parents have told me about their experiences when someone was dying and after a death occurred. I develop a narrative
describing how I see the process unfolding, exemplifying the process with extensive
quotes. These stories reflect how the bereaved created order and made meaning out
of what happened to them. Stories create pictures and make it possible for the reader
to share some of the experience in a way that no other written medium allows.

These stories describe how grief is experienced in Western society today. They
emphasize the ways in which people cope and prevail. The stories in these chapters
illustrate and validate the theories described in Part I. They describe how grief unfolds,
the nature of the changes families face, how mourners manage their stress over time,
and how they construct relationships with the deceased.

If you are bereaved, these stories may help you find common threads in the experience of others that can legitimate what you are feeling and expand your coping
repertoire. If you are helping the bereaved, these stories should help you be more sensitive and responsive to what the bereaved, who are our teachers, experience.

I begin with two chapters on what happens when a parent is dying and during
the period after the death in which the reactions of both the surviving parent and the
children in the family are described. The next three chapters deal with the death of a
child. I describe the experiences of parents whose child is dying and then discuss how
parents and siblings cope with the loss after the death. The final chapter in this section focuses on the death of a friend. Not every aspect of the bereavement process is
presented in the same depth in each chapter. To understand the fullness of the process,
all the chapters must be read. For example, how children are involved in the funeral
is described most fully in Chapter 5. This information can be applied regardless of the
type of loss.

In these stories, we hear of deaths from long illnesses, as well as sudden deaths
from accidents, murder, suicide, and acute illnesses. There are common elements in

each of these deaths, regardless of the cause. Everyone has to deal with how to tell the children the news of an illness or of a death. Everyone has to deal with a funeral. All are trying to cope with a sense of disarray and lack of control. All are trying to find new ways of living in a changed world, and all seek to maintain some sort of connection with the deceased. At the same time, each of these losses brings with it specific stressors related to who died and the manner of death.

In all the families, the mourners experienced people turning away from them, uncomfortable with the reality of death. Many mourners found themselves asking what they had done "wrong." In a sense, they felt stigmatized, their sense of self "spoiled." They were no longer the same people that they had been before the death (Goffman, 1963). When a family member dies of AIDS or commits suicide, the surviving family members may feel even more strongly that they have done something wrong in having a family member or friend die this way (Silverman, 1994). They are blamed, discredited, and often shunned, and they may feel the need to protect the reputation of the deceased. This is also true when murder is the cause of death; others assume that somehow the deceased invited his or her demise.

In the pain of each child and parent, there is a common language as they struggle together and separately to deal with the new reality that follows the death. All mourners, regardless of the nature of the death, individually and as members of a family and community, are adjusting to profound changes. They shift direction and write their stories anew many times. What follows, then, are not finished products but narratives in the making.

CHAPTER FIVE

The Death of a Parent

*Dealing with Bad News—My World Is
Turned Upside Down*

> How do you tell children their father died? When they went to sleep,
> everything was fine. I woke them up and told them Daddy didn't feel
> good. I asked a neighbor to stay with them, and I took my husband
> to the hospital. He was dead before I knew what happened.

Parents are supposed to die before their children, but they are not supposed
to die while their children are still at home, leaving them to grow up in a
single-parent family. For the most part, before the death, family life was affirming and the children lived in a caring, supportive environment. As one
widow put it:

> Before he got sick, we had a good life. He worked, he made a good living. I was
> home with the children and was beginning to think about doing something now
> that they were all in school. It is hard to believe that everything looked so com-
> fortable. We played, we laughed. We couldn't have anticipated the changes that
> were just around the corner for us.

For surviving parents, becoming single parents was not something they
chose. They must now deal with their own grief, the grief of their children,
and the need to parent in a totally transformed world. Children face their
own grief, feelings that they have never experienced before, and changes in
their world that they could not have anticipated. As I discussed in earlier
chapters, how the children cope will depend not only on their own efforts
but on those of their surviving parents. The grieving of children, parents,
siblings, and the community is intertwined. Although this chapter looks at
the death of a parent, much of what is described here is similar to what you
will see in later chapters, when a child, sibling, or friend dies.

The first thing that the surviving parents must do is take in the news of
the death. Simultaneously, the now-widowed parents must decide how to
tell the children and how to help them cope with what is happening. How
they do so depends, in part, on the degree of open communication that existed in the families prior to the death, on the amount of flexibility the families have in the face of this new reality, and on the parents' ability to understand and respond to their children's behavior. Family members will do
best if they are able to be open with each other, ask questions, and share
their pain and fears. The parents need to be aware that children's reactions

to this news will depend on their individual styles of behavior, their ages, and stages of development.

A SHARED RESPONSIBILITY: ANTICIPATING THE DEATH

When the death is anticipated, parents may have time to share what is happening with each other and make joint decisions about how to involve their children. Not every family is equally comfortable involving children and not every family can admit to itself what is happening. Often people wait until death is imminent before being open with their children. This is usually not the best choice. As was noted earlier, children can see and hear what is going on, and they often know without being told. Andrew, age 12, remembered:

> No one told me he was dying, but I could see; he was wicked skinny, and the day before, he couldn't get up, couldn't talk, or do anything he used to do.

Children need to know that what they see and how they make sense out of it is acknowledged by their parents. Ben's mother reflected on how he was involved in his father's illness from the beginning:

> Ben was 5 when his father had what we learned was a seizure due to a brain tumor. Ben saw him when he fell; he saw the blood from the wound on his face. There was no way we could tell him that this was simply an accident.

Several years after the death, Ben, then age 9, recalled:

> When my mother told me, I knew it was bad. I just knew when he fell it wasn't an accident. He was sick, but I didn't know what a brain tumor was or what it meant exactly to die. She told me she would tell me whatever she knew, and I wasn't as scared.

Ben learned from his parents' honesty that they would both be there for him as long as his father was alive. Because his parents involved him in what was happening, he had confidence that he was a respected member of the family. He also learned that while the coming times would not be easy, his mother would make sure that the family life continued. Although his world was in many ways falling apart, he felt that there were still pockets of safety.

In some situations, particularly AIDS, parents worry not only about how to tell their children, but how others in their community will react. Many children who are affected by AIDS are either infected or are orphaned when both parents die from the disease (Geballe, Gruendel, & Andiman, 1995). Their grief and the community's reaction are complicated by their own illness or by the fact that they are being cared for by relatives, grandparents, older siblings, or foster parents. It is not AIDS itself that causes their problems, but all the other issues that affect their lives.

Families in which no one else is infected do not seem to disintegrate under the impact of the illness.

Claudia's father was diagnosed with AIDS when she was 2 years old. Neither she nor her mother was infected. Her mother was concerned not only with her husband's diagnosis, but with the stigma associated with the disease:

> I didn't care for me. I had to be sure our neighbors were okay with Claudia. My husband was very protective of us. We were very careful who we told. He said, "Tell them I have cancer." Our families were wonderful; they knew the truth. But there were neighbors who might not understand. One neighbor did find out and wouldn't let her daughter play with Claudia. She was sure [Claudia] could transmit the disease. I also had to protect my husband's reputation. People who didn't know him . . . I was afraid to consider what they thought. Even now, four years later, it is still an issue if I tell people what he died of.

Most other parents do not have this worry that either they or their spouse will be seen as responsible for their own illness. Gone are the days when people thought cancer was contagious.

Often parents are not sure that the children understand what they are told. They may misinterpret the children's silence or continuing with familiar activities as an indication of the children's lack of understanding. One mother spoke very hesitantly with her children about how sick her husband was. She thought that they were not always hearing what was being said and therefore did not understand its meaning. The children told a different story. Jayne was 15 at the time. She remembered how her father was involved in the conversation as well:

> My father talked to me about the possibility of his not getting better when he first got sick. After the second operation, I figured it out for myself that he could die. I understood very well what they were saying. Neither my brother or I knew what to say, so we didn't talk much about it.

Jayne's 8-year-old brother Patrick cried as he recalled the conversation when he was told that his father was very sick and might not live:

> I understood. When my father was home from the hospital, I didn't know what to do. I just tried to stay close by him as much as I could.

News of any illness often leaves children without words and unsure of how to behave. They may feel the same way after the death. Their silence or discomfort does not mean that they are not concerned. They may simply be overwhelmed. Different children will find different ways of coping with the initial news. Staying close to a parent is one way of getting reassurance. Sometimes the children need their own space to deal with the situation. As 16-year-old Sandy said:

> I needed time to take in what was happening. My mother only made me more nervous. She looked so worried and frightened. I needed to be by myself for a while. I don't think my mother understood [my need to be alone]. I couldn't explain it to her.

We cannot underestimate the burden on parents to be patient and supportive, at a time when they are themselves in such a fragile state. Children seem to understand this burden and adjust their behavior accordingly. Taking on a helping role, even if it is not assigned to them, can help make the situation a bit more stable for them. This is not always a burden for the children. One mother saw how helpful it was to her 18-year-old son:

> As my husband got sicker, I think my son lost his role model. It was a very hard time in his life for this to happen. After school he helped his father bathe and shave, and I think that was good for him. I think his helping to care for his father got him through.

Today people can live for a long time with a terminal illness. The information that a parent will die may change day-to-day routines, but for the most part, people live in the present. Living in the present makes it nearly impossible to keep a constant focus on the fact that Daddy or Mommy will die at some time in the future. The day-to-day issues of life remain the main part of the family's conversations. As discussed in Chapter 1, the focus needs to be on how to live with this news and how to involve the ill parent in the family's life as much as possible.

Billy, whose story I told in Chapter 3, lived from age 2 with a father who was gradually becoming more and more debilitated from cancer. When his father first became ill, he and his wife told Billy and his older sister that their father had cancer and that eventually "daddy would die." Yet their father continued to work for several years. When he could no longer work, he stayed home and cared for the children while his wife worked. Finally, five years after his original diagnosis, the cancer impaired his ability to function physically and cognitively. Although the children had become accustomed to seeing him in an increasingly debilitated state, the original news that he might die had long since been forgotten. In the last few weeks of his life, they had to be told, as if for the first time.

Sharing bad news has to be done in ways that are consistent not only with the children's ages, but with the reality around them. Thus, what is talked about has to change over time as the possibility of death becomes more real. It may seem that children's knowledge of the impending death from the outset has little impact on them and that only what is said in the present is relevant. But children will understand in different ways as they get older and as their parent gets sicker. Telling them the truth from the beginning sets the stage for an openness that needs to be there throughout the illness and afterward. When they are involved in this way, they will always be certain that they are part of the family. They will know that there are no family secrets that isolate them from each other and that do not honor what they see, what they know, and what they feel. As Claudia's father's disease progressed to end-stage dementia, her mother's openness made it easier for her:

We decided she should know what her father was sick with. As she got older and went to school, everyone, even her teachers, knew. They were very supportive. I don't know how much she understood about the disease when she was so young, but we always answered all her questions. When [her father] was in an in-patient hospice, she really liked visiting him there.

Claudia was 7 at the time. She described these visits:

I liked going there. I knew what was going on. I liked going up to his room and knowing they were doing the right thing. They were very friendly.

She was not frightened by his illness, but rather took it for granted as the way things were. The support and care she received sustained her. She never felt alone or left out.

Children need information that their parents have to be prepared to give them. Parents sometimes look to their physicians for guidance about how to tell the children. Sandy's mother, for example, was not clear how to tell Alice, her 8-year-old, that Alice's father was dying. The mother was furious with her physician, who told her on the phone that nothing more could be done for her husband. When she asked him how to tell the children, he did not answer. She needed to be given the exact words for talking to an 8-year-old. She was worried, since she interpreted Sandy's earlier withdrawal as indifference. The nurse at the hospital recommended that she call the local hospice:

I knew I had to tell her, but I didn't know how. This is what the lady at hospice told me to say. She said, "You have to tell her exactly what's happening," and she gave me the words. I told my daughter that Daddy had something growing inside of him that's called cancer and that sometimes people can get better from cancer, but most times they don't. And we really didn't expect Daddy to get better.

This mother found that her daughter became much more relaxed and less demanding when she got accurate information, in words she could understand, about what was happening. Sometimes children themselves initiate the conversation. Eleven-year-old Christian knew it was all right to ask for the information he needed:

My father thought it would help if you had a positive attitude. My mother talked about stuff like not to worry about the financial situation, and that's about it. That did help because I worried about how we would manage. I didn't know as much what cancer was. . . . I was going to ask my father what it was. But he got too sick, I guess. But I asked my mother.

In the end, his mother had to tell him that his father was not going to make it. There are no elegant words for making such an announcement:

My mother told me when I came home from school that Daddy wasn't doing too good and he was going to pass away in the next few days. We came to see him just before he died, so we were there. I was scared, but I was glad, too, that I was there.

Anticipating Living as a Single Parent

For many families, the period before the death is a time for preparing the future widow or widower to deal with a new reality. Sometimes the dying parent is involved, passing on important information and giving last-minute guidance. For many women, this preparation involves learning to manage the family's finances. Sandy and Alice's father was insistent that his wife needed to know certain things. Sandy and Alice's mother recalled:

> When he first found out, he said, "You know, you're going to have to go to work; I'm sorry I'm not leaving you with more." And I would just say, "Stop! What are you talking about!" He finally said: "There are things you have to know." I didn't want to talk about that. He made sure I knew about insurance, whatever resources we had. He made me write it all down in a notebook so all this information was in one place. We signed a will in the hospital. Now I appreciate what a gift he gave me.

Claudia's mother went back to school while her husband was still well enough to take care of Claudia. She knew it would help her support them after his death.

When it was the mother who was dying, the conversation took a different direction. The parents spoke less about money and more about the children. Duncan's mother talked to her husband before she died about the children's ongoing need for care. She told him to remarry so he would have a wife to help him care for Duncan. Duncan's father said:

> She knew she was going to die. Our older children were already on their own. She told me that she wanted me to remarry and all that usual stuff. She said make sure I watched over Duncan; try to keep the family together.

Fathers may need to begin taking a more active role with their children. The father of three children, the oldest of whom, Rachel, was 16 when her mother died, recalled:

> We talked to the children. They all knew. When it was clear that there was no hope, I told the children that now their mother was dying and that they should be on extra special behavior around her and not to try to pin her and me into an argument—not to ask me and I say no, ask her and she says yes, or vice versa. I asked them to be more cooperative around the house with chores.

It is important to recognize the difference between these last messages from dying mothers and dying fathers. These dying parents at some level were aware of the major issues their surviving spouses would have to face—each would have to assume responsibility for an aspect of family life largely the domain of the other partner. These responsibilities are clearly different for most men and women.

Yet knowing that a parent will die is not the same as the fact that a parent did die. No matter how much is said or done before the death, until the door is closed, none of it is real. Knowing that death is imminent does not necessarily make grieving easier. As will be seen later in this chapter, all the plans and considerations that were made before the death may be forgotten when the death actually occurs.

THE FINALITY OF DEATH

It Really Happened

When a death occurs, children find out about it in several ways. Often they are there when it happens. When a parent dies at home, the children are not always present at the death, but may be in the house. In such cases, they are often invited to see their now-dead parent and to say good-bye. Other children are at their parent's bedside, even in the hospital.

There are often concerns about children's presence at the death. Adults are often more anxious than are children about their seeing the parent in the end stage of the disease. If children are supported and do not feel alone, they seem to be comfortable being present at the death. Ben, who was 7 at the time, visited his father the day he died. He remembered his last visit:

> I said all those things to him, and the doctor said it was no use, he wasn't going to hear and I wanted him to hear. . . . I think in some ways he did hear. I wanted him to know that I love him. I think he already knew but. . . . I remember my uncle was with me. We went outside. We cried, he bought me some candy, and we walked around for a while. My mother stayed upstairs for a while.

Luke was 17 when his father died from a short and debilitating illness. Despite the difficulty of seeing his father in this condition, he talked about how important it was to be present when he died:

> My father was very religious. He thought he was seeing God. It was important to him that we be there and pray with him. We think it made the end easier for him. It was easier for us not to have to imagine what was happening. That would have been worse.

More often than not, children are told the news of the death almost immediately after by the surviving parent. Gone are the days when parents fabricated stories to account for a parent's absence without telling the child of the death. One father I spoke with put off telling his children, but only for two days. He saw his wife's death as unexpected and needed time to absorb it. She had been severely ill in the hospital for several weeks, awaiting an organ transplant. The doctors had given him some hope that she would recover if she got the transplant in time. He was sure his children were not aware of how ill their mother was. His 11-year-old son Judd said:

> I guessed that there was a danger my mother could die. She looked so sick, and everyone was walking around looking very sad. Maybe I even guessed when she died, but I didn't say anything.

In the end the stark words had to be said: Daddy died or Mommy died. Sometimes such phrases as "passed on," "passed away," or "gone to Jesus" are used. No matter what the words, the message is the same. Some adults and children talked about feeling relief when there had been a long and painful illness. Sixteen-year-old Rachel, whose mother had been ill for a long time, said:

> I certainly didn't want my mother to die, but I am so relieved she is not in pain anymore. All I remember after they told me was that I just sat down in the living room. I couldn't cry any more and I just watched people taking care of things around me. . . . I just sat.

Relief can come in many forms. This is a time when the nature of the relationship before the death can have a great impact. One 13-year-old boy whose father died suddenly in an alcoholic stupor said:

> Now we don't have to worry about Daddy coming home drunk anymore.

Sometimes when a difficult marriage ends, the relief a parent feels can make it easier to help the children:

> We were talking divorce. He was very depressed. I was so grateful when they told me he simply had a heart attack; it looked as if it might have been suicide. I was relieved. I started to feel guilty, but as I thought about it, it was true I wouldn't have to face a divorce and it was also true that now he was at peace. It somehow made it easier for me to talk to the children about all his good points.

This is also a good example of a mother who was quickly able to see what her children needed—to remember the good in their father—and to help them despite her own sense of the situation.

Sudden Death

The actual death always feels sudden, even when it is anticipated. But when a parent simply "drops dead," the assault on the family cannot be overestimated. A mother of two children, Seth, age 8, and Mandi, age 16, remembered:

> It was all so sudden. The children found him after he collapsed. They saw the EMTs work on him and take him to the hospital. It was almost as if they knew before I got home from the hospital to tell them. What could I say? I just blurted out . . . Dad is dead. Who could believe it—he was out running the evening before.

Most children will cry when they are told, and most can talk about their sense of sadness as well. Yet just sitting with their feelings is not something children find easy to do. Some need to go for a walk or a bike ride or retreat to their rooms, and being with a friend can be reassuring. All these activities help children feel secure in a world that has turned upside down. Often an observer may not know how discordant the news of a death can be for a child. Fourteen-year-old Dean was able to say it clearly:

I went to my friend's house. We went for a bike ride along the beach. Just looking at me, no one would have guessed that my mother just died in an automobile accident. It was good that my friend was there. We didn't say much. I like to listen to the ocean. I went home when I realized my father would be worried about me.

Dean found comfort for himself in a familiar activity he could share with a friend. At least this did not change with the death. Parents also find it difficult to stay with their feelings at this time. They often feel grateful for all they have to do right after the death.

When the death is sudden, children are more likely to use the words *shocked* or *stunned* to describe their reactions. Most say they cannot believe it. One teenage boy, when told by his cousin that his father died, thought it was a cruel joke. When he realized it was true, he said he became confused and not sure what to do. He was probably speaking for most children and most parents at this point. Jayne's mother reflected on her reactions:

> Who would have thought, at our age, that we would have to be dealing with the death of one of us? It just didn't make sense.

Initial Reactions

Whatever the cause of death, many young children cannot use words to put things into perspective. They need to express their confusion and fury more actively. After his father was murdered, David's mother recalled:

> [David] was only 9 years old. When I first told him that Daddy was dead, he beat on me. All I could do was hug him. Later every time someone mentioned what happened, he ran into his room and hid under his bed. I felt like hiding myself; . . . it was so hard to take in.

Young boys especially seem to show their distress in their behavior. Eight-year-old Seth sheepishly told me:

> I showed my feeling by swearing, saying the "F" word and words like *crap*. I wanted to break something, but I didn't. My mom didn't care at the time.

He was able to use angry words to express what he felt, even when he could not verbally elaborate on the experience in a more coherent way.

Outbursts of anger are not reserved for children whose parents died suddenly. Nine-year-old Duncan, who was in bed when his mother died at home in the early hours of the morning, stated:

> My brother came in and he said, "Ma died" and he just started crying. Then I started punching walls and stuff. I was punching stuff all over the place. I broke one of the pictures in my room. I smashed it all over the place. I was mad. I just went around the house punching everything. Getting mad and freaking out, punching everything and just crying and stuff. I cried the whole night. I didn't even sleep. I guess my father would have liked me not to be mad and stuff and punch things, but I couldn't stop.

Sandy talked about her angry feelings after her father died in the hospital:

> I walked down the hall to the nurses' station. I was mad. There was a wheel-chair there. I wanted to kick it. But I controlled myself. No one knew how I felt.

Because she was older, she was able to restrain herself from acting on the anger. But it was still very much there. Sometimes children's reactions may be mixed and not understandable to the adults around them. One mother, who recognized and understood, observed her 6-year-old daughter's reaction to her father's death after a long illness:

> Barbara saw her father right after he died. She cried and said how sad she was. Then when my parents arrived, she was so glad to see them, she said, "I am over it, now I am happy." I guess at this age she hasn't quite got it together that she can be both happy to see her grandparents and still sad about her father.

Funeral Arrangements

Once the death has occurred, the arrangements for the funeral must be made, as well as decisions about how to involve the children. This is a time when family and friends come together. Children need as much support and care as the surviving parents. At this time, they often need to hear again and again what happened, especially when the death was sudden. David's mother remembered:

> I had a lot of people in the house, so there was someone to take care of and play with my children—the youngest was 2 and David was 9. I had to take care of all the details for the funeral. Every time I went by where the children were, they asked again what happened. We must have gone over it at least 100 times that day.

The immediacy of making funeral arrangements takes over. To some extent, involving the children in this ritual may be the most reassuring thing that a parent can do for them. It brings them into the family circle and identifies them as mourners. It is clear that, like their parents, children are dazed and unclear about what is happening at this point. The activity in the house is often not responsive to their need for comfort or their level of awareness of what is going on. Some children feel lost in the crowd. As 16-year-old Mandi explained:

> So many people around. For a time I felt that no one realized that I lost my father, too. One of our neighbors came over and took me out for a walk. That felt better. I told him I understood what my mother was going through, but I guess I needed something, too.

Children may not always be able to say what will comfort them. For many children of all ages, diversion and distraction can help for the moment. Other effective ways of coping at this time include an extra hug, acknowledging children's grief, and finding appropriate ways for them to help.

These days, few people exclude children from a funeral for one of their parents. Depending on the type of service, some parents may be unsure about including a younger child, under age 4 or 5, feeling that the wake or graveside service may be too frightening. Taking a child to church or synagogue or to a funeral home for a service seems less threatening, and most parents feel comfortable including younger children in this ceremony. Many parents find ways to help their children participate and feel comfortable:

> I really thought that they should be there. Sandy hadn't gone to her aunt's funeral. Now she kept saying that she was too young to come to the wake. I didn't agree. I told them that this was their father, and they should go. I was pretty clear about that, and that made me feel good about myself. I said, if they couldn't stay, that would be okay. Sandy lasted 20 minutes, and my brother took her home. Alice stayed another 10 minutes and she said she had to leave. The next day they were fine.

Sometimes, even when a parent is prepared to take a child, the child can change his or her mind, as did 8-year-old Patrick:

> We were all set to go to the wake, and he just said no, he wants to stay at his friend's house. I didn't think it was time to pressure him. He did want to go to the church service, and he did.

Eleven-year-old Judd's father had not been prepared to take Judd to his mother's wake and funeral. Judd was so sure of what he needed to do that he prevailed. Judd reflected:

> She was my mother. I would have felt weird not to have gone. I had to see her for the last time.

Nine-year-old Russell's father gave him a choice, but his ambivalence is reflected in his words:

> I gave him a choice. I told him it was an open casket, so I preferred that he did not go to the wake and as far as the funeral mass, I gave him a choice. He chose not to go.

When families take young children to the funeral home and to the cemetery, the children need someone other than their parent to stay by them, to support and comfort them. The surviving parent is likely to be distracted. Jenny's father described how she responded to the funeral service at the chapel. She was 5 at the time:

> I asked my cousin, whom she knew very well, to sit by her. I didn't know what to expect. Several times my cousin offered to take her out, especially while the rabbi was giving the eulogy—but Jenny wouldn't go. She clung to my cousin and sat there wailing into her lap through the whole service. Some people were bothered by this, but I said, if she wants to be there, this is where she belongs. It's her mother lying there. Maybe she was wailing for all of us; that's how we felt but were too self-conscious to express it. When she went to play with her cousins afterwards, and I could see a smile come back, I knew she would be okay.

Seeing their children behave in an age-specific way by playing or getting involved with friends can be reassuring for parents. Turning to play can reflect the children's sense of security, although at this point still quite tentative, that the world does continue.

Some parents have little memory of how they prepared the children for the funeral or if the children even participated. Alex was 13 when his father died of a heart attack. His mother reflected on what happened at the wake:

> I know I went with the children in the morning, when no one else was there, to see the body. That was the funeral director's advice, and it was good advice. They could look and ask questions, and we didn't have to worry about how they reacted; we could pay attention to them. They were in the building during the wake, but it is all a fog to me beyond that.

Shortly after the death, children may have difficulty talking much about the funeral (Silverman & Worden, 1993). They may not be clear about what has taken place. Some talk about the "box" and cannot remember the correct word for the coffin. They, like their parents, walked through the service in a daze. Most were not given any detailed information beforehand about what a funeral is like. Alex's mother asked a neighbor whose father was a funeral director to explain to the children what would happen. The children (ages 7 to 13) remembered that she talked to them, but they were not clear what she said. In preparing children for a funeral, what is said may be less important than creating an accepting atmosphere. Christian's mother did instruct her children:

> Be polite, greet people, and if anyone tells you that now you are the man of the family, just ignore that advice. You can't take your father's place, nor should you be told to.

Concrete guidance seems to be helpful, especially for older children. They then feel they know what is expected of them and how to behave. Letting a child participate in planning the funeral can also be helpful. Age is not always a factor. A mother of two girls, ages 11 and 13, involved them in each step of the process after their father's sudden death:

> The girls wanted a retired priest who had been in the parish. He was like a grandfather figure, and they were pleased when he said yes. They also wanted the music to be happy. Their father was a cabinetmaker and loved cherry wood. They wanted the coffin made out of that wood, too. I didn't have any problems with any of this.

Children feel better when they are involved—if not in planning, then in having some task to perform. Mandi was grateful that the rabbi came to talk to her:

> He said it was important that we be at the funeral, and he wanted us to tell him about our father—what we thought he should say. I appreciated that.

Some parents invite their younger children to draw a picture and put it in the coffin. Alice asked to put a teddy bear her father had given her in his coffin.

Several years after the death, it is often easier for children to reflect on their experience. Ben recalled his father's funeral:

> I was glad I saw the body at the wake. It made it more real. I didn't see the ashes after he was cremated. After the funeral we went to our church for a meal. I played outside with friends in the playground. We played for a long time; I needed that. I was tired afterwards, exhausted, and that felt good. But I didn't feel any better.

He recognized that he could both feel good and still feel bad.

These children are clear about the importance of being at the funeral. Not only is it important for their role as mourner to be recognized, but it helps them to be involved. Rachel, now 18, talked about her mother's funeral:

> It helped me realize that she was not coming back, and I appreciated seeing all the people there who knew her and liked her. I realized how special she was.

Many children say it is hard to believe that it is their parent in the coffin. Mandi recalled:

> I kept expecting the cover to be pushed open, and my father would come out alive. At that point I could not believe he was really dead.

The feeling that this was not real was often unspoken but shared by both children and their surviving parents. The funeral is the last public ritual in which the deceased has a central role. After the funeral, the family has to begin to deal with the real impact of the death, their feelings, and all the changes in their lives. Fortunately, for most people, the numbness and disbelief stay with them for a while, protecting them from being overwhelmed.

Newly widowed parents are often forced out of this numbness rather quickly. When there are children to care for, it becomes difficult to ignore their demands and needs for an extended period. Whether they are ready or not, the surviving parents have to begin to design for themselves a new role as single parents. How they deal with this new role has direct consequences for how their children will cope.

REDESIGNING THE ROLE OF PARENT: WHAT DO MY CHILDREN NEED?

Being a Single Parent

The role of parent cannot be separated completely from that of husband or wife. The spouses' identities as part of a couple give meaning to their daily lives, providing a framework and focus for how they relate to each other and to each member of the family. Just as the surviving spouse will no longer be husband or wife to this man or woman, the way he or she defined the role of parent in that relationship no longer exists. The surviving parent now must parent alone without the balance offered by the other parent. Ben's mother talked about these changes:

> Some of the life went out of our family. I was always more earnest about things. He was the one with the humor and was always finding fun things to do. They also had a father-son thing going, doing fun things, that I can't replace. I enjoyed a lot of what we did, so I have to take some initiative now. I didn't know this for a long time.

For this woman, her husband represented a contrasting force to her own nature and brought a lightness into the house that she is worried she cannot replace. Her memory of these qualities in her husband gives some direction to the changes she is making as she redesigns her role as parent. As the surviving parents do this work, they need to be in touch with what their children are experiencing and what their children's needs are. They need to be able to set aside their own concerns and look at the needs of those around them, at a time when they are least able to do so. Ben's mother talked about her feelings during the first months:

> After he died, I was like numb, in a crazy funk. I felt like I was chronically jet lagged. Fortunately, my son didn't feel much better most of the time, but he still needed my attention. I'm not sure what he got. It was school vacation. He watched TV while I stayed in bed. Sometimes a friend came to visit and got us out. School pushed us into a working routine.

The Children Need Care

Having dependent children who still need care and attention pulls the parents out of their initial numbness. Responding to the needs of others helps keep them at least partly grounded in this world. After his wife's sudden death from what was seen as a chronic but not terminal condition, Russell's father said:

> If I didn't have children, sure, it would have been easier. But really, knowing that they were there and needed me kept me going, sort of pulled me through.

This would be equally true after the death of a child who is survived not only by grieving parents but by siblings who still need the care of their parents.

Being needed helps focus the parents' attention on what else is going on in their families. It is not always easy to keep focused, to make the connections between the death and their children's behavior. Alice's mother recalled some of her daughter's behavior just before and after her father died:

> It started while he was sick. She was awful; she wouldn't get dressed to go to school some days. One day she was at a friend's and this friend's father came

to tell me he didn't want her around his child. He had just come home, and Alice started to hit his daughter. I told him it wasn't right for her to hit, but her father is dying and she may be having trouble because her friend has a father. Once he knew, he was very helpful. It made a big difference for her. Boy, was I relieved that I could put it together. Then after he died, she started yelling and screaming for several months; nothing I did seemed to help. Finally, she burst out and said I didn't love Daddy because I wasn't crying. I explained that I am a private person and cry when I am alone. It seemed to reassure her, and she did calm down. I am always having to learn how to say things to her in a way she understands. I never put things together by myself like this before. It's hard work.

The Impact of Gender

As was described in earlier chapters, men and women have different roles and different styles of relating. They therefore have different adjustments to make after the death. Most men have to consider how to nurture and take care of their children, whereas most women have to begin to focus on "getting the job done," on the more instrumental parts of family life (Silverman, 1988).

When a mother dies, the loss is accompanied by more dramatic changes. Mothers are often the glue that holds family life together. What is lost is the homemaker and caretaker of the family, and so children experience much more disruption in their daily lives. In addition, children of all ages report that it was easier to confide in their mothers and talk to them about feelings (Silverman & Worden, 1992). For the girls they were role models, to buy them their first bras and to help when they began to menstruate.

Some men know immediately that they will have to alter the way they are involved in parenting. They change jobs to make themselves more available and find others to help them with the children during those periods of the day when they are not home. Russell's father moved quickly:

> I changed my job immediately to be closer to home and to be available during the day if I was needed. I was lucky, my mother was able to take care of the baby and be there when Russell came home from school. I was able to do the housework because I had always helped my wife who never had a lot of energy.

Some men try to go on as before, maintaining their previous routines at work. They keep themselves busy outside the home and leave the care of the children to others. Eventually, something will remind them that their children need them. A year after the death, one father recalled how his children put pressure on him to come back into the family:

> It was my daughters, Lian was 17 and Janice about 14, they called me on it four months after their mother died. They reminded me that I was needed at home, that this was not a good time to be working overtime and on weekends. I had to explain that I wasn't sure what needed doing, that I was a man, I was the only parent they had, and they had to accept my limitations. My oldest finally

got me to see that she would be going off to college and it really wasn't her job to "mother" her younger sister.

Many fathers are used to seeing their role as mainly being the bread-winner for the family. Caring for their children in this way is a new experience for them.

Part of the adjustment involves recognizing that there are some spaces that no one can fill. The father of 11-year-old Darin said, several years after his wife's death:

> My son was always very close to his mother. They could talk to each other in a way that I couldn't. It was nice to watch. He won't have that again. I was forced to retire because of my health. I was home; that was no problem. I had to learn to be more open and to listen better. I am impressed with what I have done. We seem to be managing and even having some fun.

The mothers, in contrast to the fathers just described, went on doing what they always did—taking care of the house and children one way or another. Nonetheless, many mothers worried about keeping the household going. Alex's mother recalled her fear:

> My husband knew how to take care of all the little things in the house. He was always there to back me up. I don't know how I can be alone. I think there is always the worry. Can I hang on to the house? Am I going to raise my kids well enough? Can I get a job with mothers' hours and health insurance to carry us through, so I can be with the children as much as possible?

Although their role as mother remains unchanged and they carry on as before, women also have a lot of learning to do. They are challenged from the beginning. Mandi's mother described her determination:

> I didn't like it; I didn't want to be here, but I was determined to do whatever I needed to be sure we would make it. I never lived alone. I went from my parents' home to my marriage.

Women, for the most part, could work part time to be at home, so that on a day-to-day basis there were fewer changes in their children's daily routines. Andrew's mother remembered:

> I wasn't sure where I was at. I decided whatever energy I had, I had to be home for the children, so I changed my hours and my boss was very understanding when I couldn't make it in. I was scared. I wasn't sure I could handle everything by myself.

Her fears about her ability to make it made it difficult for her to relate to her children's needs. She had a hard time seeing that their needs had changed in light of the new situation. She stayed focused on their need for structure and discipline and had difficulty relating to her younger daughter's mixed messages, which reflected her inner turmoil after the death:

> I was sure my little girl was mad at me. She wanted to be with anybody else or anywhere else.

In the same breath, she said that her daughter insisted on sleeping with her each night since her father's sudden death. This mother could not understand her child's need for comfort or the meaning of her anger. She understood that some of what her children were doing was related to their grieving, but her own grief interfered with her ability to understand their behavior. In a sense, she became more and more parent centered as she focused on her own grief and her doubts about her ability to cope. Her very sense of self was challenged. Over time, she was able to learn new ways of coping. A year and a half later, she recalled:

> I got to the point where I wasn't sure who I was. I knew I was my children's mother, but if I wasn't my husband's wife, then who was I? This made me think. I realized that the house wasn't falling apart. I found a part-time job I really liked. I began to think that my husband would see me as a good manager and have faith in my ability to take care of our children. I started to feel in charge. I began to believe that we would make it. It seemed easier to look at my kids' needs.

Although she still had to keep the family going on her own, she began to see that she could. Reaching a place where she could allow the supportive and positive aspects of her relationship to her husband to emerge also helped her to move ahead. Claudia's mother had gotten used to being on her own in the last months of her husband's life. Then and afterward, her family helped with babysitting and taking care of the house. But being a single parent meant she had no one with whom to share the tensions of daily life. Four years after her husband's death, she described how being a single parent felt:

> Being a single parent . . . I am ashamed of myself sometimes. I'm tired after work. I might be shriller than I like. I try to lay down with her before she goes to sleep. During this quiet time, if I need to, I can say I overreacted, I'm sorry. Then we each look at what is happening, and she finds it easy to see her part and we try to change. I'm sometimes so tired of making all these decisions by myself, but I do, and we are really doing okay.

After any death, how the family lived and did business together crumbles in many ways. A key member has "disappeared." The deceased parent's role may have been supportive, or she or he may have been the primary caregiver—and there is a big void. The depth of the loss cannot be underestimated. David's mother looked at what she had gone through since her husband's murder:

> So what parents need is to be there and to listen. But it usually is a time when we may not know which side is up. Children may be young, but their feelings may be more powerful than anything we will ever hear. . . . We are all grieving. Learning to listen, however, may take longer than we like.

CHAPTER SIX

Death of a Parent

Making an Accommodation

> At the beginning I thought a lot about the sadness and pain she felt
> and then the sadness we felt afterwards. I don't think of her every
> day, I'm not sad every day. I don't like it when I feel sad. I feel hap-
> pier now more often, and I guess I'm not depressed anymore. I go to
> the cemetery by myself on the way home from school, and I tell her
> what is going on in my life. I like to think that she or her spirit can
> see and hear, I don't know how, but it is comforting to me.
>
> —18-year-old Rachel, 2 years after her mother's death

Children eventually arrive at a place and time when they are carrying on
with their lives, making an accommodation to their parent's death. It may
take a long time of traveling on a bumpy road for them to live comfortably
in a single-parent family and build a comfortable relationship with their surviving parent and the deceased. For both the children and the surviving parent, dealing with the death, their grief, and the many changes in their lives
is an ongoing, unfolding process during which they learn new ways of being with each other.

Children's work is to grow up, to go to school, and to continue to learn
new social and emotional skills. In fact, as I discussed in Chapter 3, this is
the work of all children. The stories presented here reflect how this work
changes as a result of a death.

LIVING IN A NEW REALITY

Developing New Routines

After the funeral, the family returns to a home that may no longer be familiar to them. There is an emptiness in it that they are only beginning to
understand. Mandi remembered the day her father died:

> We had just moved into the house. The new washing machine arrived the af-
> ternoon he died. He had decided he would install it himself. It was sitting in
> the back hall, looking out of place, just like we all felt. It was chaos. I guess Mom
> took care of getting it installed eventually, I can't remember except I kept wor-
> rying about how we were going to manage.

The family must find new routines, to build around the space left by the death. In most instances, the surviving parent does not sit down with the children to plan how they will manage their affairs. From the children's point of view, things often happen by default. Nine-year-old Russell remembered:

> I went back to school the day after the funeral—that seemed like what I should do. Most kids in the class didn't say anything, although I think the teacher told them. They looked uncomfortable, but no one knew exactly what to say.

In elementary school, the class most likely knows what happened. In high school, where not every classmate is in the same homeroom, some teachers and students may not be aware of the death.

For many children, changes are quickly apparent. After his father's sudden death, 13-year-old Alex recalled how empty the house felt:

> It was strange coming home from school. Mom was usually not there. We stayed with a neighbor until she came home from work, or I had to babysit my kid sister.

For other children, the routine is the same, but the players are different. In Russell's case, his grandmother was now present:

> My grandmother was always there after school. I'd help her with the baby. Playing with him made me feel better and helped me not think so much about my mom not being there.

Vickie's father died after a long illness. She observed how her mother changed after his death. While her mother reassured her that, in the long run, everything would work out, Vickie found it hard to believe:

> Mom yells a little more now, but she was always stricter about our doing well. She says we will be okay, and I know her—we'll be okay. She says I have to get used to the fact that it is different now. I'm trying. It sure isn't easy.

My Parent Isn't Coming Back?

All bereaved children have trouble putting together a picture of their family in which one parent is gone. There is a cognitive dissonance they cannot reconcile: He was alive yesterday, where is he today? It takes time for them to learn that their parent really will not return. Children of all ages experience this dissonance, not just young ones. Nine-year-old Jason remembered how startled he was about a month after his father's death, when he thought: "Oh my God, he is not coming back."

When asked about his mother several months after her death, 14-year-old Dean said:

> I don't want to think about her; it hurts too much to think that she isn't here anymore.

He is not alone. Children often say that they do not want to talk about their deceased parent because it hurts too much. However, as you will see later in this chapter, this is also exactly what they want to do. They prefer not to talk about their parent as dead, but they do want to talk about him or her as a person. They are aware of the facts, but it may hurt too much to be reminded of them. To the extent that they remain numb, their feelings can be contained and they can let things in slowly so that they are not overwhelmed. The strategy of distraction can mediate the pain to some extent. Getting involved in school is an effective distractor, just as work is for their surviving parents. For Mandi, the everyday activity of school helped:

> Going back to school made it easier—at least for part of the day my mind was occupied with things I could understand.

Their dead parents are never really far from their thoughts. A year after her father died, Vickie, now 14, said:

> Every day I think about him. He was sick and didn't work. I got used to his being at home when I came home from school. I just wish he was here. Sometimes it's an excuse. During a test, when all is quiet, I think about him and then I get a C. I can blame it on the stress, but I can't use that excuse to myself.

Children need to learn to accept what they are dealing with. They need to learn that for a while after the death, it may be difficult for them to concentrate. Few people give them this permission. Her mother's reassurance that the family will carry on may give Vickie a sense of support. She also needs to know that her pain and discomfort are appropriate. Thoughts of their dead parent seem to come in and out of consciousness—almost with a life of their own. Fifteen-year-old Thea talked about going to a school concert, something she used to do with her father:

> I was just sitting there thinking that I am here without him. Then I realized that my mind was just floating in and out; I wasn't listening to the music. Ordinarily I wouldn't miss a note.

It Hurts So Much: New and Strange Feelings

The feelings that accompany facing this new reality are new for most children. They have never experienced anything this intense. Young children may not have words to articulate the pain and their reactions to it. They can stay with their grief only for short periods. Eight-year-old Seth told me, not long after his father's death:

> Let me play the piano for you. I know how to play Mozart. My father liked that I could do that. He won't hear me now. I like to read books. I'm learning to write on the computer. My friend's waiting; I can't talk to you anymore.

If we listen carefully, we see that, in his own way, he is telling us about his father and what he has lost. Alex's younger sister, 7-year-old Sophie, could not talk about her father's death, but instead talked about her bird that her father liked, focusing on the tricks the bird could do. She used the word *shock* to describe how she felt when she was told of his sudden death.

She was torn between trying, in concrete ways, to recognize that her father was not there anymore and her need to emphasize his involvement with her through the bird. Her sadness was almost palpable, but she could not talk about it except to acknowledge that "yes," she was sad. A year later talking about her father as dead was still not something she could easily do. Two years later, she was much more comfortable talking about him and his death.

Anger. In the previous chapter, I described how some children react to the news of the death with angry outbursts that may continue for some time after the death. School-age boys, in particular, seem to let their feelings out in their tone of voice, restlessness, and lashing-out behavior. It is not clear whether this behavior reflects anger or their confusion and uncertainty about what they feel and their lack of words to describe it.

Fighting is one way of expressing what they are feeling, but often brings them the opposite of what they want. Ben recalled what he was like a year after his father's death:

> I was always angry at school. Kids thought I was stuck up, but I figured I had better stay out of their way to keep from fighting. I didn't connect this to my father's death.

This behavior is not exclusive to boys, as you saw in the last chapter when Alice lashed out at her friend. Unless the parents put this behavior in the context of mourning, their own and their children's, they are likely to worry about discipline and their ability to control their children. A similar understanding is required of others, such as teachers and friends' parents, who interact with the children. Ben's mother explained her dilemma:

> His teacher kept saying he was looking for a fight. When it finally happened, Ben kept saying it wasn't his fault; he didn't start it. The principal wouldn't listen and said Ben had to change. I finally started to listen to what Ben was saying and I understood that he was right. I was able to change schools. The new school said, okay, he is grieving—what can we do to help? What a different attitude. Ben began to relax immediately.

When parents make this connection, they can act to obtain more appropriate resources for their children. Duncan, now 11, described the trouble he had in school the year after his mother died. He attributed part of this difficulty to the fact that he did not have a sense that the world would continue after she was gone:

> I didn't think that I would ever feel better; when I went back to school I couldn't concentrate or think about anything but my mother. I thought that the world was going to end without her. I was yelling at everyone. I wouldn't talk to anyone. I can't believe that one year later, I can study and I'm getting along with my friends. I'm lucky they stayed with me.

In the period right after the death, Duncan did not try to talk about his feelings; he acted on them. The change in Duncan probably related to the wide range of support his father was able to access and utilize once he changed his own behavior. Since Duncan's father was home more, he was paying more attention to Duncan and giving him a good deal of support. He also encouraged a hospice volunteer who had visited when his mother was sick to continue to visit, and allowed Duncan to visit a favorite nun in a nearby convent whenever he felt like it. His father helped Duncan learn to ride his bike, enabling him to move about the neighborhood more freely to visit friends. A year after the death, Duncan seemed more grown up. He was not simply acting on his feelings; instead, he could reflect on what was happening to him—to look at his own reactions and feelings, as might be expected of a child approaching preadolescence. His father's return to the fold had been a turning point. Although the father was not facile with words, he had found ways to be there for his son:

> I'm not good at talking about feelings. But I am good at just being there and helping out—doing what needs doing when I know I'm needed.

Most children, especially as they get older, can name what they feel and have the ability to let out their feelings in a more controlled fashion. Vickie talked directly about what makes her angry:

> I don't cry too often. There's no real reason for crying about my father; it won't bring him back. He was such a good guy. I am still angry because I don't understand why he had to die.

Parents are not always aware of their children's anger. Vickie's mother said she never thought her children were angry.

Anger is rarely directed at the deceased. It is an anger with God, with a world in which this kind of thing can happen. This anger seems to develop as children consider, over time, what happened. Sometimes they couch their concern in philosophical terms about the nature of a belief in God: "If God is good, how could he take my father?"

Sadness and Loneliness. Probably the most difficult feeling for all involved was sadness. This was a feeling that prevailed after the tears had subsided and even after school and family routines had been reestablished. Thirteen-year-old Terry, Rachel's younger brother, reflected on his reactions to his mother's death two years before:

> At first I was shocked; that was the only feeling I can remember at the beginning. Now it is just sad and angry. . . . Angry because she had to go and sad because I loved my mom more than anything.

Often parents do not know what to do about their children's sadness. They want their children to be happy at all times and do whatever they can to alleviate the pain. Jason's mother, whose children were 9 and 6 when their father died suddenly, recalled:

> I would look at their faces and see their sadness. I couldn't refuse them anything. My heart broke for them. You want a chocolate bar before supper—eat a chocolate bar!

Shortly after the death, children often describe an amorphous emptiness that seems almost bottomless. It takes a lot of support to learn to live with this pain, to feel it, and to accept it as part of dealing with what is lost. We have seen that this pain is no less intense in young children, but it may be more difficult for them to put it into words. Four years later, 11-year-old Claudia remembered how she felt just after her father's death:

> I don't know . . . I was kind of sad . . . kind of a lot of different things. . . . Sometimes I just sat in my room or laid on my bed. Some nights I just lay down with my mom.

Their pain and sadness come not only from their sense of what is lost, but from the absolute silence of death. The temptation is great at any age to run from these feelings. Most children turn their energy into sports, schoolwork, and other after-school activities. Sixteen-year-old Christy struggled with her pain over her father's death from an industrial accident. For a while she flirted with drugs. Six months after he died she recalled:

> I was really hurting. I couldn't tell my mother. It was so easy to go off with my friends. It felt good to be away from the sadness and to forget he was dead. One night I had a few drinks and then someone offered me a "smoke," and then I realized it wasn't going to work. I began to think about my father, how he wouldn't like my getting into this kind of trouble. He wanted me to go to college. I was out all night. I had to deal with my mother's anger. She was also so worried. Somehow she began to listen, and we both had a good cry together. It still hurts so much but not as much as when I felt so alone. I think that talking about it helps a little—it helps me see that running doesn't help.

Guilt. Although clinical studies have emphasized guilt as a main feeling of bereaved children after a parent dies, this is not an issue for most children. It may be a particular issue in those families who seek psychiatric treatment (Altschul, 1988). It may also be an issue with very young children who think that they can cause things by thinking them. This kind of magical thinking generally passes by the time a child is 6 or 7. For example, a 7-year-old thought that she had caused her father's death because they had a fight the night before his unexpected heart attack. Her mother took her to the doctor who, in simple language and with pictures, showed her what causes heart attacks. She was reassured. Children have to be taken seriously and given as full an explanation as possible of what happened.

There can be elements of "survivors' guilt" if the children survived an accident in which their parent died. A 17-year-old reflected on the circumstances of his mother's death three years after she died:

> My mother fell asleep at the wheel, I think I was asleep. It was at night. When I woke up, the police were there. She was dead. At first I thought *if* I had stayed awake . . . and I felt guilty. It took me a while to sort it out. I got some help. I understand now that sometimes things happen, and we can't control everything. It is not okay that she died, but I know it wasn't my fault.

It is not easy for a child to come to this kind of understanding. It requires time, patience, and a good deal of support. Sixteen-year-old Antonio's father died of the effects of a severe drinking problem. He learned that his wish to be helpful did not mean he could change the outcome:

> Sometimes I feel guilty. Maybe I should have said something to him about watching his health, but part of me knows there was nothing I could have done.

On the whole, guilt is not an issue for most children. It simply does not come up.

Talking About the Deceased

Not Talking—Protecting Their Parents. Feeling alone with their feelings can be one of the worst things that can happen. However, talking about their feelings may only partially ease the pain. Sometimes children do not share these feelings because they do not want to make other people sad or burden their parents. Siblings report that when they lose a brother or sister, they try to protect their parents in the same way. Mandi was careful about what she told her mother:

> My mother was having a hard enough time. I would cry when I was alone so as not to upset her. I try to keep my fears to myself to make her feel better. She is all I have now; I need to take care of her, too.

We tend to think of adults as protectors of the children, but children also see themselves as needing to protect their surviving parents. Often parents, because of their own pain, do not invite talk (Silverman & Silverman, 1979). Children can tell when they should be quiet. Dean observed his father:

> I just knew when it wasn't a good time to ask any questions. My father would have a short fuse on some days. I would then decide the best I could do was behave myself and be quiet. It wasn't as if he said, "be good" or anything.

Parents may or may not be aware of their children's efforts to protect them. Claudia's mother knew what her daughter was doing:

> I know that she goes through these times when she doesn't want to tell me she is sad because if she sees my eyes fill up, she wants to protect me. I told her that there's nothing wrong with feeling sad. I would feel that way even if she didn't say anything.

Other children do not share their fears and their feelings because they do not feel understood. They may feel this way because their parents' pain gets in the way of their parents reaching out to them. This feeling may also be due to the fact that neither they nor their parents have a vocabulary for talking about what they are experiencing. One year after his mother died, 17-year-old Tony said:

> I always think no one understands. I can talk to my godfather; he understands more than most, but even he was grown up when he lost his mother.

Finding Ways to Talk. Parents may encourage their children to talk about their feelings. Seth's mother worried because he was reluctant to talk to her:

> They say it is important for children to talk about how they feel. Sometimes I worry as he gets older that he will break if he doesn't "let it out."

Talking about feelings, however, is not always what children want. They will talk much more readily about the qualities and personal characteristics of the deceased. As 13-year-old Chris noted:

> I like it when my mother talks about my father and how he liked helping other people. My friends and I like to share things they remember about him. She [mother] sometimes pushes on me because I don't talk about my feelings. What can I say about them?

Here we see the paucity of vocabulary to describe the sadness and pain children experience. But this is also a developmental process. The children's ability to experience and articulate feelings changes as they grow, just as does their ability to understand who died.

Talking about who died and all the changes in their lives may be more important than talking about feelings. It may be an important part of keeping the deceased in their lives and can bring them comfort and reassurance. This point is illustrated by the advice children of all ages give: "Try to remember him [her]"; "talk about him [her] when you can."

There Is Such a Big Space

As the family settles in, it becomes important to understand who is missing in the children's lives. The death leaves a gap caused not only by the lack of the dead parent's physical presence, but by the part this parent played in framing and directing the family's life. As was discussed in previous chapters, parents are role models, nurturers, and carriers of the family tradition. Each child loses someone different, depending not only on the parent's role in the family, but on the child's relationship to this parent and how the child made meaning out of this relationship.

One thing that is not always appreciated is the importance of a parent simply being there. Most children take for granted this sense of security and certainty in the world. After a death, children recognize how important it is. Alex considered what he lost:

> It hurts the most in the beginning. It's two years now. You get used to it, so it doesn't hurt as much. You have to get used to the idea that he is not there anymore. That was hard because I could always count on his being there. It is hard when you go over your friend's house and their father comes home and asks how you're doing and then you go home and your father isn't there. It's only your mother. And then you hear kids like say they hate their parents and stuff. It's like you don't know how much you like them until you lose them.

Young children do not have words to express what they have lost. They may be able to use the word *dead* or *all gone.* They may use words like *sad-*

ness and show a sad face. They can feel the emptiness and longing. They know something is missing. Legitimating their experience is important. It can take many forms. One mother recalled:

> My 2-year-old would get excited when a man entered the house, until he realized that it wasn't his father. There was no way to really explain dead. I could see the disappointment in his face. I held him and tried to make him feel safe. After a while he started talking to his father's picture, and that seemed to feel okay with both of us.

As the children approach school age, they have words for what they lost: the parent who bought them toys, who did things with them. They talk about what the person looked like, in concrete, specific language, for example, he had brown hair or she wore turtleneck sweaters. They describe their parent in simple statements, using words such as *nice* or *funny*, as a person who was important in their lives because he or she did things for them. Two years after her father died, Sophie had these words for what she lost:

> I was lonely. There was no one to snuggle with watching TV. It was empty. So I had to watch TV by myself. He used to have a surprise for us when he came home, like candy or a special toy. I miss that.

Russell missed his mother's attention:

> What I miss most is she was always there when I got home from school. She wanted to know what I had done at school, and she always had a snack for me.

Younger children focus on the loss as a deprivation: This person is no longer there to do things for them. As they get older, children begin to appreciate that their parent did things *with* them as well. Eleven-year-old Jason lost someone who was teaching him new skills. One year after his father's sudden death he said:

> My father kept a garden, and I was trying to keep it up. He was teaching me, and I try to remember what I learned. I have his tools, and it is a lot of work. I did it after school and on the weekend. We had some nice vegetables last summer. I'm not doing it any more; it is too hard alone.

Jason wanted to do things as his father had done when they were working together. Now he had lost his partner.

Most boys seemed to focus on sports that they shared with their fathers. David remembered that playing baseball together was as important to his father as it was to him:

> I miss him, too, sometimes on regular days (not just Christmas) like when I'm playing softball or basketball. I'd like for him to see me play. He had taught me how to do most of it. . . . He would be happy to see me play, see me play and how good I was.

Depending upon their interests, the fathers were teachers to both their boys and girls. Girls, however, focused more on help with homework and remembered family outings. When their mothers died, both boys and girls talked about the mothers taking care of them. Their mothers were the parents they could most talk with.

Children in their early teens emphasize the less tangible aspects of the relationship. Vickie lost someone who could understand her:

> I think about the things my father and I used to do when I was younger. My father understood me. I could really talk to him about anything. I miss that very much. My mother is not as understanding. He had more patience than my mother and was more encouraging when I didn't do well in school.

She was able to describe their relationship on the basis of some of her father's unique qualities. Andrew, who was 12 when his father died, lost someone who encouraged him and was supportive:

> He always wanted to help us so we could do better. Like if I wanted to build a magic trick, he would always help me with that. He was sometimes strict, but that's how all parents are, I think. He wanted me to get involved in anything I could.

Andrew recognized a quality in his father that he could generalize to all fathers and accepted that this was an appropriate thing for a father to expect of his children.

Tony talked about what he missed about his mother and how he remembered her:

> She was nice all around. She brought us up well. She was always there when we needed her. I miss most how nice she was. If she was here, everything would be going good for me, school and everything; I'd be a lot happier. My father always gets angry when we don't react like he wants. I don't want to make it sound like I'm never close to my father, but he never lost his mother.

For Tony, what was lost was the person who could make things right in the family because of her qualities as a person. In contrast, Tony's younger sister Melissa missed her mother's ability to discipline her:

> I don't listen to my father the same way I listened to my mother. I wish my mother was here to yell at me. I need discipline. When she yelled I felt that she cared, my father can't do that in the same way.

Melissa had some perspective on her own needs so that she could describe her need for someone to help her keep her life in order, which a younger child might not be able to do.

Seventeen-year-old Rachel recognized her mother's qualities in herself. She was beginning to see her mother as a person in her own right:

> I'm like her, I have her ability to listen and reason things out. Actually I'm a lot like both of them, but I have my mother's self-discipline.

Thea, now 17, had a fuller sense of who her father was. This sense of him did not change over time. She lost not only a teacher but a relationship with a friend:

> He was a very gifted, intelligent, loving person, liberal. He never tried to judge people. He was very open-minded. We were very close. We always knew what each other was thinking. I respected him very much; he taught me a lot. I really miss being able to share what I'm learning, his not seeing how I'm growing up.

Thea lost a person with unique personal qualities. She could describe what she lost in terms not only of her needs, but of who her father was and what he had lost by dying so young.

What is important is to recognize that as children grow, their sense of what they lost changes. They begin to see and understand more about the person who died. They will continue to connect and reconnect to the deceased in different ways, so that the deceased is always part of their lives.

School and Friends

School is a central part of every child's or adolescent's life. In this setting, they have to deal with the reactions of friends and teachers to their loss. Often others are uncomfortable or unsure how to deal with the death. Sophie's teacher was upset with her when she would not participate in a Father's Day project. She was a new teacher who did not know that Sophie's father had died the year before. A child of this age does not necessarily know how to tell her teacher that her father is dead. Sophie assumed that the teacher would automatically know these things. Children need their parents' help to learn how to negotiate such situations. After Sophie's mother came to school and talked to the teacher, the teacher was glad to find an appropriate project for Sophie.

Because of their own discomfort and that of others, children have mixed feelings about sharing the death with friends. Most children have one or two friends who they think will understand. Alex's father is buried in a cemetery near his school. He described his routine:

> On the way home from school, when my friend and I ride our bikes, we stop to visit my father. Sometimes I bring flowers, but mostly I just tell him about how good I did in the hockey game that week or if I had a test that day and how I did. My friend knew him, and we just talk about him.

Other children know that some friends will listen, but they prefer not to talk to them. Older children sometimes worry about crying in front of their friends.

Some children, especially in the lower grades, were teased by their classmates. Claudia confided in one classmate that her father was dead, and the friend told another. Claudia learned that she had to be careful because she was not comfortable with the whole school knowing about her father's death. In addition, one friend's father committed suicide, and both Claudia and the friend were taunted by other classmates. As Claudia put it:

> The kids said we didn't have a father. We thought about that, and I said loudly, "Yes, we do, only he's dead." Kids don't tease me too much. I stare them down, and they know I have friends who will get after them. That was last year, in fourth grade.

Claudia also considered what to tell people about how her father died. She described how this felt:

> This year, I'm kind of careful who I tell how he died. It's not that they would judge me. I think they would be frightened of me—like I could give it to them.

At the same time, however, Claudia was comfortable asking her classmates for pledges for the AIDS walk-a-thon and explaining that she participates in it in her father's memory. Although this lack of consistency may seem odd to an adult, it felt comfortable to Claudia. Her sense of self was not challenged by others' discomfort with her father's illness.

NEVER FORGET: CONSTRUCTING A RELATIONSHIP TO THE DECEASED

Two years after the death of his mother, 16-year-old Dean said:

> I feel good that I remember my mother every day. You keep going, but it is important to remember.

Most children have not read the books that say they should give up their ties to their dead parents in order to move on. Children advise that you go on living and never stop remembering. Johanna (quoted in Silverman & Silverman, 1979, p. 437) talked about her father's death four years earlier:

> I don't know if I had much of a philosophy in the fifth grade. But now it seems if something is taken away from me, if I lose someone close, I just still go on living. The whole world doesn't end. I should go on doing whatever I was doing. You shouldn't let it change everything. It's not going to correct itself. Like if somebody dies, they can't come back. So it's not going to correct itself, so I have to learn to live with it.

We carry many relationships within us. A person does not always have to be present for us to feel connected. When the absence is the result of a death, it is necessary to change the nature of the relationship and find new ways of staying connected. As in life, relationships change shape and form as time passes but do not necessarily end.

Children find many ways of staying connected when one of their parents dies. Their parent is no longer present in their lives, and they cannot interact with him or her on a daily basis. They are, however, continually constructing and reconstructing a new or altered attachment to the deceased. They find a place in their lives for the deceased in a way that gives them comfort and frees them to go on with their lives. The past serves as a prologue to the future. It gives it direction and roots.

As noted in Chapter 2, Normand (1996), in response to the question about whether children's connections to the deceased changed over time, found that change did take place. Qualities of the relationship can place a child, at any one time, in more than one of the clusters that Norman identified. There also does seem to be a progression. Thus, when children fear their parents' ghosts, within a year, they typically move on to thinking about memories of their parents. Eventually, many children come to a place where they see themselves as giving their deceased parents life through their deeds and activities. The process of connecting to the deceased begins shortly after the death. As discussed in Chapter 2, children dream of the deceased, talk to them, feel watched, and sometimes are even visited by the spirits of their parents.

Dreams of the Deceased

Mandi had this dream shortly after her father's death:

> I dreamed he would be with us for a few days and then leave, that he had come back and had to leave again. He had this suitcase, and he'd pick it up and leave again. I'd wake up in the morning and think he'd been there. It made me feel good, but it stopped after two weeks though.

Jason remembered that he dreamed, but not what he dreamed:

> I forget right away when I wake up. But the dreams make me kinda happy because I get to see him but sad when I wake up because he is not there.

Dreams can also be opportunities to interact and experience the deceased, as well as to receive reassuring messages. Thea recalled:

> I dreamed we met on my way home from school; he hugged me. I kept some of that warmth after I woke up.

In most societies, children are taught that there is some form of life after death. In the Western world, the bereaved usually locate the deceased in heaven, as Rachel did with her mother:

> I think of my mother in heaven—at the beach with all her relatives who have died. My mother loved the beach.

In other traditions there is no heaven as such. Dean, whose mother was from Japan and was raised in a Buddhist tradition, thought of her as a spirit who is often present in their lives. Two years after her death, he said:

> When she first died, I had a dream in which she told me she didn't die. It felt good. Now I think she is probably in Japan . . . helping my Japanese grandmother get over my grandfather's death. Sometimes it is really hard, but I know that her spirit will be there to help us get through. In the spirit life she can make herself available to people having a hard time.

Experiencing the Deceased

Regardless of their religious orientation, it is not unusual for children to experience the deceased in their lives. Some of them wondered about their parents visiting as ghosts who, they felt, were moving about the environment. Sometimes they experienced these visits as friendly. One of Duncan's older sisters talked about her mother this way:

> I waitress at the same place where my mother worked before she got sick. Sometimes when the door blows shut, everyone jokes and says, "That's your mother's ghost visiting." We talk a lot about her, and we all like thinking of her spirit being here.

Everyone in the restaurant sees this "ghost" as a friendly visitor, much like the Buddhist who was thought of as a supportive spirit who was always present in her family. Judy, Antonio's younger sister, had a different reaction. Their father had been an alcoholic and, shortly after his death, she saw her father's ghost as an unwelcome intrusion:

> Me and my brother think about him. We get nervous. What if he is watching; that's scary. Sometimes I think I shouldn't take a shower. I don't dream, and I don't like to talk about him. I guess I do talk to my mother. I like to remember when he would give me a piggy back ride.

This ghost or spirit offered them no comfort. Judy and Antonio were able to diffuse this fear with help from a therapist with whom they could talk about these experiences. As part of this therapy, Judy could also remember some of the nice things her father did with her.

Children who enjoy the visit use the word *ghost* in a light manner to refer to their sense of their parents' presence. A woman of 35 whose mother had died when she was 15 told me of how she had experienced her mother's presence:

> When I had my first child, I really missed my mother. I visualized my mother, that same comfort of her hands. I remember her hands as if they were right in front of me. I woke up crying, wanting her arms around me. It was interesting, I felt cheated, I felt sad, but thinking about her and talking about her made me feel good. I had to believe that she could see her first grandchild.

Talking to the Deceased

A relationship is also constructed by talking to the deceased and talking about the deceased. Dean's conversations with his father were described earlier in this chapter. The sense that the children are interacting with their parents is another part of their experience. Sometimes they get advice or guidance. Thea experienced her father as helping her with her sadness and the pain of missing him:

> He talks to me. He said, "Just get yourself together." He said, "I know you miss me. I know it is hard. I miss you, too. But I care for you. I am waiting for you,

and just try to get yourself back together as much as you can." I know I am not imagining him, consciously imagining him. I just see him—I don't see him standing on the lawn or anything. I feel his presence.

It Belonged to My Parent

Having something that belonged to the deceased is an important way of maintaining the connection. When his father died, Alex took his father's navy commander cap. Two years later he said:

> I still have it. I keep it in the closet now. I used to wear it more often, but now I don't. Now when I think about him, I guess I just feel him by me when I need encouragement or support like on a test or [at] a hockey game.

Eight-year-old Patrick has his father's pocket watch, which his mother is keeping for him until he is older. Sandy wears her father's school ring around her neck. Claudia's father made her an audiotape of him reading stories to her. When she was younger, she listened to it regularly.

Sometimes the family shares the possessions. David described how his mother worked this sharing out:

> We all share the tools that were his. . . . I asked Mom for them, and she said, "No, they are for the whole family." But she gave me his favorite blanket; it makes me feel close to him.

Remembering

Some children maintain a connection to the deceased primarily by reminiscing. Andrew remembered:

> Everything reminds me of him, when I see a pennant or fly my kite. My father was smart. You could talk about food, sports. We played cards, watched documentaries. We got along well, even when we disagreed sometimes about baseball.

These children hold on to memories of things they did together with their dead parents. Remembering makes them feel good. Chris described his connection to his father:

> I think about him and the good times we had. I like to talk about him to my mother. I sure wish he was here to see how we are doing. I don't dream about him or talk to him, but he is in my mind all the time. In some ways, I am like him. I like to do things for other people.

This last comment is the seed for his sense of himself as his father's legacy. He has taken some of his father into himself as he becomes more like him.

Interacting

Children who maintain an interactive relationship with their deceased parents develop an elaborate array of strategies through which they feel connected to them. They talk to the deceased, reach out to them (for example, by visiting the graves), and perceive the deceased as an active force in their lives. As Chris said:

> When I am taking a test I think of my father as right next to me giving me encouragement.

Adults may have similar experiences. Alex's mother felt she had received an interactive message from beyond the grave:

> I dreamed that he came to visit me. He was dead. He told me that everything would be all right. He was safe and okay and he was sure we would do fine. When I woke up, I felt more hopeful than I had in a long time. He wants us to carry on, and we will make it.

A Living Legacy

As time goes on, children talk less to their deceased parents, but they still dream of them and retain many of the elements of remembering and interacting. The deceased are still thought of as in heaven, and the children still feel watched in a way that is comforting. They feel less sad and are encouraged that things are getting better. Recalling the deceased and what they would want for their families gives the mourners direction and hope, as it did Jason's mother:

> He would want us to carry on in spite of the pain and the sadness. It somehow makes it easier when I think that's what he would want.

In a sense, the bereaved carry the deceased within themselves and converse often with them. The bereaved see themselves as repositories of the deceased's talents, hopes, and expectations for their children and their families. Children find ways to keep their dead parents' spirits alive. The older the children, the more deliberate they are in their attempts to find ways of remembering the best parts of their parents and trying to let these qualities influence the way they act. Now $11^1/_2$ years old, Jason described himself:

> I'm like my father in almost every way. I like fishing, I look like him, I say things like him, I tell jokes; people remember him by looking at me. I want to become a scientist like my father.

Connecting as a Family

The surviving parents play an active role in the children's construction. Without their help, it is often difficult for children to sustain this activity. The surviving parents are the repositories of memory, of family history, and of continuity in the family. They also are involved in similar activities: They dream, they ask for advice, they plan the memorials, and they remember. Vickie talked about her mother's beliefs:

> My mother believes the dead can come to you; they can come in dreams and can help. She says my father comes when she asks him to.

Her mother elaborated:

> I often go to his grave. I sit and talk. I tell him about how the children are doing. I talk about my problems. I don't know where the answer comes from, but I always get one.

Lian and Janice's father described how they talked about their mother:

> Any mention of her is brief, but it is on a happy note. At the beginning it trailed off to sadness. Then I did not try to keep the conversation going. Now if we are close to something about her, I'll always bring it up. Lian used to be the only one to bring it up, but now both of them do almost equally, although I worry about Janice. She doesn't seem to like to talk. They like to talk about food she liked and her sense of humor. When they go clothes shopping, they always ask if Mom would have liked that.

This is a good example of how different children react in different ways. Janice explained why she is often quiet:

> I don't like to talk about her in the family or with my friends. I am a private person. I sometimes go to the cemetery and sit there and think. But I wish we had a big get-together on the anniversary of her death. We didn't do anything. It would have been nice to think about memories and to be there for each other.

We see the two sides of her thinking. Keeping a sense of her mother alive is important. She wants help but not on a one-to-one basis. She also sees the value of ritual. Parents may be aware of their own ambivalence, but they need to remember that their children may also feel several ways at once. Janice's unwillingness to talk in one setting had little to do with what would be acceptable in another.

IN THE LONG RUN

There is no question that the death of a parent leads to radical changes in a child's life. We can never be sure what life would have been like had the parent lived. In a few cases, the death ended a troubled life and an unhappy marriage. To some extent, over time, this made life easier for all. Children whose surviving parents could not help them construct a connection to their dead parents had difficulty finding the good in the deceased. In this situation, they needed to have a name for the difficulty ("my father drank," for example) and to understand the family problems created by the deceased's behavior. Several years after her mother died of an overdose of medication, an 18-year-old described her thoughts:

> I used to be furious with the doctor for giving her all those pills. But now I realize she was responsible for taking them and for taking too many. As I get older, I also realize that it is a lot easier not living with someone who was al-

ways depressed. I miss her very much. I try to remember the good times, when she was feeling good.

Each child who loses a parent learns to think of himself or herself as a child with only one living parent. These children learn to deal with their feelings and with the pain around the loss, as well as with the changes in their lives. In the end, they find a way to continue to grow and develop as appropriate to children at their specific ages and stages. Claudia's mother worried about Claudia, but now sees things more positively:

> Her father's death was a tragedy, but her life is not tragic now. We had a lot of support. She is a great kid. She is very accomplished. She has friends, she plays the violin, she's involved in sports, she's going right along.

Most children do not sit and wait for their lives to come together. Their struggle to make their way is a lifelong process. Many years down the road, it looks different from the way it did at first.

Conversations with college-age women who lost parents earlier in their lives provide information on how they looked back at the deaths. Many felt that they grew up before their time. As one woman recalled:

> I was in seventh grade. I walked a little taller because I knew what life was really about. When I got to high school, I didn't always have patience for the other kids whose only worry was what to wear to the prom. I saw myself as knowing what was really important. I soon learned to keep some things to myself since very few people wanted to hear that I didn't have a mother.

These women reflected on their awareness that the world is no longer safe and their parents cannot protect them. This feeling is similar to what you will see with the loss of friends discussed in Chapter 10:

> The death brought with it an end to a kind of innocence. My parents led me to believe that they were in control and could keep things safe. I had no preparation that they wouldn't always be there.

Some of the women whose mothers had died talked of their fathers' inability to be the primary caretaker, much like the men described earlier in this chapter. Those who had lost fathers said that their mothers had been fearful of their ability to manage alone and that some had made poor choices in hasty second marriages. Some mentioned that they now look to their boyfriends for support and feel that they differ from other women their age. As one woman stated:

> I hope to marry J someday. He is the most comforting person I know. But first I have to find out who I am. I really feel out of "sync" with most people. They are like I was before my mother died: fun loving and childish. It is hard to tell them that's not life.

We tend to minimize the appropriateness of asking questions about the death many years later. As noted earlier, this is sometimes seen as unresolved grief, as if such issues should have long since been put to rest. Yet for these women, asking questions is an integral part of developing an adult identity in light of their parents' death. They ask questions about their deceased parents' interests, likes, dislikes, and temperament and how their parents died. One woman, whose mother died when she was 13, found out that her mother had committed suicide:

> I am glad that I now know the truth. It has always haunted me, that I went to school in the morning and everything was fine. When I came home, they told me she was dead. What amazes me is that this whole town colluded to keep the secret. Now that my father and I talked about it, we feel much closer to each other.

In a sense, they were also searching for roots to which they could tie their own interests and development:

> I was excited to learn that my musical ability came from my father. But my mother was now able to tell me something I was too young to understand before. The night he was run over, he had asked her for a divorce. That helped explain a lot of her reactions that I couldn't quite put together over the years.

Some of these women continue to dream about or have images of their dead parents. As they mature, they revisit the reality of their lives and the loss as part of who they are. They can acknowledge what they missed and accept the differences in their lives:

> Sometimes I think I have missed out on some of the things which make childhood enjoyable. My mother had to work to support us. I learned how to cook and clean when I was pretty young. We always knew we were a family, and my mother found things we could do that didn't cost money. Now that I am older, I realize that the death of my father, and the fact that I had to grow up a little quicker than most people my age, has made me a much stronger person and has given me the ability to deal with a greater amount of responsibility and maturity and that's okay.

CHAPTER SEVEN

My Child Is Dying

> Something is very wrong here! Children are not supposed to die before their parents. How could I take in that this was happening to our child and to us?

Children are our link between the past and the future. They are reflections of our self-images, of ourselves as caring people. Raising a child is not always easy or carefree. It can bring out the best and the worst in us. Overall, however, what we get back can be greater than what we give. We gain pleasure watching children grow and following the rhythm of the life cycle through their lives. For parents in the late 20th century, to consider that their children may die before them is a traumatic violation of their sense of order.

This chapter looks at families who are living with the fact that a child will die. As they integrate this fact into the life of their family, parents simultaneously need to focus on life continuing. They need to find a vocabulary for talking with each other and with their children about this shadow that now hangs over their family. They need to be tuned into the ill child's changing needs during this period, as well as their own needs and those of their other children if they have any.

As is true when a parent is dying, each family does this work in its own unique way. There is a gradual progression that takes the family from the time when they must first deal with the news of a potentially fatal illness to the time when they must surrender any hope of control (Davies, Reimer, Brown, & Martens, 1995). Each day is different. Every time the child's condition changes, the family is affected differently. As the child grows, there are differences in how he or she copes and interacts with the family and the disease. Families have to find the resources to deal with this complex process on a daily basis. They may have little preparation and have to learn a good deal as they reshape their lives to deal with this new situation. Although each family goes through this process differently, all are changed by it in ways they would never have anticipated or wanted.

GETTING BAD NEWS

One of the first things parents must do is take in the fact that their child has a serious illness that will lead to his or her death. The messenger with the bad news is typically the physician. The parents' stress may be increased if they sense that the physician is not telling them everything. Josh was diagnosed with a brain tumor when he was $4\frac{1}{2}$. His mother talked about how difficult it was for their physician to be direct:

> There was nothing in his manner to alarm us. When they finally got the results, there was this terrible silence. I basically had to scream at them, "Tell me what is going on." It was very strange . . . being told that my child had a tumor and then being held by strangers.

At this time, parents may feel that they have been knocked down and are not sure how they will ever stand up again. In the clear face of a life-threatening situation, both physicians and parents may look for whatever hope they can, any alternate interpretation that would change the prognosis. Josh's mother continued:

> When the neurosurgeon said that maybe it could be a cyst, for a brief period we were foolishly optimistic. It was a fool's paradise. They weren't telling us everything. But we didn't question, we were too busy just surviving. After the biopsy, they said directly that it was inoperable, but they would try radiation to shrink the tumor. In retrospect we see that our hope that with treatment it would get better made no sense. But we couldn't see it any other way at that time.

The need to be direct is important. Parents may not really absorb the information at this time, but they need to know where they are starting from. Many understand intellectually what is happening, but cannot take it in emotionally.

This knowing and not knowing is common to most families who face such a situation. There are several levels of knowing. Kübler-Ross (1969) talked about denial as the dominant feeling shortly after one receives bad news. I believe that what occurs is more complicated than simply not accepting what is happening (Silverman & Silverman, 1979). Parents, whether it is one of them or a child who is dying, can take in only so much at a time. The sense of numbness and unreality may make it easier for them to modulate the full impact of the news. All their assumptive values about the world and their child's future have been disrupted. Nicole was 10 years old when she was diagnosed with cancer. Her father recalled:

> My first thought was that I would never walk her down the aisle. It was ludicrous. The doctor is talking life and death, and all I could think about was a wedding I would never arrange.

The sense of disbelief and shock is real. Even when the parents know that they are genetic carriers of a disease and that their children may be at risk, their world is turned upside down. When the child is the first in the family actually to develop the disease, it is even more disconcerting. Parents' first impulse is to distance themselves as much as possible from this news. Colin's mother described her reaction to his diagnosis, at age 5, with spinal muscular atrophy, a form of muscular dystrophy:

I got mail from the Muscular Dystrophy Society and threw it away for a whole year. I was a basket case. Although my family couldn't have been more supportive, I kept thinking, "You don't know what I am going through." In our very large families, no one had ever had anything like this happen. It was a fluke that my husband and I both had these genes. Finally I went to a parents' meeting. I met a mother who spent 13 years being a mess, taking drugs, and feeling very sorry for herself. That did it for me. I'm not going to be like that. That's not what I want for my child. I am going to be positive, to give him the best I can. I began to realize with this disease you can't really forget. I am learning that I have to constantly adapt to different changes in his body. As I became more honest with myself, I was more honest with him. The disease just progresses, and I have to make a new adjustment, and so does he. But we are living, and that is what is important.

What does it mean to accept the reality of the diagnosis? It may mean asking thousands of questions to be sure that what is being proposed for treatment is most appropriate. It means becoming an instant expert in a subject that these parents would not choose to study. It means finding a place in their world and in their children's world for the fact that this can and does happen. It means knowing when to fight for their children's lives with every tool of modern medicine and, in the end, coming to a place where they have to decide when, where, and how their children will die. As the children get older, this decision will also involve them and it certainly involves the health care providers.

Doctors' visits and hospital stays become a normal part of the family's routine. Parents learn to juggle their needs, their other children's needs, and the needs of their ill children. Maureen was diagnosed with a rare malignant tumor when she was 3½. Her mother talked about how the family managed:

> I went to the hospital with Maureen. My husband went to work, and either my mother or my mother-in-law came to take care of our other children. We were lucky they were nearby.

Family life may become a bit of a roller-coaster ride. Dale, an only child, battled leukemia for three years. His mother described this period:

> Whenever we felt he was a little better or the visit had not revealed any new problem, we found ourselves getting our hopes up. These were false hopes that would soon be smashed. It was very difficult. He was 15 when it began.

Parents find themselves stretching their vocabulary to try to find words to explain the situation, not only to their children but to themselves. This is a time that tests the parents' awareness of their ill children's feelings and behaviors. Do they recognize that withdrawal in their children is not indifference, or that anxiety may cause the children to be uncooperative? Can they see that their children are also responding to what is happening? Even when children do not fully understand, they can sense the tension in those around them. Can the parents recognize that their children's temperaments will make a difference in how they react? Some children are accepting of their situation, whereas others find it extremely difficult. Colin was in kindergarten when he was diagnosed.

> He told everyone, "I have spinal muscular atrophy, and it makes my muscles weak and if I can't walk right or if I fall, it is not my fault. If you have any questions just ask me." Now he will tell anyone who looks curiously at him in his wheelchair exactly what is going on. He has a friend who is very shy. He always seems frightened. He won't talk to anyone about what is wrong with him, and he doesn't like to let anyone help him. His friend's parents hope some of my son's attitude will rub off on his friend.

Some of how a child reacts depends on his or her age. Parents need to be able to recognize age-specific behavior. Josh's mother described her experiences in the hospital:

> The doctor wanted him to lie still on the table. He was terrified, as a $4\frac{1}{2}$-year-old might be. He couldn't sit up, he couldn't walk. I had to interpret his anxiety for the specialist and tell him that a little patience and some explanation in language he could understand would make difference. It was a large teaching hospital. They do a lot of what is comfortable for doctors but not for the patient or family.

In contrast, Maureen was in a hospital that had a program to meet the special needs of young children:

> They had pictures and coloring books and things to help them understand. All the nurses were prepared to explain to the children what was happening. I learned from them how to explain to Maureen what different treatments were for.

Many parents become the children's advocates, trying to make the situation more responsive to their children's needs. By focusing on meeting their child's personal needs, Josh's parents and others like them can become involved in specific activities that provide them with something to do at a time when their world is coming undone.

Continuing to Live

Parents have to make a decision not to assign their children to the role of dying persons when the death is still relatively far off. Living in the present and for the moment is something families learn to value. They develop a routine, compartmentalize to the extent that they can, and begin to find a flexibility that they may not have known they have. The family has to find a way of continuing to live and of including the sick child in the family. Josh's mother was pregnant when he was diagnosed:

> Josh knew about the baby, and he could understand how the baby was growing. He would feel the baby kick against his back while I was cuddling him in the hospital after he had radiation. He helped me shop for the baby, and he chose a fluffy duckling for the baby.

To the extent that it was possible, there was never a time when he was not involved in the ongoing life of the family.

Janice was diagnosed with cystic fibrosis when she was a toddler. Her mother focused on the affirming aspects of what they were living through:

> Each day was a gift that we enjoyed as much as we could. We always had to remind ourselves that we had today, for which we should be grateful. We dwelled on what she could do, not on what she couldn't do. We gave the illness a name, and everyone in the family was involved in understanding what treatment was necessary and how things had to change in our daily routine. We tried to make it as easy for her as for her healthy siblings, who had so much more energy and could do so many more things.

Explaining What Is Happening to the Child

Research is clear that children know the nature of their diagnoses and are aware that their lives are in danger, even when strong efforts are made not to share with them what is wrong (Bluebond-Langner, 1978, 1996; Waechter, 1987). Parents need to recognize that their ill children, regardless of their age, need to be involved in their own care. Helping children understand what is going on is not easy.

Hiding the truth from a child may work for a brief period, but, in the long run, parents learn that there is no benefit in trying to do so. Bluebond-Langner (1996) wrote that the openness of family members about the illness increases as they get closer to the terminal phase.

Telling the children exactly what is going on is also important when they need to take responsibility for what they can and cannot do. Children need to understand their illness in order to recognize that their behavior can sometimes have life-threatening consequences. Nicole's parents tried to be clear:

> She had to have all the details of what was happening. If someone had a cold, she needed to stay away. We explained about her immune system being compromised by the treatment, and then she understood.

Other children in the family also need to know what is going on, so they can cope with the changes as the family adjusts to these new circumstances. Ellen was born with severe brain damage when her older brother Nick was 4. Her mother recalled:

> We decided to take her off the respirator, and she lived, to everyone's surprise. We didn't know what to tell Nick. Nick would talk about when Ellen grows up and has her own children. . . . I then decided to tell him the truth, that Ellen will not grow up. She is sick. I now think that I cut off his imagination. He then gave his sister a hug . . . and said, "Oh." He just took the news in stride. I talked with people at the bereavement center, and they said that he needs the truth and to let his imagination grow into the truth.

In Josh's case there was never a time, after the first week, that his parents had much hope of saving his life. The parents had to figure out quickly how to help a 4½-year-old understand what was happening and help him be cooperative with the doctors, who did not always take his needs into consideration. His parents were aware that developmentally he was concrete and specific. His father told him:

> We explained that he had a lump in his head that was making him sick. It could kill him. He could understand then what they were doing. We made the hospital bed look like home, so he wasn't quite so nervous. He wanted to know why the doctor didn't simply take out the lump. I explained that they couldn't, but that all the treatment was to make it smaller.

Although the parents used the words *kill* or *die*, these words had little meaning to Josh at this age. Josh could understand only that there was a lump in his head. He protested that the lump was not going to kill him, but his parents were not sure what this protest meant to him. Death was too abstract a concept for him; no one he knew had died. Yet understanding the treatment, in his own way, was important to him. He became less frightened when he understood why he had to have radiation and why he had to take medicine that made his body "blow up." His most immediate need was to know that one of his parents was always with him.

The need for parental support may take different forms at different ages. Younger children need to know that they will not be left alone (personal communication with R. Drigan, Dana Farber Cancer Institute, 1995). Older children need their parents to support them as they take more active roles in their treatment. Dale, a teenager when he was diagnosed with leukemia, knew all the details of his illness from the beginning. He knew that he could die, but was optimistic that he would be cured. As a teenager, he could take an active role in his care, but he also needed his parents to help him negotiate with the medical system. His mother remembered:

> He was always very clear that I couldn't talk for him at school or with his friends. In the hospital he said, "You are my spokesman. You have to be here. I'll tell you what I think and want, and you tell the doctors."

We can assume that as a teenager, it would be difficult for Dale to acknowledge his fear of being alone. But without explicitly saying so, he was able to arrange it so that someone was always with him.

If the illness extends for many years, the parents and child will have to renegotiate their interactions as the child matures. Nicole went out of remission several years after her first diagnosis. Her mother described how both she and her daughter had to change, since her daughter was now an adolescent:

> I wanted her to be polite and do what the therapist was asking of her. She was now a teenager, and she found her voice. She wouldn't do anything until they sat down and explained all the details and what benefits there were for her. There was no fooling with what she knew anymore. I had to realize that and be sure that the hospital personnel could respect her changing needs. Actually we all worked together on this.

Regardless of age, the sense of loss is assuaged by the safety children feel when they know what is happening and trust their parents and others to keep them feeling as safe as possible in the world. Knowledge, in its way, is power. The more we can understand what is going on and what is influencing our behavior, the easier it is to be creative and comfortable in moving into uncharted territory. Zach's mother, looking back over his illness, which extended from when he was 15 months old to when he died at age 15, said:

> We never lied; sometimes we didn't tell him the whole truth. Being sick was always a part of his life, so I guess he took it for granted. As he got older, we told him more and more. Sometimes he would complain and wish he was like other children. He knew about his medications, about when he went out of remission, what every treatment involved.

Reactions of Family and Friends

When children learn that they have an illness or congenital condition, they generally have an openness and ability to live in the moment if others around them are supportive. Maureen's cousins came to play with her as they always had; in this sense, little in her world had changed, and she continued to live as before. For older children, friends play an important role. Jessica was 16 when she was diagnosed with cancer. Her mother recalled:

> Her friends were wonderful. She told them she had cancer from the very beginning. They all seemed to grow up as they tried to understand what was going on and what could happen. No one talked about death, but at the end they all knew. I was so grateful their parents never tried to stop them from visiting, even at the very end. They helped my 9-year-old son with his homework and talked to him when we were all involved in my daughter's care. It meant so much to my daughter, that one of them would come and hang out at our house every afternoon after school.

In contrast, the uninformed in the larger society, adults as well as children, can make life difficult for children at this time. Josh's neighbors would not let their children play with him and allowed them to call him a "circus freak" because he was so bloated from the medication he was taking. Other parents have had people challenge them for having their child in a wheelchair when "he doesn't look as if anything is wrong." Challenges can also come from family members who do not know how to deal with this kind of situation and cannot set aside their own needs. Nicole's mother talked about her father-in-law's behavior at Christmas:

> My father-in-law couldn't deal with this, but he didn't know what he couldn't deal with. He couldn't understand why I couldn't respond to his needs. He came first. It was the first time in my life I yelled at a parent. It was just too much. He survived my anger, and so did I. Maybe we both grew up a little bit.

Other children, at school or in the neighborhood, can make it difficult for a child who is now different from them. Colin's 8-year-old brother Adam, who has a milder case of the same condition (spinal muscular atrophy), re-flected on how mean children can be:

> Sometimes they tease me because I am slow. I don't like recess. I told them about my disease, but it doesn't help. We had a geography contest in school, and no one would believe that I had the right answer. When they found out I was right, then kids wanted to play with me.

While his parents may be concerned about the progression of the disease, what is important to Adam now is to have a respected place in the life of his peers. At this point, the long-term consequences of his illness have little meaning for him.

Parents cannot protect their children from some of the pain other children inflict on them. But they can play an important role in helping the other children learn new ways of dealing with difference. Many people need to be educated, especially in the schools, where children spend much of their time. When Nicole returned to school after a round of chemotherapy, her mother found a way to make it easier for her:

> I figured if she could talk about the fact that she was bald and show them her wig, their curiosity might take over, rather than the part of them that makes fun. So I talked to her, to her teacher, and to her guidance counselor. The hospital social worker helped me rehearse what I was going to say, and it worked.

To help their children, parents need to have command over their own feelings and needs and an awareness of their children's needs. If they did not have this command before, the new situation may prompt a move in this direction. Richard had Duchenne's muscular dystrophy. His mother developed an ability to help people understand his condition so that he would not be stigmatized by other children:

> Richard was discriminated against mentally and emotionally because of the wheelchair . . . people would just stop and stare at him. He used to get very angry at people staring. You have little kids who would say "Mommy, mommy look at that kid," and mommy would whack the child and pull him away. Boy, did I ever want to get at those parents. If kids would come near, I would explain about weakness in his legs and that the chair was his legs. Kids could understand that.

WHEN DEATH IS IMMINENT

They Know They Will Die

There comes a time when children realize that they will die from their condition:

> Richard first realized that he could die when he was young . . . 6, 7. Here he had a double whammy—first he began to realize that his illness meant he couldn't do a lot of things, and at the same time he became aware of his own

mortality. He saw kids die in muscular dystrophy camp. The questions continued as he got older. It's a hard thing to deal with when you're holding a 10-
year-old who asks, "Why am I dying?" He had what we called an old soul. His
insights were way beyond his years . . . that helped him a lot.

Parents need to be able to follow their children's emotional and cognitive
development, to realize that how the children understand death is going to
change as they grow, as will their ways of relating to the world and to their
parents and to the fact that they are going to die. Richard's mother remembered:

Richard talked about death, that he didn't want to die, that he was scared of
death itself. He would ask, "How long am I going to live?" He wanted to live
longer, he wanted to make plans, he wanted to marry. He was going through
his adolescence. He had a girlfriend. He had the same wishes as everyone else.
Not many kids his age have so many friends who are dying. Sometimes he felt
guilty, because he was glad it was a friend dying, not him. He was glad that he
was still healthy and yet very sad that friends were dying. We didn't try to shel-
ter him; we knew it was very important that he had his peers. Another thing
for me was that I wanted him around other children who were experiencing the
same things so I wouldn't have to answer all these questions.

Making Difficult Decisions

Bartholome (1995) described the difficulty that healthcare professionals have
in labeling children terminally ill. Part of the problem is that it is difficult to
abandon hope for recovery. Both physicians and parents find the decision
to withdraw treatment and provide only comfort care extremely difficult to
make. They need to recognize when they are no longer doing things *for* the
child, but *to* the child. Both parents and physicians may be working with
unknowns. Leslie was 12 when she was diagnosed with cancer. In the words
of her mother:

The more chemo they gave her, the worse she got. By the time she had relapsed
the third time, they realized that they had been giving her chemo more than
they should. When she went into a coma, we were never sure whether it was
caused by the chemo or the cancer. We had no way of evaluating what they
were doing and when to say stop.

Knowing when to stop is never easy. Communication at this stage is especially important. Yet the child, parents, and medical personnel may mean
different things when they use the same terms. After living with leukemia
for three years, Dale was clear that he still wanted to find other options that
might put him back in remission. His parents recalled his last hospitalization:

We thought we were clear that he would be intubated and perhaps this would
help him get well enough to be able to try this new treatment. It turns out the
doctors never intended to do that. They were sure that nothing would help and
thought we were "in denial." We each thought that the other understood what

was to be done. Now when someone asks if we understand, we are very explicit about what it is we are talking about.

The real issue is that it is not easy to talk about death and to acknowledge its inevitability. There is something unreal about the whole situation, and we can never assume that there is consensus on what to do. Jessica's father remembered:

> She was always clear that she wanted everything possible done that might save her life. She suffered a good deal from treatments that had no success. We did what she wanted. When it went to her brain, maybe even she knew that there was no hope. She could no longer tell us what she wanted. The doctor knew before we did. He was good; he let us come to this moment ourselves. I still can't believe we made the decision not to try anything else to save our daughter's life.

Zach's mother described the last six months of his life:

> The only time we did not tell him the entire truth was in the last six months of his life, when we knew there was nothing more that could be done. At that point he didn't really ask. We talked about death. We are religious, and we talked about God giving and God taking. He understood and had a lot of faith, but we simply could not take away his hope. We couldn't live—for however long it was going to be—with nothing else but waiting for him to die.

Talking About the Death

As noted earlier, the challenge is to live until you die. As the end is near, the pressure on the family increases. No matter how long the family lives with the knowledge that the child is dying, there is no way of making the death real until it happens. Richard's mother talked about this difficulty:

> I thought Richard would die younger, since he lost his ability to walk four years before my brother did. Once he lived past 14, we began to fool ourselves that he would live longer; we were getting more complacent. We focused on the kids who lived to be 24, 25, ignoring those who died when 15, 16. My brother was 18 when he died of the same disease. Richard died at the same age and on almost the same date. Up there, there is a power; I really feel it was destiny. When my father told me both boys were 18 . . . I was spooked.

Some parents cannot say the words. Maureen's mother told her she was going to heaven where she would be healthy and visit her grandfather. She did not use the word *dead*, and Maureen seemed very accepting. Josh's parents were advised by the hospice social worker to tell him the truth and to use the word *die*.

> After we stopped chemo, the social worker said that we should tell him that he was going to die. She felt that it would be the ultimate betrayal to let him go up to the end thinking that he would make it. Finally we agreed. We told him, "We have done everything we could, and you are going to die." "What does that mean?" he asked. We told him: "You'll go to where grandma is." He cried and

said, "I don't want to go to where grandma is; I want to stay with you." Whatever I said didn't make any difference. So I dropped it.

Finding words that children can understand can be difficult. Children
need to be told in terms that they can relate to. Regardless of what children
are told, they do not always understand in the way their parents expect.
Josh's mother continued:

> One day when I was short with him, he said, "You just want to send me away."
> We kept telling him that this was not something that we wanted, but it was the
> nasty lump. At about the same time, we heard that a boy on the ward had died
> . . . everyone knew him. I told Josh that Brent just went to heaven. Every time
> we said, "Daddy's mommy is in heaven," he said he didn't want to see Daddy's
> mommy. He had never met her. We didn't know anyone else who had died.
> Now we had a face, a name, a person who was in heaven who he knew. After
> this discussion, he sat up and told us he wanted to play with a friend who was
> living in another state. Until then, he hadn't wanted to play with old friends be-
> cause of the way he looked.

Here the truth seemed to free Josh to be more open to continuing relationships among the living, to take a chance that he would not be rejected. In
fact, these friends agreed to come, and their daughter was very accepting of
his condition. As this account shows, with parental support and a sensitivity to explain to them in an age-appropriate manner, children can participate in positive ways in times of crisis.

Unacceptable Feelings

Parents cannot always maintain a warm, even manner. They experience
anger and despair and are sometimes critical of themselves for having negative feelings about their child at such a time. Josh's mother described the
feeling that filled her one day as she looked at him sleeping in his bed:

> My little prince was lying there sleeping, and suddenly I felt betrayed by him.
> I couldn't put my finger on it until later. How could this perfect little boy have
> this thing inside his head . . . this perfect Godlike exterior, how could he have
> this?

Betrayal was the only word she could find for this fleeting feeling. For a
brief moment, she blamed him for his illness.

Other parents report a momentary anger with their children for caus-
ing them so much pain (Finkbeiner, 1996). The whole scenario is so inex-
plicable that reason cannot prevail, and for a moment they blame the victims. It is not easy for a parent to accept such an unacceptable feeling, but
it does help to know that it is not unusual, given the circumstances.

Such feelings become a problem only when parents do not recognize
them. Hospital staff sometimes see families who are ready for their children
to die before either the children or the staff feel it is time. L. Schwartz, former medical director of the Hospital School, Canton, MA (personal com-

munication, 1996) talked about her experience with families whose children have Duchenne's muscular dystrophy and how they "conduct or orchestrate their children's dying." These parents had been told that their children would die by age 15, and they find it difficult to continue interventions that may improve and prolong their children's lives. Schwartz described the all-consuming anger these parents experience which is often directed at their children for not dying at the expected time.

This behavior makes us aware how difficult it is to balance the needs of the sick child with those of the rest of the family. Family coping styles and resources may not be able to rise to the occasion. Parents can become so obsessed with their own feelings that they fail to see the impact of the disease on their child. Here again, we see parent-centered and child-centered families. The families that Schwartz described, who are angry with their children for not dying on time, could be classified as parent-centered. When both parents are parent-centered, then the child suffers. Jonathan, looking back on his difficult childhood with Duchenne's muscular dystrophy, remembered his mother's anger with him:

> My mother didn't want to see me in a wheelchair, and she kept saying I could walk if I wanted to. I kept trying, and I was falling a lot. She saw my cousins and she knew better, but she didn't want it to be happening to me. Only when the doctor got alarmed and he sat her down and made her listen, did she change. My father wasn't much help; every once in a while he would get angry and say it was her genes that caused this. It was hard on me because I knew I couldn't help myself. My grandmother and my sister helped a lot. I could talk to them.

When parents are tied up in their own feelings, they cannot help their children. They can find excuses for what they need to do and for not seeing their children's individual needs. As one parent put it:

> My 8-year-old is very demanding, but that is his nature. He has cystic fibrosis. He has to understand that his brother needs our attention and that we need to work. Work is salvation for both of us. If he gets hyperactive in school, they should be able to help. He knows we love him, that he is never alone in the house—what could he be afraid of?

This way of viewing children may work if there is no crisis in the family. Parents may need to be educated, to be given the tools to grow in the situation and become more empathic and aware of the needs of others in the family—to be aware that what is happening is not simply between them and their sick child.

Some parents will never accept the situation and will not acknowledge that it is not going to go away. In the extreme, one parent absents himself or herself from the family, leaving the more child-centered parent at home. Paul's mother described her husband's reaction to their son's increasing debilitation from cystic fibrosis:

> My husband was not able to accept it. He won't talk about it. He left us two years ago. He couldn't face the fact that his child had a disability. He said, "I

can't get over it," and just left. He felt terribly guilty that it was his gene, too. I
don't have that feeling. I don't blame God or feel guilty; I got this and deal with
it. My husband was angry with God. He just wanted it all to go away, which,
of course, it didn't.

This family situation is a good example of the crisis in family development
described in Chapter 4. In many ways, this father fits Kegan's (1982) construct of a school-age child whose world revolves around his needs and
wants. Newberger and White (1989) described this type of parent as having
an egotistical orientation.

In contrast, Richard's father reflected on what he and his wife learned
over the years as they dealt with the impact of Richard's illness on their
lives:

> When your child has a genetic illness like muscular dystrophy and my wife was
> the carrier, it becomes easy to blame her. What good would that do? We talked;
> I tried to understand the burden she felt. We both agreed that we would not
> have any more children and then we both rallied to give our son the best life
> he could have under the circumstances.

In the ideal situation, both parents recognize the need to be child-
centered and, if need be, can reconcile their differences. Often they take turns:

> My husband went to work, and I was left home to take care of Zach and my
> other children. He knew when I was reaching my limit and would try to come
> home early so I could have some time off. I liked to just go out by myself—to
> a movie, to the mall shopping. We had trained a special babysitter, so some-
> times we could just take off and try to find something special we both enjoyed
> . . . even like going dancing. We sort of learned that we needed to replenish our-
> selves to have what to give.

Learning from the Children

If they are open to their children, parents may find they have much to learn
from them. In the words of Leslie's mother, looking back on her daughter's
life:

> She was so wonderful, so open, she taught me so much. I am just glad to have
> known her.

In time, many parents begin to realize that their children's world is not always a world they can enter. Richard's father talked respectfully about his
son:

> Richard was very dependent. He learned a kind of dignity I, in a way, en-
> vied. I don't know if I could go to a restaurant and have someone else feed
> me or have a woman attendant clean me in the toilet. At the end he couldn't
> do anything for himself. What I realize now is that every time he would lose
> a function, it was a whole grieving process all over again. He grieved, too.
> He reacted through his mouth, through the words he found for what was go-
> ing on.

Parents who allow their children to grow emotionally and cognitively, who do not overprotect them, discover that both they and their children seem to grow in this situation. Colin and Adam's mother said:

> My children want to be like other children, do what others are doing. You want to nail them to the floor so that they won't take risks, but you really can't do that. You have to let them go. My husband and I learned to talk to each other in a new way. We began to appreciate strengths that neither of us knew we had. Strength didn't mean being like iron; it meant letting ourselves feel and sharing both the good and the bad with each other and with our children.

Deciding Where to Die

When death seems imminent, parents have to make decisions about where their children will die. Children sometimes know that the end is near before their parents are aware:

> We used a lot of imagery with Josh. We liked to get him to think that the treatment was like turtles going in to get the lump. One day coming home, about seven months after he was diagnosed, he said, "The turtles aren't fighting anymore; they are losing."

Richard died in his sleep at camp. In retrospect, his parents realized that he had given them many clues that he felt the end was near:

> He knew he was getting weaker. There were signs, we didn't realize until he died. It was imminent. . . . He was breathing as if he had congestive heart failure. The doctor said nothing. Richard began to be nostalgic: "Remember when I did this?" "Remember when I hurt someone?" "Remember when you wouldn't let me spend time with a friend at the mall who turned out to be a shoplifter?" We reach a time in life when we make amends, and he was dealing with some of the things that he thought were bad and making sure it was okay now with us. When he went to camp, we always left numbers where we could be reached. He would always roll his eyes as if this was unnecessary. But this time when we left him at camp, he said to make sure they have all the information about where we were. We didn't put any of the clues together.

The circumstances of Richard's death can be seen as a blessing. His parents did not have to decide when or where or how he would die.

As the end becomes nearer, some parents begin to acknowledge the need for funeral plans. Josh's father talked about planning for his son's funeral in advance:

> When we stopped the chemo, I had a discussion with the funeral people. It was probably the most unreal conversation in my life . . . to make these arrangements in advance. In the end it was very important after Josh died. We just had to make one phone call, and literally everything happened automatically. . . but to have to do that while the person was still alive was horrible.

When the family plans the funeral in advance, the child himself may be involved in the planning:

Josh had told us what he wanted to take with him to heaven . . . turtles, bunny, blanket. We had agreed that he would be buried next to his grandmother in the family plot. That seemed to be comfortable for all of us.

Parents are often faced with decisions about continuing life support, using antibiotics, and whether the child will die at home or in the hospital. In some cases, the child may be the main decision maker. Janice knew that she was totally debilitated by cystic fibrosis. Her mother described the decisions that they had to make:

> We let them do comfort measures. We had talked it over. She knew it would be easier at the hospital. After all, she was 18 years old, and, as she said, she had been living with this almost all her life. She told us she wanted us to stay with her. She got the doctor to promise to keep most of the hospital staff out of her room. She even understood that it was her heart that was going to give out. She knew she could trust this doctor to respect her wishes.

Some parents did not feel that they could ever return to their homes if their children died there. Zach's parents took him to the hospital to die:

> We didn't have hospice; that might have helped. My husband and I agreed that with all the other children in the house, it was better that way. We didn't want the responsibility at this time. Zach was used to going to the hospital.

Josh's parents resisted accepting hospice referral until they learned they had to choose where he would die. They, too, felt they could not go back into the house. His mother described him just before he died:

> I felt something changed in him because he sensed it was all right for him to die. If it is okay, then let me go, I'll be able to run and jump. . . . He couldn't speak, sit up, or walk. It was time to take him to the hospital. I remember throwing things into a suitcase and I started filing my nails. I realized I didn't know what I was doing. We had the baby with us, and when we got to the hospital, he wanted to be fed. I couldn't breast-feed at that point. A hospice volunteer appeared and took him home, where I had breast milk in the freezer. We had to tell the doctors not to give Josh antibiotics. It just wasn't fair, his body really wasn't working. We watched him stop breathing; that was very tough.

Other parents were more comfortable with their children dying at home. Maureen's parents decided that Maureen should die at home. Because her younger siblings, who were 5 and 3 at the time, had been involved all along, they were very accepting of this plan:

> We had promised her she would be at home with us. By this point, she was so sedated that she didn't know us. We tried to make things as natural as we could under the circumstances. Her younger sister and brother would come into her room and visit. They took it for granted that the nurses were coming in and out. My sister, who came to be with my little ones, brought her 4-year-old with her and they played, sometimes including Maureen. Sometimes they played music for her. Sometimes we read to her. In the end there were no big good-byes.

Jessica's parents found comfort in her dying in her own room and from the fact that she continued to be part of the family until the end:

> This was very important to us. We wanted to take care of her and know that she was as comfortable as possible. No one was going to try any heroic measures, and we could all be together. We always focused on how she would live. As long as her mind was working, that's what she did. She was still doing her homework almost to the end. None of us could imagine a time when she wouldn't be here. Sure we knew, but that's not where we put our energy.

Even though Richard died at camp, it was important to his parents that he be at home for a while. They arranged for his body to be brought back home before it went to the funeral home:

> We got the call while we were away. One thing I really wanted was to bring him home. His attendant volunteered to bring him home in our van that was at camp. It was very important to us that the three of us could be together at home. I don't know why . . . it just helped me a lot. We were always together at that house, we were a threesome. Having him there made it real.

THE DOOR IS FINALLY CLOSED

Knowing that the death is coming does not mean that you are prepared for it, as discussed in Chapter 5. Richard's parents reflected on their reaction to the news of his death:

> We realized that what we heard from other parents was true: At first when you hear, you say it can't be true—not to our son, our child. It was as if it was a sudden, unexpected death.

In some ways, all deaths are sudden. At this time there may be a fleeting sense of disbelief, but mostly parents are numbed by it all. Dale's parents thought of his death as almost anticlimactic. They were exhausted from the relapse-remission cycles they had lived with during the three years of his illness. For many parents, the disbelief and numbness serve them well as they mobilize to do what has to be done—making funeral arrangements or implementing plans made earlier. The funeral provides a way of honoring the life of this child and a way for the family to be consoled by their community. It is the last public act these parents will perform on behalf of their child.

The family's formal religious background often dictates some of the ritual, guiding the parents' decision about appropriate ceremonies at this time. Zach's family was active in a traditional synagogue. His mother described what they did:

> We didn't have to think about anything. He was buried the next day according to our tradition, and we sat shiva [a period of mourning] for seven days. Tradition guided how we should behave and what to expect from the community. All the children were home from school for the week; they were mourning, too.

My husband and Aaron, who was now over 13, helped form the minyan [prayer group] we needed every morning and evening, and men came from the community to participate.

Role of Religion and Faith

For other families, who are not religiously involved, rituals may still provide a guide for their behavior at a time when they feel afloat without direction. Dale's parents were clear that they did not find formal religion helpful and probably would describe themselves as atheists. They did not think that they would meet again after death or that Dale's spirit lived on in any form. However, when he died, they followed the Jewish burial rituals and found comfort in having their family around them for a period after the death, albeit not for the traditional seven days. In retrospect, they could see that they needed the order and direction this tradition gave them in the face of the vacuum Dale's death created.

Most parents saw the death as liberating their children from the debilitating conditions that had kept them prisoners in their own bodies. Richard's mother recalled:

> We all three of us saw cremation as very symbolic—freeing him from the body that had imprisoned him. It gave him the freedom to be where he is now. We had gone to a spiritual fair not long before Richard died. This reader said he will walk, he will be free. Then I realized she is right . . . it will happen with his death. This is another reason why it was important to have him cremated. It was about this time that I had what I call a vision, for lack of a better word, of two teachers we knew who had died. I saw the three of them playing basketball. We believe Richard will come back in a different body someplace, somewhere in this world. There has to be something else.

Whatever the belief system, it helped these parents give some meaning and direction to what they were experiencing. Josh's mother described her last few minutes with him:

> I had read all the books about seeing the light. I had been packing my bag preparing for this birth or death, treating it like I was going into labor for the first time. For me, it was an unknown quantity, whatever it was. I had decided that at the point when he died, if I remembered I would look up and say I loved him and I wanted him to see my face, and not the back of my head. He looked physically different. I don't know if it was my imagination. This was the first time I had seen a dead person, but it was as if his soul was gone.

Josh's father talked about how faith helped to give direction and meaning at a time when nothing made sense. He saw himself as a lapsed Catholic:

> The experience in some ways actually strengthened my faith. After I married I slowly drifted away from church. I wasn't even feeling guilty. We were actually looking for alternatives at about the time Josh got sick. It was around Christmas, and somewhere around there I started to go to church again and to go every week. I asked for forgiveness and then I started to bargain. I said I would

be a good Catholic if my son could be saved. Then, I prayed for enough strength to just get me through this. I got that. Then I prayed that I would be there when Josh passed away . . . and for that to have happened was a great blessing. And to me, deep down, I always realized that it was not nice to be selfish. We do not know what God's plan is. Sometimes I think that things are pretty much pre-ordained. What I can ask is to make this, as painful as it is going to be, as palatable as possible, and that did take place. Now I am still trying to decide what my relationship to the church will be.

Having a way of understanding the place of death in life is important. Dale's parents felt strongly that this life is all we get. They understood their son's illness and death as an accident of nature. They helped other parents who were angry with God for making their children ill by saying that it had nothing to do with God. God is about love; this illness is an accident of nature. Even religiously observant parents found this observation helpful. Like Josh's parents, most people were not always consistent in how they felt. However, the ability to reflect and not see oneself or one's child as chosen to suffer in a personal way, to recognize that not everything is logical and consistent, gave them comfort.

CHAPTER EIGHT

After a Child's Death
Nothing Is the Same

> If the pain went away, then it would be a real loss, a greater loss. The pain that stays with me is to honor him. I keep the pain at a level that is tolerable, but it is important to me that it is there, and it's for the same reason that we like to talk about him. We also think that our zest for life is a tribute to him. Life can be exciting. How would it honor him—and all that he lost—if we didn't go on?
>
> —Dale's father, 10 years after his son's death

When children die, they do not stop being their parents' children or their siblings' brothers or sisters. Even though they no longer fill their family's current life space or make daily demands on their parents, there is still a place for them in the family. Bereaved parents live with this paradox of being parents yet not being able to parent. The children are missing in their families and will never be replaced, but they are still very much present. Parents use various strategies to deal with this new reality, to find consolation for this irreparable loss, and to reach a place where life goes on.

DOES KNOWING IN ADVANCE MAKE A DIFFERENCE?

Parents sometimes think that if their children had died in a different way, it would be easier for them. When the death was sudden, they wonder how it would have been if there had been time to say good-bye. Peter died suddenly when he was 14. His mother remembered:

> I used to think it might have been easier if Peter died of a long disease or a bullet or an accident. But people who had that say no. For Peter, it was a good death. Everything was fine. He was having a good time, an aneurysm, we couldn't have known it was there, it was no one's fault. But these other parents are right: No matter how he died, Peter is gone and that stays with me, and that's what I have to deal with.

Sudden death does bring with it a much more intense sense of shock. Shelly's mother talked about her reactions to her daughter's death in an automobile accident caused by a drunk driver:

> How did I react? All I can say is I think I was in shock. The first night I was
> on her bed, and I said to myself, "I know that I am in shock." She was wear-
> ing a hat, and they gave it to me. I sat there with this hat in my hand, and I
> just sat there. I couldn't even close my eyes. How could it be that this hap-
> pened?

Darrell's father considered how he took in the news that his 15-year-old son
was murdered:

> When you first hear, your first response is to block it out and to pretend that
> everyone is wrong, that there is a terrible mistake here. When you are finally
> faced with the facts and you see it really is your son, you find yourself trying
> to find ways to soften the impact on the rest of the family . . . but also it is find-
> ing a way to better absorb it for yourself.

With any sudden death of a child, the parents have lost all control for
the moment. They may think that time to say good-bye would have given
them a sense of control, when, in fact, there was none to be had, or that they
would have been able to comfort their child in his or her last moments. With
this thought in mind, parents sometimes put things in their children's coffins.
Twelve-year-old Carl died in a sporting accident. His father recalled what
he did to comfort himself:

> I made a butterfly out of clay—I am a potter, and I did what I know how to do.
> I put it in his coffin. I said in my heart that it was to accompany him on his new
> journey, to ease the way, and to let him know we will always love him.

Such behaviors are not unique to sudden deaths. Both Dale's parents and
Josh's parents put things in their sons' coffins as a way of saying good-bye
and helping them on their journeys.

For a time, people thought that if all unfinished business was taken care
of and there was time to say good-bye, then grief would be easier and perhaps shorter. Rando (1993), for example, wrote that a sudden death leads to
greater trauma and stress for the family, so that they are more likely to develop serious emotional problems. There is little data to sustain this idea
(Silverman & Worden, 1993), however. Time to say good-bye does not ease
the pain. The pain may be different, but it is no less there. The suddenness
of the death and the cause of death may influence the degree of numbness
and disbelief initially, but in the long run, the emptiness and the pain are
alike. One kind of death is no less awful than another, and none is more
likely than another, by itself, to lead to emotional problems. All deaths lead
to stress, pain, and change in almost every aspect of a family's life. Regardless of the way their children die, parents speak in the same language. In
each instance, the disarray may take its own shape, but it is always there.
Richard's parents talk about their experience of knowing that his death was
inevitable:

> We never went to bed leaving things unsaid. I just think of parents whose chil-
> dren die in an accident who didn't say I love you. That would have been hard

for us, but then we weren't there when he died. Bringing his body back to our house was our way of saying good-bye. Whatever we had done before, it was different now.

Knowing that their child was left with a message of love and concern can help for the moment. On the other hand, Richard's parents still felt that the death was unexpected. Yet because they knew the death was coming, they had some control over their behavior afterward, such as asking to have his body brought home. Their pain was still real, and their grief was not abbreviated.

When a child commits suicide, parents deal with an additional issue of responsibility (Shneidman, 1996; Shneidman & Mandelkorn, 1994). If they were aware of their child's intentions and their efforts to stop the child were inadequate, then they have to deal with the weight of feeling culpable in some way. In Bruce's case, his family had no idea that suicide was on his mind. Bruce was 13 and left no note, but the way he died left little doubt that he intended to kill himself. The burden of responsibility was clear as his mother reconstructed what happened:

> Only later did I realize that he showed signs of depression, and when someone says, "The day I was born was the worst day of my life," that can be a real danger signal. This is the hardest thing in the world to face. It would have been easy to say it was an accident—but it wasn't. I have to live with that. I keep saying, if only I had known, if only I had forced him to see a counselor, if only I had gotten to his room sooner.

If there is a difference in the grief of parents whose children committed suicide and that of parents whose children died of other causes, it is the degree to which parents feel guilt and are blamed, by themselves and others, for what happened. The question of degree is important. As you shall see later in this chapter, many parents feel that they have failed their children by not being able to prevent the death. However, after a suicide the blame by others for what happened is more blatant and open.

When they have been living with any illness, parents may feel some relief that the suffering has ended, that the vigil is over. But now they face a new set of circumstances—living without their children. Josh's mother said:

> Bereavement is traumatic; it is really a crisis in your life, it is awful. It amplified all my foibles. The hospice worker had told us, "You will never be the same again." I'm so grateful she warned me. A whole different set of issues is at work; it is different than when he was sick. Then, he was here, and that's what we thought about.

When the door is finally closed, the loss takes on a new reality and a new dimension of pain. This is a process that changes with time; time may ease the pain but does not take it away.

LEARNING OVER TIME

Changed Routines

One of the early things parents learn is that the little things that happen remind them that their children are not coming back. Shelly's mother reflected on how she felt just after the death:

> Sometimes I would get scared about how I will live without her love. I expected to have my daughter's love forever; you know, you go through all that pain of having and raising that child, and now—she was only 17 and all excited about finishing high school and getting her first job. . . . My husband talks about how much he misses just her touch when they watched TV together.

Most people cannot imagine how much the little things of life will be affected. Carl's father talked about how their house changed:

> As soon as people went back to their routines and you try to go back to your routine, that's when you realize that that routine doesn't exist anymore. We now had to get used to this new reality. Nothing is the same. All of a sudden there was this silence. The expectations of waking up in the morning, of hearing your son stomping up and down stairs going to the bathroom. You never knew you woke up expecting to hear them . . . it is automatic. You never realize that they meant anything to you except to irritate you for a while. Suddenly it is too quiet, and that's when it starts sinking in.

This new reality becomes real in little pieces, over time. Shelly's mother remembered:

> This happened in the summer, and I remember at Christmas thinking—okay, you can come out now. I did a good job, it is enough . . . but it didn't happen; she was really gone.

Dale's parents observed:

> Dale was supposed to be going to college. After the funeral, all his friends went off to college. For us for a while it was as if he had gone to college, too. Sure we knew the difference. We kept thinking this is what it would have been like if he had gone to college. But then on Thanksgiving they all came back, and he didn't come back. They came to our house for leftovers. We also let each of them choose something from his room that they wanted. A part of him went with them. It was very hard for us. We laughed and got through it, but it was very hard.

The Pain Never Goes Away

Parents learn that time does not heal, in spite of what everyone says. Sam was 13 when he died in a bicycle accident. His father talked about how hard it has been:

> It has been a year, I still can't believe it. Of course, I know he is dead, but his birthday was coming and I found myself thinking automatically of what we

could do to celebrate, and then I remembered. I began to realize that you never quite get used to it.

Time may temper the pain, so that there are days when the parents can think of their child without breaking down. They no longer think of things as easier or harder, but as different. Sam's father continued:

It is never going to stop hurting. People have to understand that . . . never. . . . This is someone you brought into this life . . . you bathed him, you nourished him, and you loved him. This pain remains the same; it is constant, what do you do about it? It is like a throbbing headache: At the beginning it can drive you crazy. Then you find ways of living with it. At first we were paralyzed by his death. Just accepting that every day this pain is there was what we had to do. Then we found ways of functioning around it—we are still finding ways.

Bruce's mother's pain has another dimension. This mother had to find a way to live with her guilt. Her acceptance of some responsibility for his death has become a part of who she is:

For a while I hibernated. I couldn't face people. Even my own mother said, "If he did do this—which I don't believe—then what did you do to him?" This is a small town, and I'm sure people were pointing fingers, saying this was a family doing terrible things. For a while, I felt myself to be suicidal. Even now, I still feel some responsibility. His personality contributed, but I wasn't there. I didn't respond in the way he needed. I just live with this.

As life goes on, there will always be reminders, things that will bring the pain to the surface again. Four years after Dale's death, his dog died. His parents described their reactions:

The dog was part of him; [Dale] trained him, he took care of him. He was a part of Dale that was still here. We didn't think about it until he died. It hit us very hard because, in a sense, another part of Dale was gone, and we felt bereft again in a new way. We still miss that dog.

Twelve years after his death, Carl's mother reflected:

I lost a 12-year-old who would have been 24 now . . . so I also lost a 24-year-old. . . . You are also a different person; I understand it all differently. As I put her hood on Linda at her college graduation, I suddenly realized that I would never do this with Carl, and I lost it. That's not unresolved grief . . . it will always be there. . . . You can't lose someone who was so much a part of your life and expect to fill that up or ever be able to act as if it didn't happen.

There is no "getting over it," nor can the empty space ever be filled. The pain may be less frightening and less intense, but it never entirely goes away.

TWO PARENTS: AT LEAST TWO WAYS OF GRIEVING

One of the biggest hurdles for parents may be learning to deal with each other. When a parent dies, the surviving spouse must deal with the children and all the changes in the family's life by himself or herself. When a child dies, the parents have to deal with each other's grief, as well as the grief of their other children. In today's world, this negotiation does not occur only in two-parent families. Many people, particularly women, are raising children in single-parent households. For them, these negotiations often occur with other members of their social network:

> I was divorced before my 3-year-old died suddenly. It was a rare case of sudden infant death syndrome. My mother was very helpful, especially with my older son Dan, but then she wanted me to cry like she was, and she couldn't understand how I chose to cope. We would have the same kind of arguments I hear couples having after a child dies. After a while, we learned to accept our differences.

Most of the time, there are two parents struggling with their grief. There are many different ways in which the relationship plays itself out as they each deal with the loss. Ronald died of cancer when he was 8 years old. His mother explained:

> We have come to the realization that we can't fix it. We have to have tolerance. At times we all become intolerant. A death like this disrupts the whole family. We had to renegotiate our whole relationship.

Many couples are told that the death of a child increases their chances of getting a divorce. Studies show that there are no consistent findings to support this assumption. When divorce occurs, the marriage was probably in trouble to begin with. Three years after his son's death in a swimming accident, one father told what happened to the family:

> We had gotten to a place where we were never agreeing about anything. Our son's death was the last straw. My wife wanted out. I took care of our other children, and I said go. I guess we became a statistic. But I wouldn't blame it on the death.

Bruce's mother and her husband were trying to reestablish their marriage when Bruce killed himself. She described their marital difficulties:

> I can't say we were emotionally supportive, but we agreed to be here for each other and for our younger son. Every time I tried to talk about suicide, he wouldn't go there with me. He wanted to believe it was an accident. After a while, he changed. It was like he got jolted into a different place. We went into counseling. He became more attentive. Now he can ask about blame and his part, and we are beginning to talk about this. It is hard work.

Differences Between the Genders

At one level, parents know that the world has stopped. They try to draw on the styles and resources for coping that worked for them before their child's death, which may or may not be appropriate now. In Bruce's family, their prior ways of coping were not effective, and they were able to work toward new ones. Another factor, as noted in Chapters 3 and 4, in this negotiation is that men and women may have different coping styles. Men are accustomed to "getting the job done," whereas women focus more on emotional needs.

McClowry et al. (1987) studied different coping styles in bereaved families. They identified a group of parents who coped with their grief by "getting over it," focusing on getting on with their lives; they did not dwell on their feelings about the death. This style may be more typical of men than of women (Cook, 1988). Peter's father stated the dilemma clearly a year after his son's death:

> For me, everything in the family has changed. Now I see how we deal with difference. She wants me to be like her. I can't grieve as she does. I prefer to do it by myself. I can't keep crying and go over how awful I feel. You need to respect each other's differences. My wife and I are just not in the same place.

Peter's mother described her perspective:

> In bed, I cry . . . and if I cry too long, then he starts changing the subject. I see crying in bed as my time when the other children aren't around. I get angry at him. I want to talk about Peter and things he did and what reminds me of him, and my husband has no patience. We know we need to learn to do things differently, but we don't know how to begin.

Kevin died in an automobile accident. His mother recalled:

> My husband has always been black and white: good-bad happy-sad. This is the way he always is in our marriage. When Kevin died, my husband said, "You have another child." He said, "You have to be there for him, and that's it." He sounded almost cold and matter-of-fact. There are times when a woman just wants to be held. I didn't want to have sex, but that's what he wanted and then he was upset and hurt. Then we both pulled away from each other. We certainly weren't helping each other. That's why we grabbed at the idea as soon as we heard about this program for grieving parents and siblings.

One of the most sensitive areas in which differences emerge is each partner's approach to sexuality and its meaning in his or her life. For men, this physical intimacy can be comforting. For women, sex is often associated with conception and brings back the sense of loss. Women's monthly cycle is a reminder of what has been lost, and their menstrual periods seem to make them more sensitive. In the early months after a child's death, women often report that any sexual desire died with the child.

Negotiating Differences

When a child has been sick, parents may already have experimented with their different styles by the time the death occurs. There may have been a struggle as they found their way. Dale's father talked about how he and his wife came to realize how much they needed each other:

> While Dale was getting one of his bone marrow transplants, I started to feel very angry about what was happening to my child. If I believed in God, I would have

gotten angry with him, so I figured out the only person to get angry with was my wife. I figured out how to get her so angry with me that we could get a divorce. Don't ask me what that would have accomplished. I couldn't convince myself or my wife that she deserved my anger. She kept looking at me strangely. It lasted about a week. We finally laughed and we cried together as we reflected on what I was doing.

As parents grieve, feelings of all sorts emerge, and changes take place at many levels. It is not as if they work out their relationship once and are done with it. Their relationship will change many times as they deal with the loss over the years. Dale's parents reflected on this fact:

> I think that the reason that our marriage lasted and got better after his death was because we were pretty much in agreement even though our styles are so different. We were basically able to talk about most things, and we were able to live with each other's differences.

Openness to each other's differences is a critical quality. Ellen's mother commented:

> How do you survive as a couple? How did we work out our difference? We talked, we love each other, and we held each other and we began to appreciate that we were different and also had our own lives. I always tell people to do things separately. Each of us was grieving on different levels. I was very sad at the beginning, and he was very rational. He was the type who was always very concerned about everyone else, but now he had to face what was happening in his life. When we went to bed, I would talk about my feelings, so I could go to sleep, and then he would have it all, and he couldn't sleep. He got to the point where he said, "Don't talk," and then that would breed resentment in me. It was a while after Ellen died, but we got to a place where we could hear each other. Coming to the bereavement center where we knew our son was getting some attention helped us to break this barrier.

This kind of openness is partly the result of arriving at a place where neither parent is totally dependent on the relationship with the other; that is, both can accept each other as separate people and not be threatened by their differences. They can acknowledge their pain, but are not so consumed by it that they cannot see the other person's pain as well. As I discussed in Chapters 3 and 4, parents who have this openness and flexibility may begin with a greater capacity for mutuality. They can acknowledge their own needs and, from this perspective, can see the needs of others more clearly. They need to learn that they can help each other and now to include their other children who have also experienced a loss. Ronald's mother reflected on what she and her husband had learned during the five years since his death:

> My husband always said it is like reading the same book, but being on different pages. It takes a lot of patience. We could comfort each other, but we always knew we each had our own pain. I think everyone is different with their pain and experiences it differently.

COMPLICATED EMOTIONS

Blame and Guilt

Blame is one issue that can become extremely divisive. It can be an easy way to displace the pain. It becomes essential to recognize what can and cannot be controlled. Blame is associated with guilt. People play the "if only" game: if only I hadn't bought him the roller blades, but my husband insisted; if only my wife had backed me up about not giving him the car that night; if only we had moved out of that community, she wouldn't have been exposed to those pollutants in the water.

Guilt is a way of saying "it is my fault." When a child dies, parents feel that they have failed in some way because they could not protect their child. As the parents try to understand what happened, their own frustration and sense of futility almost always lead them to ask: "Where did I fail? What didn't I see? What did I overlook?" As you saw earlier, this is a pressing issue for parents whose children killed themselves. Rando (1993) pointed out that feelings of guilt may be a way of protecting oneself from the real sense of loss. Guilt is a way of diverting feelings. Clinging to the feeling that you could have done something to avert the tragedy is a way of avoiding the helplessness and powerlessness that everyone feels when a child dies, regardless of the cause. It can provide a false sense of control. Bruce's mother consoled herself by learning to respect her own lack of knowledge and the limits this placed on her ability to change the scenario.

Dealing with this guilt may be one of the earliest tests of parents' ability to be there for each other, to respect their differences, and to find new ways of working together for their own sakes, as well as their other children's.

Anger

With guilt often comes anger. Sometimes parents feel guilty because they are angry at God or at the fates that brought them to this place. If they feel they were singled out for this fate, it can make the situation worse. Several years after Ellen died, her mother talked about this feeling:

> I have to get angry at something because I am so sad. . . . Why me, why am I the one? Why can't I be normal, mainstream like everyone else?

Some, like Josh's mother, simply get angry for what they lost:

> Sometimes I get angry when I see a child who is not very nice. Josh had so much more to offer, and he is not here. Luckily I'm getting over this. I don't ask as much why was he taken when he had so much to offer. Also for a long time, it was very hard for me to realize that friends' children are growing up. I don't know what it means to have a 9-year-old. . . . Now I can listen to friends who talk about their 9-year-olds without getting angry.

It is important at least to acknowledge the anger, the sense of assault on one's very being. Even years after the death, the anger may come back, usually when things have not been going well at work or when a parent is feeling down for one reason or another. All of this is very normal under the circumstances and people need to know that.

Anger can become pervasive when the death is the result of a criminal act. Stephanie was killed in a drive-by shooting. Her mother said:

> You are angry at yourself for not being able to prevent this; you are angry at the system around you for not being able to prevent it. You are also confused because what you thought you could do to prevent it didn't work.

How can parents reconcile their sense of loss with the fact that the murderer still lives? Will the death of the perpetrator ease this anger? When David's father was killed (see Chapter 5), his mother was clear that she would not allow herself to be consumed by a need for vengeance. This was not the message she wanted to teach her children, and it would not be true to her husband's memory. When a child is murdered, is it possible to feel the same way? Darrell's parents put it clearly:

> For a year after he was killed, they didn't know who did it. We didn't let that consume us. There was never any vengefulness. The media tried to fan our sense of vengeance . . . but what good would that do? For myself, I needed to step back to ask what would I get out of it? So yes, I was very angry. We are looking for solace, for a way to appease the pain, even something to feed the pain. Some people think vengeance will do that for them, then that's what they seek. At the trial, after it was over, we heard people saying, "Now you can have closure." We said no; it is closure for the detective, for the district attorney, and it is closure for the media. But we continue to live, and there will never be closure. We still have to find ways of living with our son's death, but vengeance won't help.

Releasing the Tension

Parents often talk about the need to "let off steam," to let out the tension and pain in them. This is a different feeling from anger. Dale's mother recalled:

> If I was driving, I sometimes would pull over and just scream. I didn't bother anyone, and I felt better. I had a friend whose daughter died and she had young children at home. She couldn't simply leave. So she had a pillow in her basement where she could bury her head, scream as she needed to, and go back to the children.

Everyone needs ways of putting grief on hold from time to time. For parents who work outside the home, work may provide some escape. It is another way of shrouding their feelings, but like screaming, it is only temporary. Carl's mother said:

> Work was very important after my son died. It was a place where he wasn't present all the time like at home. I was just existing. All I could hope to do was

get through a day where I had five minutes' relief from thinking that my son was dead—without thinking about how can I survive without my son.

Mothers who are at home full time with younger children have to find other outlets. Leslie's mother talked about her life as an army wife who moved every few years:

> When we moved this last time, I began to realize that I needed something more than being at home with my other child. I could have gotten a paying job, but I wanted the flexibility to be home for my son and my husband. I joined every community group that seemed to have any interest to me, from the garden club to raising money for cancer research. I needed to be with people, so I pushed aside my shyness and my sadness and I reached out. It's working. I don't get so impatient with my son or worry about him so much. It seems easier to be there for both my husband and my son when I feel good.

OTHER PEOPLE DO NOT ALWAYS HELP

Mourners often talk about the need to deal with other people's reactions. Every mourner has stories about inappropriate comments from others. More often, others avoid meeting them face to face. Any mention of a child's death can be a conversation stopper. At a time when parents need all the help they can get, they are often aware of how other people's attitudes toward them change. This may be especially true of new people who ask how many children they have. Peter's mother was angry that she had to be concerned not to hurt other people's feelings:

> What should I say when someone asks how many children we have? Sometimes when I see how people react, I wonder if I am too blunt. . . . I say two living and one dead. Now I think maybe I shouldn't use the word *dead*, maybe I should say, one passed away. . . . Would that make it easier for people to hear?

In fact, short of confronting these people with their own fears and discomfort, there is little she can do. It is not really her responsibility to help others feel better. This kind of exchange often leaves parents with the feeling that they are being criticized because their children died, especially if the children were murdered, committed suicide, or died from sudden infant death syndrome. In these situations, people react as if the parents did something to hurt their children or that the parents or their children must have done something wrong to put themselves in harm's way. Darrell's parents remembered how criticized they felt by hospital personnel and, later, by the police who investigated his death:

> The way they asked questions, it made us feel that he was just another African American kid in trouble. We found ourselves defending him, to be sure they knew he was a good kid, never involved in gangs, and from a very caring family.

People who back off at a time when you need them the most add additional stress to the situation. Bruce's mother talked about her younger son's teacher:

> His teacher the first year after Bruce died was wonderful. He was also a good little boy. By the next year, he decided it was time to show how he felt. This new teacher kept telling me, "We have big problems." I kept saying, "Let's figure out what is going on and try to help him." But she never called me. Once I overheard her tell another teacher: "This boy needs a lot of attention because his brother committed suicide. This is a really problematic family. What can you expect?" She was condemning us. It helped her not to take any responsibility for her classroom.

It takes a good deal of energy, at a time when parents least have it, to see what people are saying in the larger context and to deal with their inability to cope with an uncomfortable situation.

With time, some parents develop a sense of humor about it that serves them well. Three years after Ronald died, his mother said:

> Sometimes we (my husband and I) test people to see how fast they will back off from us when we tell them we have two children; one died of cancer when he was 8.

PARENTING THE OTHER CHILDREN

Couples also have to deal with changes in the way they parent their other children. For mothers, who are often the primary caretakers in the family, their awareness of the changed dynamic is often immediate. Soon after Peter's death, his mother described the changes she experienced in her daily life:

> I went back to work. That's fine, but it is coming home that's the problem. I am used to saying where are all three of my children. Now I have to remember not to ask for Peter. We have to create a new normal. Priscilla is our oldest child now. Greg used to say, "I wish I had my own room"; now he does. I have a hard time at night when one of the kids asks for help with their homework, I find myself studying the same chapter I did with Peter: Who would dream that it was the last time I would study with him? and then I start to cry. I think that upsets the children, but sometimes I can't help it.

How can parents share grief with a child? Often this sharing involves qualities similar to those that are needed to share grief with the other parent. Parents need to learn how to include both each other and their other children. This is not an easy process. Peter's mother was aware that her children were upset by her crying, but did not know what to do about it:

> The kids come in. They say don't cry. I guess it upsets them, but if I didn't cry, it might be worse. I am not sure what I should say. It is all so turned around. I am the one who is used to comforting them. For the moment, nothing is in place.

A Different Parent

It may not be easy for parents, initially, to experience their other children's pain and to see how to comfort them. It is too overwhelming. Children may need to hear that it is. Knowing what is going on, even if it is only that their parents are overwhelmed, will make them feel more secure. Some time after Janice died of cystic fibrosis, her siblings came to their parents and demanded their attention:

> The children were very blunt. They said: "We want our mother and father back." It wasn't easy, but we listened. They were really surprised when we told them, "Those people are gone forever; you have to live with the mother and father you have now. Everything is changed. Your sister's death has turned everything around, and we *all* need to learn new ways. We are all hurting and we are in this together." It made a big difference in the way the children, even the 6-year-old, reacted. They seemed to relax. We think it was because they felt included and began to understand what was happening.

As the parents and surviving children negotiate the changes in their lives, they begin to recognize the scope of what has happened. The change is radical. Carl's mother described how she felt immediately after the death:

> I was a fairly decisive person before Carl died. But afterward, I couldn't decide whether my 16-year-old should do certain things. I found myself phoning her best friend's mother, asking, "Are 16-year-olds doing this?" I remember one of her teachers talked to me when I was at school: "You have no idea how much Linda is trying to protect you." I looked at him, and said, "How can a 16-year-old protect me?" He said Linda told him, "I can't be late even five minutes; my mother gets upset." Then I remembered the first time she was late, and I went through the ceiling.

Continuity and Structure

As the family deals with the changes, there has to be some continuity and structure that the other children can count on. Parents provide this continuity by maintaining routines that make the children's daily lives somewhat predictable. Maureen's parents sent their surviving children to school and encouraged them to invite their friends over to play. Their mother overheard her 5-year-old tell a friend: "My big sister died. That was her toy. Let's play with it." Because others around her acknowledged the death, she was able to accept it as part of her life and who she was. There may be some things about which, under the circumstances, parents feel ambivalent, especially when their children misbehave. Leslie's mother talked about her 8-year-old son:

> I soon learned what didn't work dealing with Kyle. It didn't work trying to be angry when he did something that he knew wasn't right. . . . What worked was understanding and hugging and letting him be a kid. Sometimes I had to put my foot down. It can get very confusing; it was very difficult to sort out what is part of death and what was related to other things. I didn't want him to use

Leslie's death as an excuse to get away with things. It could also be his age, or maybe because he is just bored. I realized it was everything.

Bruce's mother's interactions with her younger son also changed. She described this process:

Parents carry this horror with them all the time, but I think it has a positive effect. I'm more conscious now of what I'm doing. I ask, what are my issues that are getting in the way? At the beginning, my 6-year-old could be loving and caring, and just like that, he would get angry. I tried to understand what a 6-year-old can understand and what he can't. I wouldn't do that before. I realized I couldn't give him enough attention. I got him into counseling. If I can't be there with him, someone else can be. I try to follow his lead more. We talk a lot about Bruce. Sometimes he will approach how Bruce died with a little openness, and ask for details. But then he says, "I don't want to talk about it," so we don't go there. I've learned we talk as much as he wants.

Community Support

How parents cope with these changes and how they involve their other children in the process are influenced by their experiences with death and illness and by the community in which they live. Darrell's parents realized that they had to respond to their 4-year-old's understanding of death almost immediately because they were sure that she did not understand what had happened to her brother. Even though they had grown up in a religious and ethnic community that accepted death as part of life, they still had to think carefully about how to help their daughter. Although she was surrounded by caring relatives whom she knew and trusted, her parents recognized that they had to involve her school as well. Several years later, her mother explained that it took a long time for the daughter to understand:

I went to school. I told her teacher and the principal what had happened. I knew they knew, but I wanted them to hear it from me. I said, "If she cries, just allow her to cry—don't tell her to stop crying. You have my permission to hold her. She is sad, and no one has an answer for what happened. If you can't deal with this, send her to the principal." I have done this every year because she still is dealing with his death. All the teachers so far have been most understanding. It is three years later, and she is just beginning to understand that he is really not coming back. She talks a lot about him, and the teachers have to understand that this is okay.

Applying Their Own Experience

Other parents may not have any experience or models to draw on as they cope with the death. For some, the death of their child is their first personal encounter with death. Kevin's mother described her experience:

This was my first brush with death; both my parents are still alive. My husband was in Vietnam, so he had a lot of experience. As I think about Kevin's death, I realize now that I had to grow up fast. I watched our son. All of a sudden, he is an only child. He seems so alone, and I am not sure we can help him.

Other parents experienced losses when they were young, which made them aware of some of the things their children were feeling. Sometimes this experience helps, sometimes it does not. Six years after Zach's death, his mother was concerned about her son Aaron, now the oldest. She was aware of how the death still affected him, but felt helpless to do anything. At age 20, Aaron was no longer a child. His mother said:

> Aaron had mixed feelings after the death. He understood his brother and looked out for him. On the other hand, he was jealous and also worried that he didn't do enough. He is very angry, not doing well at school, kind of drifting. He blames it on my not having had time for him. I've tried to explain that it wasn't up to me. I told him my own story. My little sister got polio, and in the end, she died. My mother was at the hospital a lot. I was a child, and I needed attention that I didn't get. I understand what Aaron feels. My mother didn't do it deliberately. Neither did I. I suggested counseling might be of use to him. He says no, he already knows his issues. I love him, I want to help, but he won't let me.

At this point in his life, hearing his mother's story does not help Aaron deal with his own situation. He is not able to hold both his own and his mother's perspectives at the same time, to recognize that he can learn from her experience. He seems developmentally young for his age. His mother needs to find other ways of helping him that are more appropriate to his developmental stage. As you can see, being aware of a problem does not always mean that there is an easy solution.

Juggling Different Needs

Parents need to learn to coordinate their own needs with their children's need for their support and guidance. As Darrell's parents described, this is an ongoing process:

> It is difficult for us because there are times when you want to let it all out, but it wouldn't help the kids. You need to be there for them. When they are down, you have to be there. When our daughter is feeling that way, we are there, and as painful as it is, we continue to talk, and we cry. We don't try to put up a wall. We acknowledge her pain. She is learning that there are two kinds of pain . . . pain when you get hurt that you can see and pain that you feel, that is in your heart, and she says it hurts so much—it hurts so bad and we agree with her, and it does hurt. We had to help her get to the stage where she could talk about Darrell and think about him. We were doing it for her, never realizing that we had to do it for ourselves. But we realized she needed us. In a way, it was she who helped us.

CONSTRUCTING A RELATIONSHIP
TO THE DECEASED

After the death, parents find ways to maintain a continuing relationship with their deceased child. One of the things they discover is that, in ways for which they are often unprepared, their child is still alive within them and has a role in their current life. Josh's family has Christmas ornaments that he made:

> Whenever we put up the tree, Kenneth asks about Josh. He always is sure to put up the ornaments that we saved, and he really enjoys hearing about his brother. This has become a very important part of the holiday for us. We know Josh will always be with us and is now a part of his brother's life and his sister's, too, as she gets old enough to understand.

Darrell's family has also found a way of maintaining some of his traditions at Christmas:

> He had the habit of giving out roses at Christmas. Now we give everyone in the family one rose on the holiday. It was important to him that he was going to make a difference in people's lives, and we are trying to make that happen.

Darrell is still, in an appropriate manner, part of his family and his community's life.

Talking about the child is another important way of keeping his or her presence alive. This does not always involve public occasions; small private activities count as well:

> I like to talk about Dale even if some people are uncomfortable. My stories about diapers and picking a college are just as valid. People come to me and say, "It is so miraculous that you can talk." At first I thought, Am I making others uncomfortable? but with time people got used to it. Maybe they learned something, too, about life and death.

Siblings can also stimulate the connection if the parents are willing. Ellen's mother found ways to help her son remember his sister:

> Sometimes I read books to Nick about people dying. I can start to cry, and he does, too. Then he said he wants to make a scrapbook, to collect all the pictures of Ellen. I thought this was a neat idea, and we have started to work on it.

Leslie's mother spreads her memory throughout the family:

> All my sisters were having children. We had so many stuffed animals people had sent her. I decided that I would keep her alive for their children through this collection of stuffed animals. Each time a baby is born, I send them one of the animals and so Leslie's animals become part of this new family member's world.

Dale's parents keep his presence alive on a daily basis by wearing his jewelry. His mother explained:

I wear a gold chain that he wore. He had two rings, one had belonged to my father. Now my husband wears that. Dale had bought me a little necklace with a heart on it for Mother's Day. I keep the heart on a charm bracelet that has things from him on it, and I wear it all the time.

Kevin's father wanted to give his son a posthumous birthday party. Friends and family were clearly opposed, yet he was not deterred:

I had promised him a bash, and I wanted him to have it. I explained to my wife, and she agreed. We invited neighbors, friends, some relatives, and our minister. I heard later that one friend's wife said we were nuts; we should let Kevin go. This friend didn't agree with his wife, but he didn't feel he could come alone! We had a little gathering. We didn't have a cake, just "obscene" desserts. We talked about Kevin and about his life. Our minister said a prayer. Our other son loved it. We had a birthday to celebrate the time he was here. As the minister was leaving, he said, "I wasn't sure how this would come off. This was wonderful, this was a nice evening. Now tomorrow I will be thinking about him. I know him a little better, and also that everything is going on as best it can." We felt we had a support group and that life was somehow ongoing. It was a birthday memorial and maybe we will do it again next year.

In this way, Kevin came alive for their friends. A person had died, not simply a son. His father felt that he had kept his promise to his son and perhaps had created a new ritual for remembering and honoring his son's life. Shelly's mother was asked by friends if she felt guilty about laughing:

I never felt that way. My daughter laughed a lot. . . . She had this wonderful belly laugh. I just think it is a wonderful stress reliever; it helps you make it. Plus it is more of a tribute to her that I laugh in her spirit.

Often this connection to their deceased children helps parents find new ways of living their lives. Shelly's mother felt that her daughter still played an active role in her life. She described Shelly's presence this way:

My husband and I felt the emptiness of our house and that we needed someone who could benefit from what we had to give. Two years after the accident, we decided to adopt a little girl from China. I think that my daughter chose her for us. There is no replacement, but she has given us something to live for. We see her as our third child.

This mother also has a faith system that gives some shape to her sense of connection:

I think it is helpful to look forward to being united. I don't know how people can go on if they don't believe they will meet. I never thought about seeing my father again when he died when I was young. All this came out after my daughter died. Things happen that keep reinforcing my belief. I was at a wedding two years ago, felt the wind and lots of leaves rustling. I then felt my daughter was there, and I started crying. I didn't want to cry, but when you lose a child, you feel especially uncomfortable at weddings.

Josh's mother also had a sense of his spirit living on:

> For me, I had to believe that he was safe, some place warm and safe, in the sense that heaven could be that. It was something that we could cling to. We both feel that he went on to a better place because his body failed him so terribly. We can feel his spirit around; that gives us a feeling that he is not completely gone. We acknowledge that he was a part of the family. . . . He has a place in our hearts; . . he will always be there.

Even when parents do not feel that there is something beyond death or that their child's spirit is there, they find that this connection is strong and that it is consoling and important to them. Dale's mother was surprised:

> I had a spiritual experience—in spite of what I say—several days after Dale died. I felt a spirit—no words, just that I got a feeling that Dale was saying, "I am okay, Mom." I said for a person who doesn't believe in anything, I just had the weirdest experience. I rationalize it that I brought it on myself because I wanted to have that experience, to feel that he was okay.

Some parents are also aware that their other children feel this connection and encourage them to do so. Darrell's father described his daughter's relationship with her brother:

> Her main concern was if she could still talk to him at home or in the car. She knew we used to tease him about being lazy, and so she wanted to know why God would want him and why couldn't he send him back after he finished his work? She now knows that he is an angel. She believes that he is her guardian angel. When we remember the good times, it seems to ease her pain. Remembering gives her comfort, and then she will go off and play.

CHANGED BY THE EXPERIENCE

It is clear that at each step along the way, parents have to discover new ways of living in the world. At some point they realize that they are no longer the persons they were before the death. When the death comes after a long illness, some parents report this awakening when they first heard the diagnosis. Dale's father recalled:

> I soon learned that I couldn't control the world. I found out what was important. My whole attitude toward work and family changed. I think that this all started as soon as I found out how sick my son was. I was a changed man.

As they deal with their grief, parents have to surrender their sense of order and control in the world. As they move in time with their grief, reestablishing the order and control becomes possible, but in an entirely different way. Three years after Stephanie was killed, her mother said:

> Only now can I see what it means. I was forced to grow. All of a sudden, I did feel like a grown up. . . . Until then I still felt, in part, like a teenager. It also forced my husband and me to be more introspective than we would otherwise.

One way that parents change is that they develop a new sense of voice. They develop a capacity to think for themselves and to speak out. Bruce's mother said:

> At church, I realized I was being told by my pastor that suicide was a sin and Bruce was doomed to hell. The old me would have sat there quietly and accepted what he said. The new me said, "He can't be right," and I told my husband, "I'm leaving this church." It was okay with me if he stayed. I couldn't have done that before either. I would have waited for him or been upset if he didn't come along. As it turned out, he felt the same way.

The death also has a clear impact on how parents relate to themselves and to others. After her son's death, Sam's mother spent a lot of time reflecting on her way of doing things and participated in a parent support group. She described the resulting change:

> I was raised to understand that my parents were in charge and when I got to be a parent, I would be in charge. That's what I did, and I was just like my mother. You don't challenge that order, and you don't think for yourself. I taught my children, "You don't step outside these boundaries, and you listen to what I tell you." After my son died, I realized that's not the way things are. Waiting for other people to tell you what to do doesn't help at such times. I talk differently to Barry, my other son, now. I realize that I have to hear him, too. If I let him, he has something to contribute. I don't feel so helpless, and neither does he.

Before her son's death, this mother was dependent on others to guide her thinking. Her sense of self depended on authority to maintain the balance in her relationships. As she coped with Sam's death, she began to see that thinking is not a unilateral process, but has to allow for mutuality and exchanging of ideas. She saw the value of the ability of each of her family members to think actively about and organize his or her experience and make meaning of it. In a sense, the family members began to hear each other's voices and, in listening, came to yet another way of working together to deal with the loss in their lives. She felt empowered by this shift in how she made meaning.

The death also has an impact on how parents react to death and how they educate their younger children about it. Josh's father clearly believed that Josh's death changed the way both he and his wife handle death with their young son:

> I try not to let him watch TV shows in which life is a cheap commodity. What happens when people have guns . . . guns kill people. We try very hard to explain that when you die, people are not here anymore . . . like Josh. Therefore, playing "bang, bang, you're dead" is not a game. He remembers when his grandfather died recently. He knows what it means. He will probably not grow up with the prejudices I had about death. I wasn't allowed, even as an older teenager, to visit the sick or go to funerals. Probably not until my mom passed away did death became real for me. It's different for my children.

CHAPTER NINE

When a Sibling Dies

> The worst part about my brother's death is that it is so quiet in the house and there is no one to fight with now.
>
> —Barry, Sam's younger brother

What is lost when a sibling dies? We grow up with the expectation that our siblings will always be part of our lives. This relationship is supposed to be the longest we have with anyone, even longer than that with our parents, whom we expect to die before us. When a sibling dies, this expectation is lost (Coles, 1996; Hause, 1989). What is lost also depends on the nature of the relationship before the death. As with all deaths, children lose not only the individual, but the unique relationship they had with that sibling (Bank, 1992). Just as there are many different families, there are many different kinds of sibling relationships.

A sibling relationship colors and enriches childhood in unique ways. Sibling relationships are dynamic, changing, always busy with something. Siblings grow up in the same household and, if born to the same parents, are genetically linked as well. They learn similar familial values and share common experiences. They give each other companionship and affection. They learn from each other to be dependent in a way that is different from their dependence on their parents, as well as how to accept help comfortably in a different manner (Bryant, 1982; Dunn, 1992). They provide each other with what can be called direct services—teaching each other new skills, exchanging toys, and sharing clothes (Davies, 1988).

Attachments between siblings shape personality and sense of place in the world as much as attachments to parents. Siblings can develop a special intimacy with each other. They confide in each other and share their responses to the family story. Martinson and Campos (1991) talked about siblings serving one another by challenging parental authority. Siblings learn to juggle for position and attention and to cooperate for common goals. Josh's father considered how his relationship with 5-year-old Kenneth would be different if Josh had lived:

> A lot of what I do would be done by Josh as the big brother. Kenneth would be the middle child. The whole dynamic in the family would be different. It defies our imagination; . . we have no concept.

He recognized that Josh could have taught his brother new skills and ways of getting along in the world that would be different from what a parent could teach.

At the same time, each sibling has a unique experience in the family, depending on his or her age, birth order, and gender, and each has particular interactions with his or her parents and other siblings (Dunn & Plomin, 1990). Typically, parent-child relationships are hierarchical; in most families, there is a chain of command. In many ways, this hierarchy is mirrored in the relationship between younger and older siblings at certain periods of their lives. As members of the same generation, siblings usually relate as peers. But unlike peers, their shared family ties and roles in their family may make their relationship more complicated.

WHEN A SIBLING IS ILL

When a child in a family is terminally ill, the impact on a sibling is pervasive. Parents often want to protect their other children from this painful experience. In Chapter 7, I discussed the decision parents have to make about telling the child about his or her illness. They find that their impulse to protect the sick child from the bad news does not work. This situation is true for their other children as well: They cannot protect them from their sibling's illness and impending death. In this instance, protection means involving them. Children need to be involved and seen as active members of the family, as helpers, and as grievers. Martinson and Campos (1991) found that siblings who were allowed to participate in caring for a sibling who was dying of cancer felt pride and pleasure about their ability to help. The same conclusions would be true for other illnesses as well. Maureen's siblings were young; they could help by reading to her or playing music in her room. Older children can do more. A 17-year-old described what she did when it became clear that her younger sister would not survive:

> I was the oldest daughter. I said I would be at home, after school, to take care of my younger brother and sister when they got home while my mother was in the hospital with my sister who had this rare genetic disease. I was pleased that I could help. It wasn't that it was all on me. Everyone really helped me: Mom was in and out, my father was there, and neighbors in the building came by. In the end, it brought us closer. When my sister died, we didn't feel so alone. We were there for each other.

Because she had a valued role in the family's coping with the illness, she gained a new sense of competence. This sense of competence, in turn, helped her to cope well when the death occurred.

Like other relationships, sibling roles are not static. As children mature, the nature of their sibling relationship changes. Two years after Jessica died of cancer, her younger sister Emma, now 16, recalled how their relationship changed as she matured:

> We weren't very close. There were four years between us. Actually we fought a lot . . . until she became sick. I think we stopped fighting because I became more mature—we seemed to have more in common. She was home a lot, and

so we did things together. We liked to cook, we liked to work on the crossword puzzles in the Sunday paper together, we liked to see the same movies on TV. Our taste in things became more similar. When I think of those times with her, I miss her.

Often the illness changes the course of the sibling relationship, bringing the siblings closer together or reducing tensions between them. Five years after her older brother's death, 15-year-old Jane described how things changed when he got sick with cancer:

As I look back, I used to make my brother's life miserable. I followed him and insisted that I could do everything he did, even when he was 10 and I was 5. I think now that I just didn't like being the youngest, and I couldn't believe what my parents told me, that I would get older and be able to do what he did. When he got sick and I saw what he was going through, I think that pushed me to grow up a little faster.

Children develop an understanding beyond their years as they learn to ask questions and take in what is going on. The illness pushes them to confront issues and feelings that would not ordinarily be expected of children their age.

AT THE TIME OF DEATH

Children whose siblings died have many of the same reactions as the bereaved children described earlier. When parents have decided that their child will die at home, siblings are, by default, involved in the process. In Chapter 8, Maureen's mother described her younger children's easy relationship with their sister before and after she died. For older children, being present at a sibling's death may be more difficult. They may have a fuller understanding of what dying means and have absorbed the discomfort of those around them in dealing with death. At age 14, Emma found watching Jessica die at home painful. She describes the process:

If she had died in the hospital, then I wouldn't have had to see it all the time. That was very hard. I liked that everyone always told us the truth. We knew how sick she was, but we tried to keep up our spirits and be hopeful. When she finally died, I ran out to a neighbor. I came home only when the funeral director came and took away her body. I was relieved that it was over and I didn't have to come home every day from school and worry about what I would find. But even then, it was hard to believe that she was gone.

Emma's reactions to her sister's death raise some questions about how to support children who are watching their siblings die. Having her sister die in their home raised her stress to a level that taxed her ability to cope. While her parents were honest with her and present on a day-to-day basis, she needed more support than they could provide at the time. They were under tremendous stress themselves, trying to juggle the needs of their dying child, their own reactions to the illness, and the different needs of their other children.

Like the mourners described in other chapters, children often feel a sense of shock and disbelief when their siblings die. Even when they know death is imminent, they find it hard to believe that their sibling is really dead. When the death is sudden or violent, the level of shock is deeper. Kayla was injured in the accident that killed her mother and sister. Her sense of shock and numbness helped her get through the trauma:

> I actually had a sense of peace. Reality didn't hit me until I was out in the real world. The first time I really cried was in a grief group of other kids my age, about three months later.

Jocelyn was 17 when her older brother was killed in Vietnam. She ran after the navy chaplain who came to tell the family about her brother's death:

> I just couldn't believe it. He told my mother, made sure she called another adult to be with her, and left. I needed to hear it myself. I wanted him to say it wasn't true. Of course, he couldn't.

When a sibling commits suicide, the shock has an additional dimension as the family struggles to accept this act:

> It was almost impossible to believe that my brother chose to kill himself. I knew he was unhappy, but I couldn't imagine he would do this. My mind raced with all sorts of questions about what I could have done. I was so angry. Then I just sort of shut off. Otherwise, I don't know how I would have got through the funeral.

As was discussed earlier, children need to be recognized as mourners and involved in the rituals around the death. Three-year-old Teddy was killed in a farming accident 15 years ago. In spite of his family's shock, his parents were clear that their three other children had to be informed and involved in what was happening. Alan was 11 at the time:

> We are farmers; we see death all the time, see animals die. But I don't think we even had a clue that we weren't going to get to see Teddy again. One thing about kids and death, you can see death, but it's nothing until you experience it.

Mark was 5 at the time:

> I didn't remember having anyone close to me die. I was pretty good for a couple of days because I thought after a few days he was coming back to life. I remember thinking Jesus came back to life after a few days, so I thought Teddy would. I looked everywhere for him. I didn't really understand. Now I am glad Mom and Dad explained everything about what was going on and they took me to the wake and the funeral.

Seeing the body may make the death more real. Eric, their third brother, was 9. Thinking back on the funeral, he offered the following advice:

> I remember going into the funeral home, and it seemed like we were in there forever. I had some anxiety about seeing him. I didn't want to. But I think it was a good experience—make sure everyone does it. In a way it helped make it real,

even though I kept looking for him for a long time afterward. We saw a rainbow after he was buried, and we decided that was him going to heaven.

A RELATIONSHIP IS LOST

In many ways, children's grief and the feelings they experience after the death are similar whether it is a parent or a sibling who dies. Yet in looking at what is lost, we see the different qualities of these two relationships. Kayla lost both her mother and sister in the same accident when she was 16. She reflected on the differences in what she lost:

> Individually there are different roles. With my mother, I lost the nurturing and the guidance; with my sister, I lost the unconditional love of a sister and a friend, no matter what phase she was in.

What is lost depends on the ages of the siblings and how they characterize their connection. Younger children see the loss as their lack of a playmate or a competitor. Older children can recognize that they lost a teacher, a role model, a protector, a student, a companion, and a friend. Sam's brother Barry, quoted at the beginning of this chapter, lost someone who shared his life. His use of the word *fighting* is one way of characterizing the active dialogue that took place between them. Barry has not yet developed a vocabulary to describe all the various ways in which he and his brother related to each other, so he focused on their disagreements. What did he lose with Sam's death? From his perspective, he lost someone who filled his life with noise and action without which his daily life now seemed empty.

When an older sibling dies, the younger sibling may lose someone who was a parent surrogate, a source of care and nourishment, as well as a friend. Jocelyn's brother helped her develop constructive behaviors and value her own well being. She remembered:

> I was 17 when my brother died at the age of 19. He was the one who always looked out for me, took care of me. He kept me from using drugs. There was a lot of it around in the high school in the 60s. Part of the reason I never used drugs was how hard he had worked to keep me away. His death was a terrible loss—there was no one who could ever fill that bill for me, even though I am married with children of my own now.

As I discussed in the last chapter, Darrell's sister remembered Darrell reading to her and playing with her. Later, she saw him continuing his role as a big brother by serving as her guardian angel. This guardian role is typical of older siblings. Barry recalled what it was like when his brother was alive:

> Since my brother was a year and a half older than me, he was tall so he stood up for me. If I got into a fight, he stopped people from bugging me. Now I have to learn to do that myself. He kicked butt; . . he was a good kid, very bright.

Barry lost a protector and someone who watched out for him. Justine was 16 when her older sister died in a motorcycle accident. For her, this sister was almost a parent surrogate. She said:

> I lost someone who really took care of me. Sometimes it seemed like she was the only one who paid attention. I felt like I didn't have any direction after she was gone.

When a younger sibling dies, the surviving siblings talk not about losing a caretaker but, rather, the person they took care of. Kayla's sister was two years younger than she was. With the death, she lost the counterpart to her role as the big sister who led the way for her younger sibling. She described their relationship:

> I lost a best friend. She went through a period where we would fight. Then something changed. She was always doing what I did, like a little sister, I guess. I would play cello, she played; I played softball and she would play softball. Then, just before she died, we really became friends.

Dan, age 8, lives in a single-parent family. His younger brother died suddenly at age 3, leaving him an only child. He talked about what he misses:

> What did I lose? . . . another boy in the family.

He wants someone like himself at home. One aspect all siblings emphasize is that they lost someone else in the house to play with, to talk to, to share with, and to fill their lives. As the importance of age differences fades with advancing years, older teenagers recognize that they lost a companion in life. They also lost someone with whom they could share their family history. As Jocelyn pointed out:

> There are a lot of memories that I can't share with anyone else. I'd love to sit and talk with him about old times. Sometimes I do talk with him.

We cannot predict how these relationships would have unfolded in time. The death, as in all the deaths described in this book, disrupts a relationship in process.

The siblings described up to this point now were actively involved with each other because of their youth and mutual dependence at the time of the death. However, older siblings who are no longer living at home can be just as touched by the death as those who are part of the family's daily life. Jocelyn talked about how her older brother, who was 21, reacted to his younger brother's death:

> It took him years before he really talked about his reaction; he was very deeply touched—in his way, always grieving for our brother. I could see how it ate at him. I guess he felt guilty, too. He was in Vietnam at the same time, and he lived. He was close to my brother who died, like I was, but we weren't close to each other. It took us a long time, but we finally began to talk, and now we are very close.

A sibling does not have to be raised in the same house to be profoundly affected by the death. Kayla described the reaction of her half-brother, who was raised by his biological mother, her father's first wife:

> We didn't see each other but once a year. He really liked my mother, and he thought my sister was neat. He used to tease me, in particular, a lot. After my mother and sister died, he reached out. He was very upset. It has become important to both of us that we can share our feelings about this and some of our own lives now as well.

This new liaison with her half-brother is important to Kayla. He is someone else with whom she can share memories of her sister and her mother.

COLLAPSE OF THEIR WORLD: A LOST WAY OF LIFE

These children are grieving not just their siblings, but the world in which their siblings existed. In many ways, their world has crumbled. Like others who have lost a parent or a child, changes permeate most aspects of their lives. Many things change: their sense of self, their relationships with their parents and their other siblings, and their relationship to their dead siblings. There are also changes in their relationships with their friends. Peter's younger brother Greg said this about his family:

> Our whole life as a family has changed. We were once five and now just four. So many things remind me of my brother; I hear a favorite song on the radio, I see the kind of clothes that he wore. I feel so confused and so sad.

Strange Feelings

Like other bereaved people, siblings experience strong new feelings as they deal with the changes in themselves and in their world resulting from the death.

Many siblings feel lonely. The house is quiet, and they cannot quite get used to it. Eleven-year-old Greg complained that he had "nothing to do now." Mark thought back on how he felt just after Teddy died:

> I think I was kind of lost because Teddy and I used to do everything together and then after he died, he wasn't there anymore. I had to do things by myself. . . . I couldn't do the things we used to do. My mother tells me that I came to her in tears, maybe two or three weeks after Teddy died, wanting to know what I had done that God would take my best friend away. She tried to tell me that I didn't do anything. We still talk about it every once in a while. She had not understood what it meant to me because he was my best friend. I remember she started to do some things with me we had never done before. As I think about it, it wasn't the same.

As this family learned, the relationship between parent and child cannot substitute for that between siblings. In addition, parents and children are often at different places as they grieve their different losses. It may not always be easy for parents to recognize the difference between how they express their grief and the way their children do. Kayla reflected on what it had been like shortly after her mother's and sister's deaths:

> My father was grieving over my mother a lot more because that was his life partner. I felt my sister was getting gypped—no one was talking about her. He thought I was trying to deny their deaths. He wanted me to grieve like he did. The first few months he would sleep at the cemetery all the time. I didn't even want to visit there. I couldn't, and we argued a lot about that. I had my own understanding of it. I really had to wrestle with my feelings in my way. I was angry for a long time, but I would fluctuate between very angry, rageful, and depressed in an instant. Most of that was directed at my father. I took all my aggression out on him; nothing he could do was right.

Most siblings do not experience multiple losses as Kayla did. Yet anger is a common feeling. This is similar to the anger of other mourners, described in earlier chapters. Three years after his brother died, Dan talked about these feelings that were still with him. At age 8, he could recognize that he had two different feelings at the same time:

> I'm mad and sad at the same time, even now sometimes. What do I do with this anger? You can't go around banging cars or people. I keep a lump in my throat, . . . sometimes I can even swallow it, but it comes back . . . two or three times a day.

Often these children are not sure who to be angry with. Depending on their religious education, they may question God's role in the death. Drew said:

> I'm angry at God for letting him die and that it happened to me. So weird that it is happening to you, that your brother died. I think it was God's fault. . . . Sometimes when I get angry with God, I feel guilty.

Siblings may seek ways to get away from these feelings for a while. For some, school, like work for adults, can involve and distract them. However, immediately after the death, children can be preoccupied with what happened. Barry described his feelings at the time:

> At the beginning, it was hard to concentrate in school. I didn't really listen because my thoughts were focused on something else. My grades didn't go off that much! It took longer to do homework, but I got it done. . . . I would go over the accident again and again.

As we saw in previous chapters, it may be more typical of younger children to lash out with their emotions. Older children can be just as impulsive at times, but their behavior takes different forms. Justine found the pain after her sister's death intolerable. She sought the easiest way she knew to numb it:

> I started to use drugs—it made it easier; it didn't hurt as much. One of the counselors in school started talking to me. I realized what I was doing, and I got help before I really lost it. I guess I was lucky.

Many children, like their parents, do not have words to describe what they are feeling. Ten-year-old Amanda, reflecting on her brother's death, said:

> I'm like my father. I don't cry. I am very bothered when I see my mother cry. I want to run away from the pain. . . . Sometimes I go visit a friend.

A friend can provide support and a safe place that is not centered on the death.

Older children generally are more able to give words to their sadness and anger about the death. They can also find more constructive ways of dealing with their feelings. Kayla described how she finally dealt with her anger:

> During college, I started telling my father that we have to decide that we are either going to fight for the rest of our lives, or we have to come to some understanding. We both have grown from this, even though it has been very painful. We are very different people, and now we are very close.

Changes with Parents and Other Siblings

One of the things siblings have to deal with is that their parents have changed. They have no way of knowing if this change is permanent or temporary. The loss often seems to compromise the parents' ability to care for their remaining children, who feel alone and isolated in the family. When their sibling died after a long illness, the remaining children hope that their parents' pain will end with the death and that they will be more available. This does not happen. With this secondary loss, just as with children who have lost a parent and whose surviving parent cannot be there for them, siblings lose the sense of safety and predictability in their lives. Their world has collapsed, then, not only because of their sibling's death, but because their parents have turned inward with their grief and no longer are in charge of the family. Shortly after Peter's sudden death, his siblings felt that the family had come apart. Peter's 12-year-old sister Priscilla said:

> I feel our family is not whole and never will be until we all die. We don't go out as much or go camping. We're usually locked in our rooms. I feel confused, scared, and I always wonder what will happen to us or to me. I hope my family can become whole again.

Peter's siblings cannot comfort each other at this point, so soon after their brother's death. The lack of comfort from their parents makes them fearful because they realize their parents' importance in giving order to their world. At this time, their parents are not there for the children, and the children are not yet at a point in their development where they can really be independent. Three years after her brother's death, Linda could see more clearly what had happened to her parents. She explained the changes she saw:

> I had never seen my parents out of control, and when I saw that—that really scared me. My parents had always been able to fix things for my brother and

me, and they couldn't fix this—and I couldn't cope with that. That has always stuck with me. They went from parents who were in charge, fixed my bike, put a bandage on my cut, to parents who couldn't make a decision about what to wear tomorrow.

Six months after Kevin's death, his 8-year-old brother Jay drew a picture of himself crying and represented his parents with their hearts broken in two. Jay said this about his brother's death:

> The biggest change is that I am an only child now. The house feels very strange, and my parents don't say much about all this. My folks cry a lot. I see mom crying, and I don't know what to say or do, so I just hug her. It makes us feel a little bit better, but we don't talk to each other about it. Mom says sometimes her heart is taken right out of her.

This sense of helplessness may pervade all aspects of children's lives. Losing a sibling makes them vulnerable as they become aware of the reality of death. Greg was specific about his fear:

> I am scared that someone else will die in my family. I drew a picture of my mom going to work, and I am sad because I am not with her and I don't know if she will die or not.

Until his brother's death, there had been no place in his view of the world for the fact that death could touch him personally. Now he is intensely aware that the death of someone close to him is a real possibility.

Is this loss of control in their parents different from what children see in their surviving parent when a parent dies? Not really, except that when a parent dies, the death is a generation or more removed from them and their own peer group is intact. When a sibling dies, children now understand at some level that children can die and their parents cannot protect them.

It may take the parents a while before they realize that just as they are changed by the death, so are their surviving children. Parents need to learn and accept that these changes are appropriate, not something to fear as signs of pathology. In fact, both parents and children need each other as they cope with the death. Parents of teenagers may expect them to continue trying to be independent, unaware that a sibling's death could change typical behavior. Linda described what happened in their family:

> I was 16 when my brother died. My parents kept saying that they would understand if I wanted to spend more time with my friends, as if nothing had happened. But whenever they would go anywhere, for about a year after he died, I always wanted to be with them. My parents were funny. They were always buying me something; if I said "Gee isn't that nice!" they would say, "Do you want it; we will buy it." I finally realized that they were in a way bribing me to be with them. They finally caught on, and I said I knew all along what they were doing. I told them I couldn't take advantage of them because I needed to be there with them; I didn't need the presents. I needed them as much as they needed me.

Linda was no less of an adolescent, but she was no longer the same adolescent she had been before her brother's death. Asserting her independence was less important than feeling connected to her parents. At this point, the entire family needed each other. Her parents were learning about her changed needs and their own needs to have her with them.

In other families, parents' fears for their surviving children can prevail, and they may become overprotective. In the words of a healthy 17-year-old whose two sisters died of a congenital disease:

> I can't wait to go to college. My mother is smothering me. She is so frightened that I will get into an accident that she won't let me drive, and if I am five minutes late, she is a wreck. My father lets her do the talking, but he's no better. Sure I understand, but I need my life, too.

Some parents tell their surviving children to "be good." This request may cause the children additional stress as they try to sort out what their parents mean by it. The children may interpret it as meaning that they not cause their parents any further grief. They may also try to contain their feelings, so as not to disturb their parents. Dan, age 8, talked about what it was like shortly after his brother died:

> My mother said I should listen and try to be good. I was having a hard time believing he was gone. I felt sad, but I just knew not to talk about it to my mother. She would cry, and I would feel bad that I upset her. Sometimes I would get angry and get into trouble at school and then I would feel worse because my mother would get all angry with me.

Many children try to keep some semblance of the family intact by exchanging "caretaking" roles with their parents. Some older children state directly that they see themselves as protecting their parents. Jocelyn reflected on her experience:

> The most heartbreaking thing was watching my parents because the whole thing was so unreal, just as unreal for me as for them. My father completely disintegrated; he started screaming and yelling. Those kinds of sounds I don't think I'll ever forget. . . . My mother was very stoic, and so she didn't show it as much. I started to take care of my parents. How did I do that? First thing, I didn't apply to any college outside my hometown. I stayed nearby. I always told them where I was and when I would be home, to be sure that they wouldn't be hurt again. I was not going to give them any more cause to worry. At the time, I didn't know that no matter what I did, they were going to be upset.

There are many ways of protecting parents. Jocelyn stayed close to home. Another way is to try to distract the parents. Many children find that acting out can serve this function. Another way is to try to fill the emptiness in the house:

> My role was to kind of make everyone else okay. . . make sure their life is okay and they're not missing one of their kids sort of thing. . . . Keeping excitement around the house, making sure things were always lively, other kids were always around. . . . At times I probably took on some of the roles or personalities

that [my brother] had as a teenager. I think I kind of slipped into that, as another way of filling in the absence. (quoted in Teplow, 1995, p. 67)

As this child mentioned, some children also try to lessen their parents' pain by trying to be both themselves and the deceased. These efforts to protect their parents are rarely successful. As Jocelyn learned, there is no way to ease the pain of the loss. In other families, older children try to play the parents' role with younger siblings. They learn that this does not work—that they cannot lessen their parents' burden. Stephanie's sister Enid was 12 when Stephanie was killed in a drive-by shooting. She recalled what happened to her family:

I thought it was my job to keep my little sister from bugging my parents. They seemed to imply that was what they needed when my older sister died. After a while, my sister got pretty angry with me. She would have temper tantrums and beat on me. Her teacher called and explained what she was hearing at school. My sister lost my parents and her big sister, and she was blaming me. I learned that my parents had to get their act together. I wasn't helping anyone. I finally realized I was having my own troubles dealing with the fact that she died and how she died. I noticed that after this crisis, my parents started to "wake up."

As the family adjusts to their changed reality after the death, new alignments occur. Families begin to re-form and children are cared for as parents learn to care in a different way. Most parents gradually resume their role as parents in their own way. Realignments may also take place between the siblings themselves. Fifteen years after Teddy died, Alan described relations in his family:

Another thing that my kid brother's death did, it made my next younger brother and me best friends, and that hasn't changed over the years.

Sometimes family problems become apparent only after a death. Steve's older brother died in a hiking accident when Steve was 18. Four years later, Steve said:

My parents don't think about me anymore. All I hear about is my brother and all his accomplishments. I can't tell them why I don't come home more often or why I won't talk to them about my brother. They say I was jealous, but that wasn't how my brother and I saw it. It was okay while he was alive because we had each other, and we could laugh with each other about how lopsided their ideas were, but after he died, there was nothing there for me.

In this instance, the tragic death of one son exacerbated these parents' attitudes. Fortunately, Steve was old enough that he was no longer completely dependent on them. He had more insight than they and some humor about the situation that allowed him to move on with his life and deal with his loss in his own way.

As children move away in time from the death and reach a different developmental plateau, they can think more easily about the nature of the change in their parents, and their fear is not as palpable. Linda reflected on her parents' behavior:

> I guess the most important thing I learned over the years was that my parents were not crazy . . . that this is what happens to parents whose children die.

MY FRIENDS ARE VERY IMPORTANT

Change occurs not only in the family but in siblings' relationships with friends as well. Children who are in school learn that friends can be a source of care and connection, someone to share with when their family feels uncertain. As we talk of change, we also need to consider the importance of continuity—that life can and does go on. This is something that friends, whose lives have not been shattered in such a personal way, can do for the bereaved: make some of life normal again. Jocelyn reflected on how her friends helped:

> The thing that helped me most was friends. They didn't know what to do, but they would come and include me. Sometimes they would just come and sit. That was the support I had. Things they would do normally, they just kept on doing it. Being normal with me.

Older children may be fortunate to have friends who are of an age when they are curious about death and ask questions. It can be helpful to have people to talk with who are not part of the family and so personally touched by the death. As Kayla said, however, it may take some work for friends to learn what is appropriate and supportive:

> My friends—either they didn't know what to say so they avoided me or they were very supportive. Two people who I wasn't close to became very close. They were just there. They came to visit in the hospital. They just accepted me throughout all the stages. After the accident, I told my friends, "If you have any questions, ask me; it is open." It helped me to talk about it.

Some potential friends may distance themselves because they do not know how to deal with the fact that a peer has died. Like the adults around them, they are uncomfortable with the subject. Peter's sister Priscilla talked about her experience:

> They feel sorry for us. Some friends ask how it feels to lose a brother. I say it is horrible. Sometimes when we meet kids who don't know me, if they ask how many brothers and sisters I have, if I say I had two brothers and one died, then they sort of step back . . . so it makes it hard to tell them.

Kayla had a similar experience. She recognized why it was so important to talk about her sister and learned that she could educate those who were uncomfortable:

> If I don't say I had a sister, it's like denying her existence, and that's not fair to both of us. But sometimes I hold back because it is hard for some people. I find

if I do talk about it, after a while people do get more comfortable. If I'm comfortable, then they become comfortable. Maybe it's part of growing up.

Making fun of peers who seem vulnerable because they look different or have had a different experience is not unusual. A. Cain and N. Kalter of the University of Michigan Psychology Department (personal communication, 1994) described how children whose parents died were teased by their peers. For some children, teasing can be a way of handling anxiety and feeling in control of a situation that makes them uncomfortable. In Chapter 7, I described how some parents tried to help their children deal with the meanness of other children. Sometimes children find their own way. Doing so can be empowering at a time when their world feels so unstable. When Kayla returned to school, she had to deal with a group of bullies:

> I just felt different. My hair was just growing back after the accident. I remember one of my first days back to school, some boys started throwing spitballs at me. I saw one of these boys in the hall later and, for some reason, I felt I had to talk to him. If I was going to survive, I couldn't let them get away with this. I said, "Take one good look; this is the closest you will ever get to me, and pray that you are not the one in the backseat who walked away." I walked away feeling really proud of myself. What I did sort of said, "This is who I am and it's okay!" No one ever said another word again.

When siblings are close in age, the surviving children are likely to encounter the deceased sibling's friends at school or in the neighborhood. These friends are also mourning and unsure how to act or what to say. This daily interaction is not something parents have to deal with. Priscilla talked about meeting her brother's friends at school:

> It was really hard to go back to school. I started to see some of my brother's friends. We didn't know what to say to each other. A few came around some after the death, but it was too hard for them.

A NEW OUTLOOK

Change and growth are often dramatic after this kind of loss. Kayla described how she found direction for herself:

> I had two choices, and one was not even a choice. I could sit in my room for the rest of my life and cry "poor me." But I said no. I have to go on, in honor of them.

Six years later, Kayla reflected on the meaning of her sister's death to her now:

> I think part of the mourning process has been accepting that I'm not going to have a sister. . . . What I realized was that it makes me feel sad to think about that. But I don't feel like I've run away from it. I don't feel like I fight it so much anymore. It's like that's who I am. And yeah, it really changed my life.

Change in their world includes the awareness that people can die, that life is fragile, and that there is real danger in the world (Coles, 1996). Teddy's 17-year-old aunt was living with the family when he died. She said this about what she has learned from his death:

> After Teddy died, what changed was not what death meant but what life meant. I realized that it doesn't matter how old you are, it doesn't matter what happens today—you might not be here tomorrow. It is important to appreciate everyone, no matter who they are, because they might not make it tomorrow. I try to help people see that we just don't know. His death also made me believe that everyone has a purpose in their life, and when you are born, God knows your purpose and when you finish your purpose, then you die. The sadness is for people around you. We all have a mission, and it affects how we interact with other people and who we touch, and when we finish touching other people, then we are able to die.

Children who lose a sibling often seem to grow up before their time. They become more sensitive to other people's needs and more appreciative of what they have. They discover new aspects of themselves. As Teddy's aunt noted, much of this change may stem from the philosophical questions the death raises. These questions sometimes lead children to a faith system that comforts and sustains them (Balk and Hogan, 1995).

The death may also lead them to new directions academically and professionally. Kayla began studying philosophy and religion, areas she would not otherwise have considered. Jocelyn became involved in community work and politics and found a direction for her professional life:

> I asked, is there any way I can make something good come out of this? Maybe I can save someone else's brother from being killed in this way. I started to worry about everyone killed in the war—on both sides. I think that was part of my grief—trying to save everybody. I see a lot of people not paying attention to themselves and what they need. They focus on helping everyone else, and that's what I found myself doing. I also found a church where I felt at home. That helped. I then began to work with hospice because I really needed to understand dying. This was about eight years later. I went back to school and did my dissertation on sibling death. After that, I found I was able to put things together and I could live with a new perspective on my grief.

CONSTRUCTING A RELATIONSHIP
WITH THE DECEASED

Just as other bereaved people do, siblings find ways of constructing and maintaining ongoing attachments to their deceased sisters or brothers. Hogan and DeSantis (1992) listed various ways in which this relationship is constructed, which are similar to those described in earlier chapters. Siblings dream about the deceased, think about the deceased, and talk to the deceased. Coles (1996) found that these enduring bonds with dead siblings involved ongoing conversations in which the siblings shared feelings, expressed regret about things not done, took on qualities of the deceased, and did things to memorialize the deceased.

Communicating with the Deceased

Communication with the deceased takes on many forms. As she said earlier in this chapter, Jocelyn had conversations in her head with her brother. Some children write letters to keep their sibling up to date on their lives. Jay wrote to his brother Kevin:

> I told him how I miss him, things about school, and that I changed schools so I could be with my best friends.

Kayla writes to her sister often to keep her up to date on what is happening in her life and with their father. She keeps the letters in a diary. Four years after the death, she wrote:

> I was talking about you with Joe today, and I started to reminisce about how we used to fight and protect each other, too. Here's my news. . . . I am facing new things every day. I'm off to graduate school. Since your deaths, I have come to appreciate the gifts I received from you and Mom. You loved life and appreciated it like no one I have ever met since.

When a sibling committed suicide, one of the topics of conversation is to ask *why* he or she did it. Why the sibling chose to solve his or her problems this way remains an unanswered question for the survivors.

Influence on Their Current Lives

Siblings reaffirm their love for their deceased brothers or sisters, and reflect on how the deceased are influencing their current lives. They try to make sense of the death, especially if the siblings committed suicide. Depending on their belief system, they talk about reunions when they die. These are not mutually exclusive experiences. The relationship is always changing, taking on different qualities and dimensions.

The deceased are present and in some way are influencing their lives. Speaking for his brothers, as well as for himself, Alan talked about how Teddy is still in their lives. They call on him to help and believe that he is responding:

> He always liked cows, and that's where he got killed. Sometimes when I am chasing cows, trying to get them together and nothing is going right, I ask him for help and usually about five minutes later, the cows start going in the right direction, just like someone shows up and turns them. Sometimes I think he is around like a guardian angel or something . . . keeps a guy out of trouble. If I go out at night when it's snowing, you have to think that he is sitting there, keeping his eye on things. Sometimes when you need a little extra help, it's always nice to have him up there with you.

Just as these brothers did, Kayla feels that her sister and mother are still with her:

> I feel that they are here. I just feel them, every time I feel something wonderful or something bad I feel them—is it inside me, or are they present? I don't know, yet I feel as if they are here; they make a difference in what happens to me.

Often siblings feel comforted when they realize that they look like the deceased. Barry said this about Sam:

> It feels good to look at his picture. I feel as if he is with me. As I get older, I realize that I look like him more and more. We are alike also and that makes me feel good when someone says, "You remind me of Sam."

This is similar to what I described in Chapter 6 as a living legacy. Children recognize that the deceased live on through them. This recognition works well when children come to it themselves and see their siblings as part of who they are. But if they are pressured to follow in their siblings' footsteps, they can feel uncomfortable if people make too much of their similarity to their dead siblings. Parents have to be careful not to make a surviving child into a replacement child (Rosen, 1988). Drew, who looks very much like his older dead brother, always reminds people that "I am *me*, not Ronald."

Memories

For Jocelyn, one of the most helpful things in maintaining her connection to her brother was being able to remember and share with others:

> Even on the anniversaries, for people to remember and to call or for me to feel comfortable to be able to call a person and say, "Well, I'm thinking of my brother today; do you remember that day?"

Regardless of how they connect to their dead siblings, however, something will always be missing. Mark still sees Teddy as he might have grown and been involved in his life. He cries as he thinks about it:

> For me, it is not so much outside; it's whenever I see a rainbow, whenever I win a big basketball game, a big football game. When we lose, I think it's because he wasn't there like he should have been . . . because I know he would have been the best of any of us in sports.

Drew had a similar feeling:

> I think of him in heaven, but that doesn't help because right now I miss him!

CHAPTER TEN

Invisible Mourners
The Death of a Friend

> The words come easier now. I can express what I lost. I have lost the
> validation that she provided—the voice that confirmed me to myself,
> that told me I could; I have lost her presence, her ideas, the new
> things she brought into my life; I have lost my belief in plans, in our
> ability to control our lives; I have lost the confidence that we could do
> anything, that we could conquer the world, change it, make it ours.

My daughter Gila wrote these words one year after her friend Mara committed suicide at age 24. Her words describe all that is lost when a friend
dies. Friends, like siblings, are not supposed to die young. Little has been
written about friends as mourners, yet people are clearly affected by the
death of a peer (Smith, 1996; Toray & Oltjenbruns, 1996).

What is lost when a friend dies? How do friends cope when it happens?
This chapter focuses on the ways the death of a friend reverberates in the
lives of older teenagers and young adults. This is an age when friends can
take on special significance in young people's lives. It is also an age when
young people can reflect on the relationship with a more mature understanding of its meaning in their lives.

When a friend dies, young people come face to face with the limitations
of the way death is viewed in the larger world around them. The death is
acknowledged in the school or community only briefly in the period immediately following it. There is little place in society for the grief of friends,
and they usually receive limited support and guidance. There are no rituals
legitimating friends as mourners. Friends as mourners can take time off from
school to attend a funeral, but not much more. The sadness of friends often
surprises people who do not appreciate the meaning of the loss and wonder why these young people have not gotten over the death more quickly.
Outsiders often think that because of their youth and because the deceased
was not "family," friends should be getting on with their lives. This belief
can leave them feeling alone and that something is not right with their feelings and behaviors. Joseph was 16 when his friend was killed while a pas-
senger in a car driven by another friend who was drinking. He talked about
how he felt after the accident:

> It was hard to get back into studying. I couldn't concentrate. I kept seeing him
> in school, all the places where we were together. I kept thinking it could only
> be a dream, but I knew it wasn't. Everyone kept saying, "You have to get on

with your life; you can't let it bother you so much." I was confused: Was something wrong with me that I was so upset?

WHAT IS A FRIEND?

To understand what is lost, it is helpful to define what we mean by a friend. L. Rubin (1985) saw friendship as associated with love, trust, security, and safety. Youniss and Smollar, as reported by Savin-Williams and Berndt (1993), characterized friendships as important, enduring, relatively problem-free, peer relationships in which the participants understand one another and learn new things. A high school junior defined a friend this way:

> A friend is someone who is there through thick and thin, always there, regardless of who or what you are or what your sexual orientation may be. A friend is going to be there when you need help and when you don't need help. A friend is someone you dare to be yourself with.

Friends are people who join us in the journey toward maturity, who facilitate our separation from the family. They encourage our development of a new appreciation of ourselves by providing the contact and comfort needed for the transition from child-in-the-family to person-in-the-world (Selman & Schultz, 1990). Most young people feel a different kind of intimacy with friends than they do with members of their own families.

Many of the same qualities exist in friendships as in sibling relationships, as noted in the previous chapter. Yet the age range of siblings and family dynamics can influence their relationship, so that not all siblings also feel connected as friends. Ruth, now 20, talked about the difference in her relationships with her sisters and with her friend Jessica, whom we first met in Chapter 7, and who had died three years earlier from cancer:

> When I was 15 a friend meant more. I couldn't talk to my older sisters. I was just the kid sister to them. My older brother was not even living at home anymore. You go out with friends, you do everything together. You tell all your secrets to friends, not to your brother or sister.

Some do develop this kind of closeness with other relatives who are near them in age. Eighteen-year-old Donna saw her cousin Tina, who shot herself three years earlier, as both family and friend. She explained:

> When she killed herself, I lost a friend. Yes, we were cousins, but we really liked each other and we chose to spend a good deal of our free time together. I used to think that we talked about everything; only now I realize that there was a part of her I knew nothing about.

In many ways, our very sense of ourselves is connected to our ability to negotiate the world of friendship. It is in this world with peers that we are introduced to new possibilities of relationships with others. We learn that there is a world outside our immediate family and that there are other ways of interacting than what we learn at home. The adult ability to understand others and to feel understood by others has a good deal of its origins in our relationships with peers.

Adolescent Friendships

Friendships mean different things to children at different points in their lives (Sullivan, 1972; Youniss 1980). As children develop and mature, the nature of their relationships changes as well (Selman & Schultz, 1990). In adolescence, friends are at least as important as parents in meeting many of the changing needs of maturing children. As they reach adolescence, young people have a greater ability to observe their own behavior, to reflect on who they are, and to recognize this ability in others. They are more capable of responding to the needs of others and of recognizing the process whereby they can act to meet each other's needs. Adolescents begin to value collaboration with their peers as distinct from cooperation.

Adolescence is typically portrayed as a time of storm and stress. There is little evidence, however, that this is how the majority of teenagers experience this period (Berman & Jobes, 1991; Hauser & Bowlds, 1993). For most, adolescence is a time of growth and exploration in which friends play an active role, helping each other negotiate all the changes in their lives: emotional, hormonal, and physical. It is, more often than not, a time of learning, of recognizing differences between self and others, and of developing skills for living in a more complex world and in more complex relationships. It is this view of adolescence that seems to be reflected in the young people whose stories are told in this chapter. It is not a question of being rebellious as much as learning to define their world as distinct from their parents'. Friends bring out parts of ourselves that family may not know or see. Clarisse, a high school sophomore, reflected on what she lost when her friend was shot:

> You lose a piece of yourself when a friend dies, like a piece of a puzzle. If you have only one friend and that person dies, then you ask: Who can I be myself with?

Parents cannot enter their children's immediate world in this way. They expect their children to conform to their values and to fit into their world and thus have a different view of what they want for their children in the long run. With adults, children receive approval for doing well according to the adults' criteria of what is good and worthwhile. With peers, children do not have to adapt to a system others have set up; they create their own. Together they develop an agreed-upon standard for valuing themselves and each other. Anna, another of Jessica's friends, talked about what it was like for her before Jessica died:

> We felt there wasn't anything we couldn't do. We encouraged, we suggested, and we helped each other try new things. We always made each other feel good about ourselves. One of us was always there if someone was in a bad mood, upset about something, or sick.

As they create their own world, loyalty to each other by, for example, keeping each other's secrets, becomes important. Typically, there is room for most adolescents to experiment with how and when to protect each other's privacy and to learn to understand the many levels of meaning behind what is said. When there is the possibility of suicide, there may be little space for this experimentation. Donna was very upset about how Tina's friends protected Tina's privacy:

> We found out that she had confided in several of her friends that she was going to kill herself. She never let on to me; she knew I would tell my mother. Her friends should have known better, but they kept their promise to her, not to tell. No one wanted to believe that she could really mean what she was saying. In a way, they didn't understand that they did not have the power to talk her out of it. She kept promising them that she wouldn't do anything, and they believed her.

When a friend dies, young people feel that their self-created world will never be the same. They have lost control of a world of their own making. Sean talked about his friend Corey's death from Duchenne's muscular dystrophy:

> Corey was my closest friend, my confidant, someone who I truly connected with, even when we first met in fourth grade. We just understood each other, and as we got older, it didn't change. He was someone I could talk to about girls, my parents' divorce, the struggles of being an adolescent. We knew we could trust each other; we had no secrets, and we could really work at solving problems in ways that worked. It took a long time before I found anything like that again.

Friendships are not held together by societal obligation or blood ties. Younger children may develop rituals of loyalty to each other; they are given to such dramatics and are known to make pledges for life. Usually, friendships continue because the participants wish them to. Some friendships are kept alive, in spite of distance and differences. They take different forms and different shapes as time goes on.

Some friends, like Anna and Sean, watched their friends become more and more ill. Anna felt that staying by Jessica was what friendship was about, however difficult it was:

> I have pictures of her in my mind when she was beautiful and healthy, but I also have some memories when she wasn't. I think if I hadn't been there at those times, I would be very angry with myself. I think that if you're really a good friend, you have to be there even at the most difficult times—that's when friendship is really tested.

Although these children were aware of the possibility of death, their focus was on continuing to live. Death was not in the picture. Sean remembered the period just before Corey's death:

> I don't recall any specific conversations about dying. It was something we both knew. I always knew he had a limited life expectancy. He was already in a wheelchair when I first met him. The only time it did come up was when we talked

about dating. He was interested in girls, just like I was. There were several women who would have been interested, but they were afraid of losing him. I think my role as a friend was to facilitate his living. We didn't think about the future or the past; we just tried to do things in life.

When a death occurs, the expectation that the friendship will always continue is lost. Gila reflected on this aspect of Mara's death:

I have lost the security that no matter how rarely we saw each other, she would be there and the knowledge that our futures would somehow, sometimes, overlap.

Friendship can also be our most fragile relationship. Friendships can fade and even disappear as people or interests change, as children grow and mature, or as physical distance makes it difficult to maintain contact. Anna reminisced about her high school friendship group and the impact of Jessica's death:

We were always together, we went everywhere together. Things changed after Jessica's death. I think she was the catalyst who brought us together and kept us together. When we finished high school and Jess died, we went in different directions. We don't see each other as often. The connection is still there, but it is different.

Gender Differences

By the preadolescent years, the friendship patterns of girls and boys may be different. This difference may be expected, given the differences, noted in previous chapters, in the ways men and women characterize relationships in their lives. Boys seem to be concerned with loyalty and solidarity, while girls are more involved in knowing each other and meeting each other's individual needs (Lyons, 1990). These differences may be more in style than substance. Both girls and boys are concerned with validating their sense of personal worth. Boys do so through actions and deeds, and girls do so by sharing their feelings and thoughts (Savin-Williams & Berndt, 1993).

Harter (1993) found that girls tended to describe themselves in a more integrated and harmonious fashion than did boys. Although older adolescents could recognize contradictory aspects of themselves, girls seemed less accepting of them than did boys. Girls were more interested in seeking harmony. But these are research findings. In real life people are not always consistent. For some boys, sharing is an essential part of their friendships. Sean and Corey talked about everything. Deborah and her friend Klara, who was killed in a random act of violence at age 15, enjoyed their differences. The way they fought, however, was different from the more physical sparring that is typical of boys. Deborah remembered:

We always fought about little things, but I think best friends should always fight—it makes it more interesting. That's what makes it a real friendship. Sometimes we would get so angry that we wouldn't talk to each other, and after a

> while when we saw each other, we would start to laugh and see how silly we were and everything was okay. It never mattered if one of us was right or wrong. We tried to learn from our differences. We both always felt if you agreed about everything, it wasn't as interesting.

It never occurred to these young girls that their differences would jeopardize their friendship.

Although differences between the genders are not always clear cut, boys and girls do face different societal expectations of how they should behave. By the time children enter adolescence, they have internalized many of these expectations, which affect how they react to a death. Girls, for the most part, are given greater latitude in expressing their feelings directly and in finding comfort in talking about them. Donna remembered how her group of friends coped after another classmate committed suicide:

> We talked, we felt closer, we weren't ever really alone. If someone wanted or needed to talk about it, we did.

Boys, for the most part, try to deal with the issues the death raises in what appears to be a rational, logical manner. They talk about crying not being acceptable and expect to contain their feelings. Sean talked about the difficulty he had after Corey died as he faced the contradiction between what was expected of him and what he experienced:

> Maybe it is a boy thing. I was uncomfortable crying. I worried that people would think I was weak, that I shouldn't let this get to me. I think Corey's family helped a lot. They were never embarrassed by my sadness or tearfulness. At least there I could let it out. I began to learn that I wasn't less of a man if I let myself feel. He was my friend for a long time, and I felt very lost.

Regardless of gender, there are many different grieving styles. Yet people expect everyone to grieve in the same way, to be open with their feelings, and to want to talk about them. For those whose style is more self-contained, the pressure to talk makes them uncomfortable; it contradicts their personal style. Jon reflected on how he reacted to his friend and housemate Ethan's suicide:

> I'm a more introverted type. I cried when I heard, but for me the best thing was to just get on with things. I was glad I was performing in the college theater. There was no one to replace me, and that kept me very busy and involved. I needed that distraction. People kept asking me how I was doing. They seemed to expect that I would want to talk, but that's not my way.

MY FRIEND DIED

Friends can die from illness and from genetic diseases like muscular dystrophy. Most often, though, adolescents and young adults die sudden, violent deaths from homicide, automobile accidents, and suicide (Lord, 1997). In the inner cities of America, more teenagers die of gunshot wounds than from all natural causes of disease combined (Prothrow-Stith, 1990). It is clear that the cause of death can make a difference in how friends react. This is particularly true if the deceased's behavior contributed to their death, as when, for example, they were involved in gang activities, were driving when drunk, or took their own lives. When the friend is a victim of homicide or an accident caused by someone else's carelessness, the question of why this happened is pervasive. Yet in many ways, friends' reactions, regardless of the cause of death, are more alike than not. All friends feel a sense of disbelief that this could really happen; they all feel great sadness that their friend is no longer there. Most say that this loss has led to a transforming experience.

Sense of Disbelief

Most of these young people, regardless of the cause of the death, felt that it was unexpected. Even though she watched Jessica get sicker and sicker, Anna did not think that Jessica would die:

> I don't think that I realized what she was going through until she died. It was unexpected in a way. I think that I was denying what she had. Even up to the very last days when it was clear that she was dying—I remember even then that I thought, okay, so she doesn't feel so good. I had heard of people who died of cancer, but it wasn't anyone I knew. I was just going along as usual. I didn't realize how difficult it was for her; we kept including her, and she did what she could. She even managed to organize a birthday party for me a month before she died.

Like other mourners, these young people were shocked by the death. They could not conceive of it happening to their friend at this time. When Corey's death was clearly imminent, it still had no reality for Sean. He described his experience:

> The night before, his mother called me to come over. He was out of the wheelchair and in a regular chair, which was very rare. He seemed so alive. How could I think that in a couple of days he would be gone? When it happened I couldn't take it in.

With a sudden, unexpected death, the sense of disbelief is similar, yet different. Death as the result of murder or a car accident comes out of the blue. Deborah talked about her reaction to the suddenness of Klara's murder:

> We had just seen each other at school that morning. It didn't sink in. She was so alive, so many plans. Funny, what I thought about was that I wouldn't hear her laughter anymore. She had a wonderful laugh. I couldn't believe she was gone; even now—it's been six months—it's still hard to believe. Even at the funeral I could not believe it was her in the coffin.

After a suicide, friends may realize that at some level of consciousness they knew that this might be possible, but did not accept that it could happen.

THE STORIES PEOPLE TELL

After their friends' death as their world was falling apart, many friends sought the reassurance and comfort of their parents. Jon was away at college when Ethan killed himself. He remembered that the first thing he did after he heard the news was to call home:

> I'm not sure why, but I found out that everyone in the house did the same thing after they found out. We needed to touch base, to let our families know and, in a way, to be sure that everything was okay with them. In fact, it was very comforting.

Such behavior is common to all children who experience a death, as you saw in earlier chapters. The need for comfort and a level of certainty in the world is not related to age or limited to the immediate family. Friends have this need as much as any other mourners.

The Funeral

For some young people, attending a friend's funeral is the first time they participate in such a ritual. Younger adolescents need their parents' approval to attend. At a time when they are shocked and unsure what to do, they also have to deal with their parents' reactions and discomfort about the subject. Deborah described Klara's funeral this way:

> Going to a friend's funeral, it's not something you expect or are prepared for. My mother wasn't sure about my going to the funeral, but my whole class was going, so she decided it was okay. At the funeral, I thought I could see Klara standing next to me like she always did.

In contrast, Clarisse found it too difficult to go to the funeral:

> I couldn't go. My teacher had just died, and then my great aunt and a cousin were killed in a car accident. I don't regret it. Now I am beginning to find my way. My mother took me to visit her mother, and I could handle that.

As a friend, she had no obligation to attend the funeral. Not attending worked well for her. She could put off facing the loss until she was ready to do so in a way that felt comfortable.

As discussed in the previous chapter, seeing the body after a sudden death can help make it real. When violence is involved, however, it may not be possible to do so. When viewing is traditional, not being able to see the body can cause a great deal of additional pain and add to the disbelief. This was a problem for Donna:

> You never want to believe that anyone you know would deliberately kill themselves. She shot herself in the face. The coroner said if I was a relative I wouldn't want to look. So it was really hard to believe. It would be easier if I could say that I saw that she was not breathing anymore.

At such times, friends may draw on the support of their peer group. Jon talked about how humor helped him and other friends get through Ethan's funeral. On the way to the cemetery, they were telling jokes in the car. It was truly black humor but typical of their group. Just like calling home, this type of continuity was comforting:

> Ethan would have appreciated the jokes. The last remark someone made when I got out of the car at the cemetery to be a pallbearer was "Don't drop him!" A lot of people probably wouldn't understand that. I actually mentioned this to someone; he was sort of aghast, but it helped us get through.

The tension was tremendous, and the routine of their usual humor provided relief.

Having never experienced such a situation before, young people may not be sure how to give expression to all their feelings at this time. The funeral is one event at which it is acceptable to let out feelings. Yet even there, tears may not come easily. Sally, another of Ethan's housemates, said that only as they began to recite the mourners' prayer at the cemetery did she give in to her tears. And Donna gave in to her feelings when they played the music she had chosen for Tina's funeral:

> I know now that I tried to be real tough. Her brother and I said, "No one will see us cry." We were going to put up this front that we could handle this. I don't know why we thought that's what we should do. Then we got to the funeral. My aunt had asked me to help pick out some of the music that they played. It was the music that really set us off, and then it was like we couldn't stop crying.

For some children, just being at the funeral is difficult. Like children whose parents or siblings die, friends may also want to run away, as if doing so would make the situation not true. As teenagers, self-control is particularly important to them. Ruth talked about her reaction to Jessica's funeral:

> The first time I saw Jess's father crying was at the cemetery. Suddenly I felt all the pain. I felt like running, but I controlled myself.

When parents invite friends to participate in the funeral, it can help them feel respected as mourners. Friends need this opportunity to share their grief. Sean participated in Corey's funeral by reading a poem he had written:

> When we were young, that seems so long ago,
> I just never thought you would really have to go . . .
> When he was here he taught me to live everyday
> As if it were the last. . . .
> Because before you know it
> Your present is your past.
> . . . I hope I made your stay here more enjoyable and free.
> When we were young, not so long ago,
> I guess I really knew that you would have to go.

Many families welcome the friends' participation because friends can provide memories and tributes that are different from those of the family. For both friends and family members, sharing their stories with each other becomes an opportunity to learn more about the deceased. Gila recalled how important this sharing was for both Mara's friends and parents:

> We exchanged stories with her parents. They told us of her illness, we told them stories from better days. Together we wove a portrait of this woman who had left us and the tremendous impact she had on our lives.

NEW AND UNUSUAL FEELINGS

Shock and Sadness

The feelings that friends experience are no different from those of any mourner. Jon described his initial feelings during the first days after he learned of Ethan's suicide:

> It is difficult to explain what I felt. It was like a leaden feeling, a numbness so it was very hard to do anything, to even talk. There were things to do, and we did them because we had to. It was very hard to interact with anyone who didn't know Ethan and didn't have some of the same feelings.

Sally talked about the things they had to do, such as calling others on campus to tell them what happened, making arrangements to go to the funeral, and being involved in planning a campus memorial. As with parents, these concrete tasks provided a framework at a time when they were "in a fog." Sean recalled how he felt for many months after Corey's death:

> People say that at the beginning, you don't feel it, you don't believe it, and then little by little, the feelings come out. That was true for me. The sadness was always there. I would watch TV or try to read something that would bring me up or go see my friends. On some occasions when it was more overwhelming, I would stay alone and be sad. At the beginning I couldn't talk much to others. I found it mattered to me if people knew Corey or not. Then again, sometimes it is easier to kind of be in denial. Keeping my mind busy works at such times.

For some, the word *denial* has a negative meaning. It should not. Distraction and keeping busy are ways of buying time as they get a handle on all that is happening. Ruth and Anna both agreed that getting back to college and a life they had not shared with Jessica helped them cope.

Anxiety and Fear

Other feelings begin to emerge as well. Sally began to feel an anxiety she had never known before. She began to feel unsure of the world and her place in it as she realized that people her own age could die suddenly:

> I found myself being scared. It started right after he died and lasted for about five months. I was scared even crossing the street. I had never lost anyone close to me before. I was frightened in the sense that this thing that had taken over

Ethan so fast, could it take me over just as suddenly? I felt so vulnerable. Things are so fragile. I wasn't one to hurt myself, but a car could come along and hit me. I was at my folks that summer, and one of my favorite movies, *The Big Chill*, was on TV. I used to have this fantasy that all of us would be like the people in that movie. I forgot it was about a suicide. I just started to cry and cry, and after that I didn't seem to have the same fear.

Donna experienced two suicides within months of each other. Shortly after her cousin Tina's death, a classmate, Ken, killed himself. She and her friends felt a pervasive anxiety. They had the sense that the next disaster could happen at any time. They also feared that people who had been close to Ken, who were having trouble dealing with his death, might try to harm themselves. She described how they coped:

> We went everywhere together. Nobody went anywhere by themselves. We never left Ken's former girlfriend alone. She never ate alone; if she went to the mall, someone went with her. We were frightened for her that she might do something. There was no real danger, but at that point everything worried us.

Anger

Like all mourners, friends experience anger as they try to understand the death. When their friend had been sick, anger was less of an issue. If they felt anger, it was with God. Ruth described her feeling about God:

> If he is a good God and really cares, how could he have allowed Jess to suffer so and to die so young? I was pretty angry with him for a while.

When suicide is involved, friends can be angry with their friend for killing himself or herself. Yet they are not usually consumed by the anger. It rarely becomes the main focus of their grief. They see it as, in some ways, appropriate under the circumstances. Sally remembered that she and his other friends felt extremely angry with Ethan:

> We were angry. We said, "What a stupid thing to do!" and asked, "Why did you do this?" It would have been easier if we knew that he didn't see any alternative.

Donna described her anger with her cousin Tina:

> Oh, I was angry. I would talk to her and say, "You didn't have the right to take that away from me. Why should you be able to do that, it is not fair." And, of course, it is sad. It is not fair to my mom, to me, to her family, that she didn't let us say good-bye to her. Even her mom is angry because she didn't let her see what she was feeling—like she had no faith that anyone could help her.

Suicide: Special Issues

In addition to the issues that are typical for most mourners, there are special concerns when a friend chooses suicide as a way of dealing with his or her problems. The surviving friends need to understand and reconcile the death with the friend they knew. As one friend said:

> Just think: one day your best friend is standing next to you, and the next day he's not. And you thought you knew him, inside and out; obviously you didn't know anything. There is the sense that I should have known my friend, and I really didn't. In a sense, there is a feeling of betrayal.

Why? If they were good friends, many young mourners, like parents and siblings, ask themselves why they were not aware of what was going on and what the real dangers were. As both Sally and Donna said, they also look for an answer to why anyone would kill themselves. They may try to get inside the head of the deceased, to understand what happened to the friend they thought they knew. Sally explained how she looked at what Ethan did:

> I said to myself, that person wasn't really Ethan. After he died, I learned that in high school he had been diagnosed with clinical depression. I prefer to see it in medical terms.

She could disassociate the Ethan she knew from the Ethan who killed himself and attribute his actions to an illness that consumed him. Donna talked about her frustration as she tried to answer her own questions:

> Of course I keep asking WHY. . . . I can't find a good reason for why she wanted to die. I have never been at a place where I felt I wanted to be dead, so it is hard to understand. I don't know why I feel I should have an answer. If it had been a car wreck, it would have been different.

Could We Have Helped? After a suicide, friends often realize that they did not take the early warning signs seriously. Donna described Tina's mother's feelings, which she shared:

> Her mom is also angry with herself because she didn't understand the signs. Tina was spending a lot of time alone in her room, and she gave away all her new clothes. We just didn't realize what it meant.

Only after the death do they piece together what happened. Donna also learned more about her friend Ken's death:

> We learned that Ken had slit his wrists a while ago. He told them in the emergency room that he fell in the shower when he cut his wrists, and they believed him. They sewed him up and sent him home. It's hard to believe they accepted his explanation. Then he wouldn't go to school. He wanted to be caught, but no one picked it up. In the end, you have to accept that it wasn't anyone else's fault. No one shot him but himself.

As friends try to understand, they may also ask themselves if they could have done anything to prevent their friend from committing suicide. For Donna and her friends, this was a real question:

> Ken wasn't in school that day. I was in a class with him, and he wasn't there. So we all asked what if someone had forced him to go [to school]? What if someone had happened to call at the moment it happened?

Ethan's friends came to the conclusion that there was nothing they could have done and that no one was to blame. Jon explained:

> We never felt that we could have done anything differently, although I think we all asked ourselves that question. He had talked to me about losing his sense of direction, but I would never have thought that his moping and withdrawing were signs of danger. I listened; I tried to understand, but I guess I couldn't. We were really relying on the professionals to help.

Is Someone to Blame? There are those in any community who find it easier to cope if they have someone to blame. These are not necessarily people who were close to the deceased. They find simple solutions to what are, in fact, complex problems. Parents of children who killed themselves often blame themselves for what happened (Aarons, 1995). For both friends and family members, this sense of blame is only made worse by people in the community who accuse them. Donna saw the consequences of this kind of behavior. She described how other students tried to find someone to blame:

> Ken and his girlfriend had broken up just before he died. It was easy for everyone to blame her. She was devastated. I told her that it was not her fault. I explained that it is easier to blame someone when this kind of thing happens. We kept those kids who wanted to point fingers away from her.

In times of stress, finding a scapegoat may be a way of avoiding a sense of helplessness. Finding someone to blame can give a sense of control when, in fact, there is none.

Helping Each Other

As they cope with the death, friends need each other. They join together to provide support and to protect each other when they are frightened or worried about their ability to handle all that has happened. Although the stability of their home lives has not been disrupted by the death, young people who lose a friend still feel that their world has fallen apart. Together they find ways of dealing with this new insecurity. Donna described what happened in her school:

> There is a kind of bond. We had kids leave class sobbing, even months afterward. They would sit in class and think, "He is not there," and start to cry. After class we would try to get together to talk. Me and my friends formed a support group from our high school and the other high school in town.

As described earlier, in addition to talking, they also stayed close to each other and watched out for each other, thus creating a sense of community and safety. Donna went on to describe how she and her friends were able to work through some of their questions after the death:

> After this happened we just realized that it was very sad, but if everyone just sits here and says, "What if," it is going to kill you. We decided that we can't go through all the what ifs. This did help, and it brought a lot of us closer together. We had to just accept what he did.

LEARNING FROM THE DEATH

Experiencing the death of someone close is often transforming for friends, as it is for other mourners. The death leads the mourners to question how they see themselves in the world. They are often propelled to a new place developmentally as they allow themselves to experience the full meaning of the loss.

A friend's death is often young people's first encounter with what Sally called, "your own vulnerability." As Gila said at the beginning of this chapter, the world is not as safe and predictable as they thought. In the words of 16-year-old Terrence, whose friend was killed in a drive-by shooting:

> When you lose someone close, who is your own age, it shows you your own mortality, that you are not going to live forever. This is someone who is your friend, someone you were cool with. Just like that, you're never going to see that person again. You could die.

It also adds to their sense of helplessness. Terrence continued:

> We all knew about different gangs in the neighborhood, but we thought if we stayed away, kept our noses out of other people's business, we would be safe, but now we know that's not how it works. It makes you want to go get a gun, but that's not the answer.

Friends are challenged to find better ways of coping that may give them back some sense of control. Sometimes they regain their sense of control as a result of a parent's initiative, but often the challenge comes from the friends themselves. Some of these efforts are described in Chapter 12.

Appreciating Life

Friends now are not only more conscious of the fragility of life, but they develop a new appreciation for what they have. Ruth reflected on what Jessica's death has meant to her:

> I think I was younger then; I looked at life much more dramatically—everything in extremes. Then you see someone dying in front of you; it makes you see how much you have. You say to yourself, "Wow, how lucky I am that I'm living, that I can go on with things." I think her death gave me a lot. I started to look at life with a different perspective. I sort of grew up fast. Before, every little thing—like being fat, doing bad on a test—was the end of the world for me. After Jess died, these things seemed so small. I tell myself: Think about Jess; she's not here anymore. Her life stopped. There were so many things she didn't manage to do. I don't have to be perfect.

For Sean, Corey's death helped him be less fearful of death and more accepting that it is a part of life. He explained:

> To see his strength, to say, this is the deal, and he didn't flip out. He had a presence, he knew what it was all about—he was ready—he didn't appear to be out-

wardly afraid. That gave me the calmness to say that I'm not going to be afraid of this. I think I was afraid of death. I don't know if I ever expressed that to Corey. I think that I have a greater peace about it since I went through this with him. I am very different now than I was before.

The difference is not only in the way he looks at death, but at how he approaches life:

I think that I started several different journeys that I would not have gone on before or would have started much later in life. I didn't have a lot of friends. I started seeking out people who I thought could really support me. I had to learn to be more social.

Corey's death opened Sean up to experiment, to try new things—to move beyond the world he had constructed with Corey and find a new place for himself.

Donna talked about the impact of the deaths on her life. She was grateful for what she had in a new way. She also found herself taking other people's comments about dying more seriously:

Now that this has happened to me, I realize you have to take these things more seriously. Now even if someone just says, "I could kill myself," I ask more questions. I say, "No, that's not funny to me." I've become an expert on suicide prevention. I've learned a lot.

Jon felt that the experience alone was not what changed him. He recognized that he is going through a process and that, in some ways, everything is changing in his life:

I rarely thought about how things were different. I just went on from where I was at the time; so much was going on in my life it is difficult to say. I don't speculate on what it might have been like if Ethan hadn't died; it's all part of the process.

Faith and Religion

Teenagers often reflect on their beliefs and the place of faith in their lives. The death of a friend gives these questions new meaning and new importance. Anna, now doing graduate work in biology, knew that faith can help some people, but this was not a direction that was comfortable for her:

I think religious people accept it because they believe in life after death. I'm not sure about that. I think that we become—this is my biology perspective—organic garbage. I don't know how much we have souls; maybe because of that, it's hard for me to accept that something happens after we die.

In contrast, Donna finds great comfort in her religion, and reading religious poetry makes her feel more comfortable about what has happened. One of her favorite poems talks about the need to accept the thorns as well as the roses in life (Hoff, 1991).

CONSTRUCTING A RELATIONSHIP
WITH THE DECEASED

Like other mourners, these young people discovered that their connection to their friend did not end with the death. Deborah said:

> It's not something you choose. You don't choose to remember; you just always carry it with you.

Friends remain connected to the deceased in ways similar to what has been described in other chapters. Some feel that their friend is visiting. Sean feels Corey's presence and his influence on things that are happening in his life:

> At the funeral, there was this balloon, his favorite color, and it separated from the other balloons and floated away. I thought that that would be Corey doing that. Things like that happened in several situations. I don't know if they happened or I wanted them to. Now it is more like a thought or feeling, almost as if he came to visit. I have a sense of his presence. It is a synchronistic thing. His mother is part of this. For example, I begin thinking about Corey, and then his mother will call.

For friends and parents, being in touch with each other is an important component of maintaining a connection to the deceased. Staying in contact with these other people who were close to their friend or child is another way of keeping his or her memory alive. Most likely, this independent relationship with a friend's parents is not something that would have happened if the friend had lived. Yet it now provides meaning and support to both. Deborah visits Klara's parents. She described their relationship this way:

> I go visit a lot, I don't want them to be alone, because then they think about what happened. They need people around. I'm her age, and we laugh, we talk about her, we cry. We feel like she is here, but she can't speak. That feels good.

Not all parents are comfortable seeing their children's friends. As Dale's parents described in Chapter 8, they were glad to see his friends, but also found it to be a painful reminder that he would never do the things they were doing.

Sorting out or keeping their friend's belongings can be another opportunity to remember and to maintain a bond with the deceased. Gila recalled that during the shiva (the week of mourning in Jewish families), Mara's mother wanted her friends to have some of her things:

> We took turns trying on her clothes, remembering when she bought each thing and how she looked in it. I wasn't ready to accept that she really wasn't coming back and would not need these things anymore. Now I'm glad her mother insisted. It made her parents happy to know her things went to people she loved, and I always have something of her with me.

As was mentioned, in Chapter 8, Dale's parents felt the same need to give some of his things to his friends. They found it very meaningful.

Remembering

Friends remember and carry the deceased with them in many ways. Anna enjoys being reminded, in spite of the pain that sometimes accompanies these memories of Jessica:

> There's a song that reminds me of her. Every time I hear it, I think that it's her song and I remember—then you feel the pain. When I wrote something for the memorial at the first anniversary of her death, it was hard. I realized then that crying can also be comforting.

Other friends also discovered that religious rituals provide an important framework for remembering. Sally described her experience this way:

> I said Kaddish [the Jewish mourner's prayer] the first year during the memorial service on Yom Kippur. If I am in synagogue on the anniversary of his death, I also say Kaddish. I did it this year. This ritual has a lot of meaning to me. It affects me to say it in his memory; it feels good.

There are few public rituals that allow friends to remember, to give concrete expression to their thoughts and feelings. Sometimes the family can help by asking friends to participate in services they organize. Jessica's friends were invited to talk at the service on the first anniversary of her death and were grateful for the opportunity. Anna found that speaking at the memorial service gave her an opportunity to remember. She wrote:

> You are gone. You withered away before my eyes, and at 19 we buried you. You became my hero, even though you were only human, with good and bad sides. You taught me to feel, to experience life in the moment, and to appreciate the life I've been given.

Still a Part of My Life

Even though their friend is no longer a part of the world that they created together, friends find other ways to keep their friend part of their life. Sean said:

> I still use him when I meditate, and when I pray, I talk to him. He is still very much a part of my life.

Ruth often thinks about Jessica when she does things that they would have done together:

> Only with time did I begin to understand that at the holidays or when I see something that reminds me of her, I will remember. Sometimes it's a shock to realize that she's not here. When I went to Europe last year, I said this is for Jess. She wanted to travel so much. Thinking of her wasn't easy, but it felt good to think she was seeing Europe through my eyes.

Sally thinks about Ethan a good deal and is aware of what she has lost because he is not in her life. She lost the potential they had to grow together. In some ways, he is still a guide to her:

When I think about him, I think, where would he be now. I am in New York, and I am sure that's where he would be. I keep expecting to see him out of the corner of my eye. He was my conscience, my role model, alter ego—not on personal matters, but on philosophical and social issues. He would be the person asking, "If you are still thinking of doing that, why aren't you?" No one has taken that place; I do it, in part, for myself. I just recently got in touch with someone who worked with him on a project in college. It felt good to know how much she missed him, too.

Talking

Talking to their friend is another direct way of keeping a connection. Deborah said:

> Every night I talk to her. I look up at the sky. I say "Hi, Klara." I also write to her in my diary. I write, "You are in heaven with others where you belong, and I am sorry that I didn't get to say good-bye." I tell her things I want her to know.

A similar way of remembering the person is by talking about their friend to others. Jon reminisces with friends:

> A lot of people I know knew Ethan. When we get together, we talk about him, things that happened during the year that might have interested him. We don't talk about his suicide. We often recall things we did together. We don't talk about his having been depressed or go over what anyone should have or could have done. Sometimes we talk about how hard it is to believe that he is gone and not some place where we can call him up.

Another aspect of talking about their friend is to tell people who did not know this friend about him or her. It is a part of their personal biography that is important for them to share. It is not only that they want others to know about their experience. It also becomes a litmus test for choosing friends. If new people cannot deal with this death, bereaved friends often back away. Anna tells people about her friend who died of cancer. Sally recognizes that the death will always be with her, and new people need to know it:

> It got to the point where anyone who knew me had to hear about it. I felt I needed to tell people even if it didn't come up, people who I thought I might be interested in getting close to. Partly this was so if they should ever be some place with me, if *The Big Chill* came on or something reminded me, they should know that I might break down, that I had this vulnerability, that I might need them more than normal.

Living Legacy

Yet another way of remaining connected to the deceased is by choosing a life work in their memory. In a sense, this is part of their living legacy. Donna is going to study psychology in college:

> I found that helping others was a good way to help myself. If I learned anything from Ken's and Tina's deaths, maybe I can help so other suicides can be pre-

vented. Becoming a psychologist is a good way to keep their memory alive and a way of honoring their lives. My aunt still can't talk much about what happened, but she does like to hear what I'm doing, my work with suicide prevention, and she encourages me.

As friends move on with their lives, we see that, like other mourners, this loss has changed them. They carry with them a new appreciation and sensitivity for life, and their friend remains an important part of who they are. They learn to live with the paradox that their friends are gone, yet still live on. Gila described this paradox:

> It is never really over. She is never really gone. In life and in death, she is so much a part of who I have become. A piece of her will live on, and a piece of me will always be missing. Mara, I have let you go, but I will always miss you.

3

On Helping

INTRODUCTION

I would tell a kid whose parent died, "It happened to me so I know how you feel. It's all right to think about it, to be sad, and to cry—but you have to get on with it. It doesn't help to keep it bottled up; try to be open with friends. It doesn't get better right away but it does get better with time." I would tell an adult, "If you want to help, you should ask if the kid wants to talk and what she wants to talk about— just don't start off."

—*15-year-old girl, two years after her mother died*

It is clear that we cannot protect children from the pain, sadness, and stress that fol- low the death of a loved one, whether a parent, sibling, or friend. Nor can we protect them from the disruption they experience with this death. The death will continue to contribute to who they become and how they grow for the remainder of their lives. The way they live and negotiate the various stages in their life cycle will not be the same as it might have been if the person had not died. They now look at their lives through a different lens, a lens to which a different layer of life experience has been added. The death becomes part of their life story and who they are.

From the stories in the previous chapters, you can see that there is no one way of doing things that leads to a good outcome or a better accommodation. Just as each loss is unique, so each mourner copes in his or her own unique way. Therefore, help is not a matter of providing the bereaved with a clear formula for what to do; rather, it means giving them options and information that they can refer to as they learn to cope. Help is about supporting the bereaved in ways with which they feel comfort- able, not in ways that *we* think appropriate. It is also about expanding their options by opening new doors for them.

In Chapter 4 I referred to a group of women whom Belenky and her colleagues (1996) identified as without a voice. Belenky et al. saw these women as silent. I think of the bereaved, regardless of their age or gender, as, at least for the moment, without a voice. They are silent not only because they lack words to describe what is hap- pening to them, but because their experience is often not legitimated or heard by those who are ostensibly listening. They are stigmatized and silenced both by their own grief and by society's reactions to them. Following the message they receive from the non- bereaved, their world becomes dichotomized: They expect that they will recover and carry on as before or not recover at all. They look for the right way to mourn, for someone to make them better. As they coped with their loss, the people described in this book found a new voice. This section focuses on what helped them do so.

As you have seen, most people are not alone on this journey. Family and friends accompany them. Clergy, funeral directors, health professionals, teachers, and counselors are among those who can be involved. Although there are always many helpers, children need a consistently available parenting figure to process the loss with them and from whom they learn how to cope. Nevertheless, one of the bereaved's most important resources is their own energy and imagination. Both parents and children find themselves developing creative solutions and ways of being in the world that they would never have imagined for themselves prior to the death. New aspects of themselves often emerge as a result of their experience and of the help they receive from others they meet on their journey.

Most parents and children learn that just as there is no one way to mourn, there is not one kind of help that makes everything better. They learn, if they did not know it before, that they need others from whom they can learn and that their willingness to learn and change eases the process of accommodation. One of the first things they come to understand is the fullness of what they are experiencing. What they can do about it depends on the resources available to them in their family and community.

Defining Help

What is meant by help? *Help* is defined in Webster's Third International Dictionary (1967, p. 1052–1053) as

> giving of assistance or support, a remedy, cure, to provide relief, extricate, benefit, to be of use, change for better. It is an act of giving aid or support and the resources employed in giving assistance.

Help, then, should, first of all, improve the situation—make things better for the recipient. Yet help is more than someone giving and someone taking. Help is an interactive process with many aspects to it. To be useful, help must be responsive to the needs of those toward whom it is directed; there has to be a match between the particular problem, the solution, and the help offered. Any help offered has to be experienced as helpful by those to whom it is directed. It is important to learn what people see themselves as needing and what they would consider to be helpful. Helpers have to learn to listen and to recognize that they are participating in a relationship. They need to be open to the fact that in the process of giving, they may also be helped.

A good deal of attention is usually focused on helping the bereaved talk about how they feel. Although recognizing and experiencing feelings may bring relief in the short run, generally it is not sufficient to help with all that the bereaved are dealing with. Talking about their feelings does not lead to more effective ways of responding to the impact of the death on their lives. Appropriate help should provide mourners—both adults and children—with opportunities to learn new ways of thinking as well. New ways of thinking enable them to move from a simplistic view of grief as something from which they will recover to a place from which they appreciate the complexity of what they are experiencing and their own role in coping. Both children and the adults around them need to learn to recognize more clearly their ability to effect change. This recognition may lead them to develop a more complex view of how they relate to themselves and to the world. As they find a new "voice," they may bring about changes in their community as well.

Learning Styles

People learn in different ways, and the services they find useful will be those that match their learning styles. Some rely on their intuition to guide them and take in new information as they find it. Others consciously seek out new information in an organized, systematic fashion. Teachers or helpers have to be aware of these different styles and their relationship to developmental stages (Belenky et al., 1996) and adjust the pace and content of the help accordingly. As a helper, it is important to know when to be concrete, when to generalize, when to draw on your own experience, and when to bring in the experience of others, as well as how to involve learners in the very process of learning. As we see in the subsequent chapters, all this applies to adults as well as to children (Elbow, 1973).

Gender differences also influence what kinds of help men and women, boys and girls, seek and how they utilize it (Cook, 1988; Silverman, 1988). Women and girls are generally more comfortable in acknowledging their need for others and reaching out to talk about what is happening (Belle, 1989). Young boys have similar qualities. However, teenage boys and men seem less interested in processing what is happening to them and are more likely to seek others to share concrete activities or look for information that will explain what is happening. Yet there are girls who do not find talking helpful and boys who seek out opportunities to talk.

Openness to Help

Not everyone is equally receptive to being helped or to seeking help. As I described in Chapter 4, some families invite others into their lives, while others want to do as much as they can for themselves. There are families who close off their options and close their doors. Some people manage well in this closed context; others may suffer unnecessarily, with help just around the corner. It is rarely an either-or situation. There are many variations. For example, some people may find it easier to accept some forms of help from relatives than from professionals. Others may be more comfortable seeking assistance outside the family.

Antonovsky (1979) identified family resources that he associated with the ability to utilize help and with the family's adaptability. These resources include a basic flexibility in how the family views the world, its members' sense of connection to themselves and to each other, and how these come together in their psychological and social makeup. As noted in Part 1, both Antonovsky and Reiss (1981) found that these qualities frame the sense of coherence that enables families to find means of coping that are affirming and adaptive. I suggest that families' sense of coherence may be related to where they are developmentally. The more developed their sense of coherence, the more likely they are to have a perspective that allows them to give voice to their experiences and be more receptive to making the changes that are needed at this time in their lives. They may also be able to create resources when none exist. Therefore, what help is provided, and by whom, has to be respectful and compatible with the family's style, resources, and developmental level.

SOCIAL SUPPORT

Certain conditions make it easier to learn and change and to use the help that is available. Connection and care between people are essential components in this process

(Belle, 1989; Sandlar et al., 1989; Silverman, 1994; Vachon & Stylianos, 1993). Only because of their relationships to others do children grow, develop, and adapt. This is the process of giving and receiving that has come to be called social support. The word *support*, as we have seen, is used by both children and adults to refer to some behavior in others that makes things easier for them. As we see in Chapters 11 and 12, although the nature of the support needed may change over time, the underlying need for support is constant. The presence of others who are there for the children and who can teach them gives children a sense of their own ability to control what is happening. Part of this sense of control comes from being given accurate information about what is going on in words they can understand.

Support is a complicated concept and, as I see it, is essential for all life to flourish. In many ways, support is a synonym for what we mean by help. Research has demonstrated that support mediates stress and facilitates effective coping (Sandlar et al., 1989). Cobb (1976) defined *support* as information that leads people to believe that they are cared for, loved, esteemed, and valued. Caplan (1974) talked about a support network that provides individuals with opportunities for feedback about themselves and for validation of their expectations about others. Feeling supported results from being involved in a network of others with whom it is possible to communicate and with whom one shares a sense of mutual obligation. When people feel supported, they feel that they are being treated in a personal way and that they are talking to people who speak the same language, guide each other in what to do, offer feedback about what is happening, and provide material help. Sometimes simply feeling supported is enough; at other times, the concrete things that are provided or exchanged are the most helpful.

Vachon and Stylianos (1993) defined *support* as a transactional process, requiring a fit between the donor and the recipient. Since grieving parents and children are not always at the same place at the same time, this can be a problem for both of them. Being aware of this discrepancy can help parents understand additional tensions they may be experiencing. It can also be another reason for parents to seek outside help that can be responsive to their children's needs when they are least able to do so.

What does support or help that specifically considers the needs of bereaved children look like? Support for children comes from providing them with *care, continuity,* and *connection.* These three are important in all children's lives, but become more critical when children are dealing with a death. *Care* literally means that children are fed, clothed, and loved. It involves not only giving physical and emotional attention, but being responsive to where children are developmentally and providing them with information and resources. After a death, part of caring is saying out loud that while parents may be physically present, go to work, and put food of one sort or another on the table, the pain of the loss changes everything. This acknowledgment can help children recognize that they are not to blame for what is happening and understand that everyone is experiencing the pain and disruption in the family.

Children not only need care, but they can give it to others in their family, although they may need some help to learn how. Denise, Maureen's 5-year-old sister, talked about what helped after Maureen died:

> My mother told me after my sister died, even when she was very sad, I should come and hug her. She was always hugging me, too, when I was sad or sometimes scared. They explained how much it hurt them, too, that my sister was dead and it was going to be hard for everyone. It was okay to cry. My father said I should try to help: not nag, put my dish in the sink, pick up my room. I could do that. We helped each other.

In an age-appropriate way, Denise was reassured that she would be taken care of and that she was, indeed, connected to this family; that her feelings were appropriate; and that she could also provide comfort, as well as be comforted.

Continuity is the need to know that there is some stability in the world; that life will continue, to the extent possible, as before; and that family members, friends, and others who are involved in children's lives will be there with them and for them. Children need to know that the family will carry on, that life is ongoing, with both a past and a future. Duncan, whom you met in Chapter 5, was 9 when his mother died. At that time, it was not clear to him that the world could continue afterward. It took him a year before he understood that there was life after his mother's death. Regardless of the child's age, an explanation about how the family will manage is reassuring. With older children, the surviving parent can be more explicit about how they will manage financially and deal with the family's daily routine. As one mother explained:

> I told my children [all of them teenagers] that Daddy left us with just enough money, but I would have to go to work if we wanted to continue to do all the things we were used to doing. They were old enough to consider working for some of the extras they wanted. It wasn't going to be easy, but we would still be a family.

Connection relates to children's need to feel a part of the family drama, to be connected to their families and community, and to be connected socially and emotionally to those whom they care about and who care for them. It involves acknowledging children as mourners and involving them in mourning rituals, as well as in managing the changes that occur as a result of the illness and the death. In addition, children need to construct a relationship with the deceased through which they connect the past to the present and future of the family. Fifteen-year-old Alex talked about how his family remained connected to his father:

> My father loved to play golf. They named a tournament after him. I get to give out the trophy. When I see my dad's name, it makes me feel good. My dad was somebody, and it feels good to remember him.

Constructing a new relationship with the deceased is not something children do by themselves. Parents play an active role in this process. They help by respecting their children's need to remember, by talking about the deceased, and by finding a place for the deceased in their current lives. Parents are also engaged in the same process, and this connection becomes part of the shared life of the family (Nickman et al., 1998).

Parents, too, are experiencing new and strange feelings. Their world has been turned around, and the way they make meaning in it has been challenged. They also need care and attention to respond to all the changes in their lives and to take care of themselves and their children. Parents need to take their children on the journey with them and let the children join in defining the problem and finding solutions. If parents do not do so already, they need help to learn how.

THE NEXT CHAPTERS

In this book, I talk about two kinds of help: helping people cope when an actual death occurs and helping children integrate into their lives the fact that we all die.

Chapter 11 focuses on people who have experienced a death, are in pain, and have a whole world to reorganize. In this chapter I examine the help that the bereaved with whom I talked identified, sought out, and considered the most useful. This includes help at home; in the community; and from friends, schools, and their faith communities. While many of the people I mention in this chapter appeared in earlier chapters, others appear for the first time.

Chapter 12 describes examples of formal programs and helping techniques that have been developed to meet the needs of the bereaved, including those developed by the bereaved themselves. I do not attempt to include every program that has merit. Rather, I try to give a representative sample of what is available and what the people I talked with found the most helpful.

Chapter 13 focuses on how to teach children about death in different contexts. Such initiatives help to promote a certain way of thinking in children and provide them with a context for understanding death. The programs that are described in this chapter can also set the stage for changing society's attitudes and reactions to death.

CHAPTER ELEVEN

Help Over Time
Meeting Changing Needs

> I don't remember ever thinking about not having a father. I always
> knew about his death. I was surrounded by relatives who cared for
> me and did things with me and for me. My father's best friend took
> me out on a regular basis and my mother was always there for me. I
> never think of her as someone who dwelt on what she didn't have,
> but on what she did have. In the world as I knew it, I never felt
> cheated or deprived because I didn't have a father. I guess you can
> say I felt supported all along the way.
>
> —a 17-year-old whose father died when he was 3 years old

Help is never a onetime offering or always the same. Both the goal and
the nature of the help change as both children and adults change. Over time,
mourners need different kinds of help as they adjust to the all-pervasive
changes in their lives. The goals of help at each stage will be different, depending on what mourners feel they need and where they are in the process
at that time.

Often mourners themselves are not clear what help they need. After a
death, both children and adults are in a new situation. They discover, as
they go, which coping strategies and types of help work best for them. It is
important to keep in mind that help children receive is usually related to
their parents' view of their needs and what their parents consider appropriate. Children's needs for care, continuity, and connection are more likely
to be met if parents feel supported and cared for. This chapter describes how
the help the bereaved needed changed over time and what resources were
available to meet these needs. As in other chapters, much of this story will
be told in the bereaved's own words.

WHEN A DEATH IS ANTICIPATED

When a child or a parent is dying, families need to mobilize help from many
sources and make this help work for them. At this stage, family and friends
are usually the primary source of support. They help with the details of daily
living: shopping, being there when children come home from school, doing
laundry, babysitting, and the like. Claudia's mother reflected on how much
her family helped while her husband was dying from AIDS:

> My family was always there, his parents, my parents, our siblings, and their children. They accepted that he had AIDS, they stayed by him, and they did whatever I needed. I see other families where people are rejected by their families or they have no family. I don't know how they get through this. I think their kids suffer. No matter how bad it got, Claudia always felt cared for.

For children, the school is always a central caregiver. Some families find the school staff helpful. For example, teachers can help an ill child stay in school as long as possible and provide support to healthy siblings and classmates during this period. Sometimes the hospital staff reach out to the school to work together to keep a child in school. The hospital staff may visit the school with the parent, to help a class understand the needs of a child returning to class after chemotherapy or to integrate a child with AIDS into the classroom. Some schools have counseling services, and some children, whether it is they themselves or a family member who is ill, find the opportunity to talk helpful. Most children are grateful when a teacher is understanding if their schoolwork suffers from time to time.

During this period, families are intimately involved in the healthcare system as they first seek a cure and then have to recognize that there will be none. Although the hospital staff can never respond to the entire range of needs families have at this time, they can play an important role in supporting the family in meeting its own needs. For example, they can provide written material for parents who are taking a dying child home (Pazola & Pugsley, 1992). They can provide guidance about what dying will be like and help identify other resources that the family may need. The doctor's involvement can make a big difference for the family. As one parent said:

> I've heard parents talk about doctors who walk away once they cannot cure the patient. We were very lucky. Our doctor continued to visit and then to call. He knew we were being cared for by the hospice doctor, but he was always ready to answer our questions and to show concern for how we were doing. We were people to him, and that meant a lot in helping us carry on.

When a family member is seriously ill, families spend a good deal of time going back and forth to the hospital. Hospital policies can have significant impact on the quality of the experience for both the family and the ill family member. Many parents appreciate policies that allow healthy children to visit, let parents stay in a sick child's room, or encourage the family to decorate the hospital room. All these efforts help children feel more connected to what is happening around them.

When hospice is recommended and available, it becomes an important aid for the family. Hospice staff help in many ways. They provide nursing care in the home and physical and emotional support to the family. Whether it is a child or a parent who is dying, families often feel less frightened when they know concrete help is available, when they learn what to expect as their child or spouse gets closer to death and what they can do to ameliorate the situation. Hospice staff may also encourage the family to make funeral plans in advance, as Josh's father described in Chapter 5. This planning can make their lives much easier when the death occurs.

Beyond nursing care, hospice social workers or psychologists may offer assistance with other family issues. As we saw in Chapter 7, both Maureen's and Joshua's parents thought this service made a big difference in their ability to talk with their children about the illness and dying. When her husband was dying, one mother found her extended family eager to help, but her family's ideas of help did not coincide with what she and her husband wanted. She described how the hospice social worker helped the family come together to find mutually acceptable ways of coping:

> The hospice social worker said we should have a family meeting. She met with us and our extended family, who were all living nearby and were here all the time. She helped us explain our need for a bit more privacy. We talked about our children's need to know what was going on, that trying to cheer them up was making us uncomfortable. We didn't want them to be out of the house so that they wouldn't be there when their father died. The children were young teenagers, and they didn't know how to deal with these different messages. Our family needed to hear all this. She helped them to listen and helped us to talk. Some of them felt hurt, but then they began to listen to each other and to us. They were able to change and were so good through it all.

Having someone outside the family system to talk with can be helpful. Some families turn to mental health professionals in private practice for support and feedback. Maureen's father recalled the value of such a meeting:

> I talked to a child psychiatrist. We wanted to do the right thing in how we involved our younger children. He said, "Don't push." We knew that naturally as parents. He just reinforced what we knew. He pointed out that having my sisters and their cousins there also gave the children's life a little continuity and made them more secure.

In contrast, Dale's parents thought that the psychologist they consulted privately was not helpful. The psychologist wanted to know about their own childhoods, which was not responsive to their needs at that time. They had more success finding a therapist for Dale, who felt he needed someone other than his parents and friends to talk with. Dale found the staff psychologist at the hospital helpful and talked with this therapist on and off until he died.

Healthy siblings and children whose parent is dying often find it useful to talk with other children who are having the same experience. As one father explained:

> The hospice nurse told me about this program, Kids Can Cope Too! that the American Cancer Society was sponsoring. Children came together to talk about what was happening in the family when someone was dying. My kids were delighted to be able to share, I guess the little ones did a lot of artwork. I also had a chance to talk with other parents about how to keep the children posted about all the changes in my wife's condition. I realized there were people who understood and we learned from each other. It helped me think through, as painful as the thought was, how I would manage after she was gone.

There are times when the family's own creativity is needed. Zach's mother realized how important it was to him, as he got sicker, not to feel cut off from his peers. She talked to neighborhood parents and encouraged their children to visit, play computer games, and just be there. She felt that everyone learned something from this experience.

As I noted earlier, when a parent is dying, she or he can help the family make some plans for the future. One father found a creative way of helping:

> My husband worried that the children would not remember him. We had just gotten a video camera. He had this great idea, while he still looked okay, to tape him talking to the children. He told them about himself and his growing up. They were old enough to ask questions, and I put my two cents in. There we were a family.

This father was anticipating his children's need for connection and found an effective way to help them with it.

THE EARLY PERIOD AFTER THE DEATH

Shortly after a death, practical assistance may be essential to sustain families so they can survive through the first months and even the first year. Although parents may be feeling numb and have difficulty functioning during this period, the presence of children, whose needs cannot be put on hold, creates a certain urgency. For example, many families found offers to play with the children or to babysit helpful. Families need to eat, and bringing meals to a newly bereaved family may be just what they need immediately after the death. Later, the family will not need this kind of help. Both adults' and children's learning during this early period often focuses on simply knowing that they can and do survive. Most adults are grateful that they can hold their own in whatever way possible and that they can provide for some of their children's needs. Concrete assistance that helps the family maintain a sense of care and continuity is the most appreciated.

How to Tell the Children

As I discussed in earlier chapters, telling the children about the death is one of the most difficult things a parent has to do. Parents often need help, especially when the death is sudden, in how to explain to the children what has happened (Parkin & Dunn-Maxim, 1995). Such help is generally not available. When the cause of death is suicide, sharing the news can be even more difficult. Twelve-year-old Nathan's mother was fortunate that her city had a children's bereavement program that advertised its hotline. The coroner suggested that she call for advice on how to tell her young son what had happened to his father. The mother recalled:

> I was surprised. They told me to just be honest. They said to say his mind wasn't clear. He was having problems that had nothing to do with anything we

did. To even say directly, "Daddy hung himself" and use the word *suicide*. It worked, and it was much easier at the funeral because I didn't have to worry that someone would let it out.

In contrast, after Bruce killed himself, his mother discovered that there was no place in her community that provided this kind of help. Like most parents, regardless of the cause of death, she and her husband had to rely on their own intuition to explain to Bruce's younger sibling what happened. In addition, instead of feeling helped by their families, they had to deal with family members, including their own parents, who would not believe that Bruce had really killed himself. This disbelief added even more stress to an extremely difficult situation and made it harder for their younger child to understand and to feel he could rely on the accuracy of what his parents were telling him.

Help from Clergy and Funeral Directors

In the period immediately after the death, many families find that funeral directors are an unexpected source of help. Shelly was killed in a drunk-driving accident. Her mother reflected on what helped at the funeral, when she had no idea what was happening:

> I've never been so concrete in my life. I was always very independent and liked to find my own solutions. Now I was so pleased that the funeral director and our minister were very specific that I needed to do this first and then that. It seemed to me that I needed their help simply so that I could walk. I couldn't even do that by myself.

The support this mother received was literal as well as figurative.

Some funeral directors have a place in the funeral home for children and their guests who come to the wake. Some families find this special room helpful. Fourteen-year-old Alex, whose father died suddenly, recalled:

> The funeral director had what he called a children's room, where we could be with our friends. It was good to be away from the wake and from the grownups for a while. No one got mad that we were being disrespectful when we made a joke about something or got a little noisy.

In addition, funeral directors often distribute pamphlets on grief and on community resources for the bereaved. Although families may not be ready to take in this information at the funeral, they have it to refer to when they are ready.

Even though the death may raise questions about aspects of their religious theology, most families feel comforted by the presence of the clergy. Some mourners are not comforted by such statements as "It is God's will," or "The good die young." These statements can be frightening to young children, who are quite literal in their understanding (Fowler, 1996). In the long run, religion and faith are important sources of comfort and support, regardless of whether the family is affiliated with a faith community (Morgan,

1993). For most families, religious practice and rituals give their life some order in this chaotic time and help them make some sense out of what is happening (Bouman, 1993; Cook & Wimberly, 1983). Shortly after Nicole died, her mother said:

> We do believe in God. I am Christian. God is in control, and there is a better place. I think that's why we can deal with this, even though it is enough to make you not want to be here. I have days where I don't want to even bother. We had both the priest who married us, from the church I grew up in, and the minister from my husband's church involved in the funeral service. That was very important to us.

Members of the church or synagogue may also offer other kinds of help. At this stage, this help tends to focus on the family's concrete needs. In one church, members set up a fund to help defray some of the family's medical expenses. In another, members sent food during the illness and after the death; the "casserole brigade" can be a real source of support. Maureen's mother recalled:

> The women's group from our church arranged for someone to bring a casserole every day for about a week after the funeral. I found out later that each person deliberately brought the food in a good dish that she wanted back. This gave each of them an excuse to come visit some time later to get back their dishes. It really was an excuse to talk, and I appreciated that.

Some congregations have formal bereavement committees that provide information and coordinate help. Billy's mother recalled how this helped after her husband died:

> Our synagogue has a bereavement committee. We had prayer services every night here at our house, during the week of mourning. They brought food. It made such a difference to know we weren't alone. Billy's Hebrew school class came. It meant so much to him. When I first heard of this committee, I could not imagine why it was needed. I couldn't imagine anyone being as out of it as I was, even though I knew he was dying.

Help from Family and Friends

During this period, mourners, still numb, often give the impression that they are fine. Since most family members do not in fact feel coherent at this time, appearances are deceptive. The most meaningful help is from those who can look beyond this surface impression and offer concrete help in meeting the family's daily needs. They provide food for the family, attend to the needs of surviving children, and generally function as gofers as they are needed. Alex's mother recalled the role her brother played shortly after her husband's sudden death:

> My brother kept saying, "We will get through it." He was shattered by my husband's death, but he was still my big brother. I didn't have to say a word, and he understood what I needed. His family came over, and somehow we got

through the funeral and we had food on the table. They were around all the time for the next month. Alex needed his cousin, too; they were the same age and very close.

Having familiar faces around serves a dual purpose. It both takes some of the pressure and responsibility off the parents and supports the children and gives them a sense of continuity when their friends are available. Sixteen-year-old Linda remembered the period immediately after her brother's sudden accidental death:

> My best friend Arlene went with me to the wake. I remember telling her every-thing I knew about what happened. We kept going over it to try to understand. Maybe three years later, my parents and I were talking about what happened. They told me they couldn't remember much about that period, but they re-membered calling Arlene to be with me. It makes me feel better even now to know that they were thinking of me then.

With her friend, Linda was able to revisit her brother's death to try to un-derstand how the accident happened. She also had support when her dis-traught parents could barely function.

Andrew's mother talked about how important it was that her family was nearby. They helped take pressure off of her and were able just to "be there":

> My 16-year-old nephew came over whenever I needed some relief. Andrew had company when he wanted it. It was good to know there was someone else he could count on besides me. I know they talked a lot about his father's death. For me, it was like putting a knife in me when I talked about my husband, so I was glad he had someone else to talk with, and it was someone who knew and loved my husband and missed him very much as well.

Even if parents cannot talk about the deceased, they may find comfort and feel helped when others do, which sets the stage for keeping a connec-tion to the deceased. As I discussed in Chapter 6, children find it easier and more consoling, at this point and for some time to come, to talk about the deceased, to "remember when," rather than talk about how they feel about the death. Andrew described how talking about his father helped:

> People kept coming up to me to ask how I felt. What could I say? I tried to be polite, but I didn't know what they wanted to hear. They could see how I felt. I was so glad when my cousin came over. We would just talk about things we did with my father.

One problem created by family members and friends is that they often want to make the mourners feel better. People are most helpful when they can just listen and try to hear what the bereaved are saying. In the words of a father whose child died:

> What we didn't need to hear was that we were spoiling our other children. We let them sleep in our room when they needed to. They needed to be reassured that we were there.

Help from family members and friends is informal and spontaneous, often an on-the-spot response to what is happening. It is out of these informal helping networks that we build community, and it is these networks that make it possible for the family to get through the first months. With support, people can often find their own solutions, as did Jason's mother:

> My sister called every day the first month. She and a friend would come by occasionally and take me out for coffee and just let me talk. We talked about my fears of making it alone without my husband, we talked about the kids, and we talked about my husband. I needed to work, and they helped me work out how I could manage a job and a home and have some energy left over for my children. They were surprised after a while at my own ideas about what to do. I didn't know this part of me existed.

School

Being busy with other things can be helpful. For many parents, going to work is not only an economic necessity but serves as a diversion and a place where they are not constantly reminded of the death. Going to school can serve the same purpose for children.

Some children are not comfortable with any extra attention, and some teachers' level of discomfort makes their response sound awkward and off-putting. Yet teachers and school personnel are a central part of a child's ongoing life and always part of children's helping network. In the lower grades, more often than not, children appreciate some recognition of what happened. Eight-year-old Seth talked about his first day at school after his father's sudden death:

> My teacher told my class that my father died. The class decided to write me letters about how sorry they were. Some kids made pictures for me, and they said welcome back. They were all on my desk when I came back to school. I was scared about what the other kids would say; sometimes kids can be mean. It turned out everyone really tried to be nice.

Many schools, especially in the upper grades, have crisis teams to help staff members and students deal with a sudden death immediately after it happens. These teams are particularly active if a fellow student commits suicide. Donna talked about what happened in her high school:

> We had an assembly after Ken committed suicide. The principal told us what happened. He explained that if we had our parents' permission, there would be a bus from the school to take us to the wake and later to the church service. They were going to meet with our parents that evening. The guidance counselors said they would be available to talk in the faculty lounge any time we wanted to come by for the next few days. Later I realized it wasn't enough. It doesn't make sense to think that we can get it all worked out in a few days.

Hospice Bereavement Services

For those who were served by hospice, the contact does not end with the death. Hospice is mandated to provide bereavement services to families they have served for a year following a death. Some simply send out information packets about bereavement; others offer support groups that reach out to the bereaved in the community, including those not served by the hospice, thus expanding the pool of resources available in their communities. Some hospices offer time-limited individual counseling specifically for their constituents, including play and art therapies for children (Gaines-Laine, 1997). Maureen's mother took advantage of this. As we saw with Alice's mother, hospice has also become a general resource for the larger community, providing both information about and referrals to other bereavement services in the community.

Whatever the source of their help, most families do find their way during this early period after the death. They do manage to keep their heads above water. The families talked about thus far are good examples of how the sense of coherence referred to in earlier chapters helped them cope. These families were able to find resources within themselves and their communities that they could call on. They were not afraid of their pain, nor did they have to have everything worked out in advance. However, their needs did not end within a few weeks or months after the death. They continued to require help for a long time.

AFTER A WHILE: OTHER HELPERS ARE NEEDED

Over time, the numbness lifts, feelings become clearer, and the pain is more real. Most family members and friends, though still available, return to their own lives. Often they begin to wonder how long this grief is going to last. Both they and the mourners start to realize that they may not be able to meet the continuing needs of the bereaved. Parents may need to look for other sources of help when they realize that the pain is not going away, they are not going to get over it, and it is not possible to resume their "normal" way of life. That is gone forever. Many parents now face the dilemma of figuring out what kind of help they need, and then of finding it in their community.

Some parents find resources in unanticipated places and at unexpected times. A bereaved mother described how she discovered new resources:

> I went to the library one day with my son who was doing a project for school. I never talk about these things to people I don't know, but one of the librarians saw me waiting. I guess I looked like I felt. She asked if I needed help. I laughed and said, "What I need you don't have." She took me to the computer and said I would be surprised, people don't appreciate what you can find in a library. She asked for a subject. I said "death." The first title I noticed was *The Bereaved Parent* by Harriet Schiff. I said that's me. This got me going. I found all kinds of books and then I realized there were books for my kids also. My husband started to read, too. Things started to make sense. We didn't feel so odd. I began to feel that there were things we could do.

Sometimes parents are directed to resources by their employers, clergy, funeral directors, teachers, and school guidance counselors. Others learn about programs from newspaper articles or supermarket flyers. Some are fortunate when the school itself has a program, as described by a widowed mother:

> The high school guidance counselor set up a group for children who had a death that year. Kids could come when they felt like it. My son went reluctantly. He had a friend who was killed in a drunk-driving accident that year, too, in addition to his father dying. He said it helped to just shoot the breeze for a while. He wouldn't say much about it, only that he liked the guidance counselor, who had also lost her father when she was a kid. He felt she could understand.

Shelly's father talked about finding a mutual help organization:

> I didn't expect to hear from the funeral director, but he called about two months later. He wanted to find out how we were and to tell us about the Mothers Against Drunk Driving organization. It took a few more months, but my wife and I went to a meeting. Suddenly I didn't feel so alone. This organization was doing things that might prevent other parents from going through this hell. After a while, I wanted to get involved and see some results in stopping drunk drivers. I joined the committee on legislation.

Finding Others Who Had the Same Experience

Programs and groups for the bereaved offer participants a supportive environment and the opportunity to learn from others in a similar situation. This is an important first step in learning to think differently. Kathleen was 17 when her mother died. Her father saw an ad in the local newspaper about a bereavement program for children. Four years later, she described her experience:

> It met in a local church. I found myself in a room with kids my age, more or less, all of whom had lost someone close. I was very nervous. It felt safe to talk, and I started to cry. It was the first time I was really talking about it. I didn't feel as alone.

The feeling that they are the only one who experienced such a loss can leave children feeling isolated and vulnerable. Participating in a group for the bereaved can help them feel less alone as they quickly discover the value of finding others who have had a similar experience.

A 10-year-old girl contrasted her experience at the bereavement center with her experience at school:

> I have only one friend in school who doesn't tease me. They pick on me and say, "You don't have a father," and they laugh. No one teases me here, and that feels good.

In this setting, bereaved children feel accepted and safe. They learn to talk about the death and to be less fearful of its consequences in their lives and, as a result, feel more in charge.

Often these programs help children correct misconceptions about the death. For example, some children, and even adults, have the feeling that since only bad people get murdered, their sibling or parent who died in this way must have been bad. Karin, age 11, reflected on how the group helped after her father was murdered:

> I never knew anyone in the same situation. I used to think my father had done something wrong that he was murdered. I began to understand that he was in the wrong place at the wrong time. Then I could compare my feelings . . . sad feeling and glad feelings. The leaders really understood my feelings, and they didn't make faces. My friend doesn't understand my feelings that much. She always feels bad and she has a sad face, and that makes me feel bad and I don't like that. I don't like people feeling sad for me. It shouldn't be a big deal; people shouldn't feel bad if I want to cry in school. That should be okay.

Friends, like family, may not always be as helpful as they wish. Karin found that her friend's sympathy made her uncomfortable, but she could not easily explain why. In the bereavement support group, she learned how to put her father's murder into perspective in a way she could understand. She learned that not everyone reacted as her friend did. She did not have to deal with her feeling of responsibility for her friend's sadness.

A 7-year-old learned to reflect on his experience in a bereavement center program. In a way, he seemed mature for his age as he described his experience:

> I liked the volcano room where I could jump around and throw things, and no one could get hurt. When I was angry, I wasn't so angry after that. I liked the art room, where I could get messy, paint on my face, like a clown. I learned from the talking circle that it was good to talk about what I remember about my dad. We made Father's Day cards, and I put mine on my father's grave.

Many children find that they prefer to be in a group composed of peers, not only in age but in terms of the cause of death. This may be especially true after a suicide, since children learn that it is not always safe to talk about how their parent or sibling died. Donna learned the importance of support when she joined the only group in her community dealing with suicide. However, its members were parents whose children had committed suicide. Although the group gave her an idea of what might be helpful, it did not really meet her needs. In the words of another teenager whose older brother killed himself:

> My mother found this group. I wanted to go with her. She took me, but I found that after one meeting I was bored. My mother still talks about it as a lifesaver for her, but I needed kids my own age.

Another 16-year-old found such a group, for children whose sibling or parent had committed suicide. Although the group was composed primarily of teenagers, children as young as 8 were involved. He reflected on what he learned:

> At first, I hated coming here. I was very angry and in lots of trouble. I learned a lot in the two years I've been coming, and I really appreciate that my mom and school made me come. I can now understand why my father killed himself.

I don't feel so alone. I met lots of other kids who this happened to. I know that I both love and hate my father, and that's okay. Now I want to help start a group in my school for children who had a death in the family. My guidance counselor is going to help me.

Coming to a group can become a very important part of a child's life. A mother talked about her children's reactions after they went to a bereavement center:

The kids were so excited. There is a quietness and safety about this place. The longer we have been coming, the more they seem to talk about their father. I had to find some of his things they wanted to put in a memory box. That helped me, too.

Often parents focus on finding help for their children. Sometimes, if the only help available is for adults, they decide not to participate. It may take a while for them to realize that helping themselves will help their children as well. They discover how useful it is to talk with other parents who had similar experiences. They learn from each other new ways of coping, including new ways to parent. Barbara was 6 when her father died. Her mother recalled:

Here were other young widows. We talked about how to deal with lonely evenings. They understood, and we began to share ideas. We exchanged phone numbers and now there was someone to talk with when I thought I was going to blow my stack. We arranged to do an outing with our children. That was very successful. We went bowling; that made it easier for the kids to get to know each other.

Different people may seek different kinds of information in the group. A widower talked about his need to learn to keep house. He had also begun dating and was finding it difficult:

I wasn't so sure this group was for me. I'm not a big talker, but once I got myself there, I was glad I came. I was feeling so helpless, and I learned that most widowers have the same difficulty when faced with trying to care for their children and hold down a job. The women got a kick out of teaching us. I was dating. They said to remember I had to learn a whole new way of doing things and to tell the kids that they weren't in any danger of losing me. No one would take their mother's place. It never occurred to me that they would worry about that. It made sense. Maybe that's why they never like anyone I date.

The group can help parents learn to understand how their children's ages and stages of development affect their feelings and behavior. One father described how the group helped him help his daughter deal with her grief:

In the group, as we talked, we came to realize that we didn't always understand our children's behavior. My daughter was only 8. Sometimes I would find her crying, other times she would just get so angry and then she would cling. I needed to learn that 8-year-olds can't always keep things together. In some ways, she was so grown up, and that's how I wanted her to be. But in fact she is still a little girl.

The reinforcement from other bereaved people can be especially important when the expectations of family members and friends do not coincide with the bereaved's experience:

> I thought I was crazy because I wasn't getting over it. Our family liked to remember Bobby. We talked a lot about him. My friends told me that it's six months; we should be getting over it. Here I was, at a Compassionate Friends meeting, in a room full of parents who all were doing the same thing, and many of their children had been dead for a long time. For the first time in a long time, I felt normal.

Individual Counseling

Often people turn to individual counseling when groups are not available or when they are not comfortable in a group setting. Sometimes they turn to a therapist they had consulted before the death. Individual counseling can serve the same purpose as a support group, in providing a safe place to talk and have feelings legitimated:

> My mom took me to see this shrink [psychiatrist] she is seeing. He was nice, and I didn't have to worry about upsetting him if I cried.

Several months after her daughter's death, Maureen's mother consulted the social worker at the hospice program:

> I needed a professional to listen to me. I didn't want anyone who would try to make me feel better like my family did. Knowing she could accept my pain was what I wanted.

Other families need more intensive care that focuses on their individual psychological problems. These problems usually existed prior to the death, but the death brings them to the surface and exacerbates them. Bruce's suicide made his parents confront their differences in a new way:

> My husband and I had a lot of serious differences. He always said therapy had nothing to offer him. After our son killed himself, my husband realized that our problems could have contributed to our son's unhappiness. My husband agreed that to save our family, we should go for help. A group couldn't help us. We found a good marriage counselor who had worked with other families where a child had committed suicide. It is taking a long time, but we are in a much better place.

Special Needs of Widowed Families

Many widowed parents need additional assistance in certain areas, such as financial planning and learning to manage their money. Sometimes these issues come up in a support group for widowed people; sometimes parents must look for individual assistance. No matter how limited their financial resources are, they need to make long-term plans for the family's economic needs. Often with their spouse's death, they lose a second income that the family depended on. They are often surprised that their local bank's financial adviser is willing to help, no matter how small their account is. Some widowed parents take courses on money management at the continuing education program at a local high school. Widowed parents also have to learn about the benefits their children are entitled to under Social Security. These benefits can make a big difference in their ability to manage. As one widower said:

> I found out I was covered under my wife's benefits. That gave me money to help pay the babysitter I needed after school.

If their health insurance was part of the deceased's benefit package, the family may lose coverage when the spouse dies. For many, primarily women who did not work outside the home, the loss of health insurance forces them to consider finding work that will provide some benefits, including coverage for their children.

Sooner or later, both widows and widowers have to think about who will take care of their children if something happens to them. Some children prompt this decision by asking their parents directly. The children become more relaxed when their surviving parent talks with them about what will happen if she or he gets sick or dies. Children of all ages need to participate in this decision and know that they will be cared for. Thus, surviving parents need appropriate legal advice to help them prepare a will and make sure that their wishes will be followed. This is not easy for most parents, and it often takes several years before they are ready to act on these issues.

Not All Families Change and Grow

Some parents are not responsive to their children's needs and, in essence, are not "there" for their children, neither initially nor later on. Tony, as reported in Chapter 6, felt alone with his grief after his mother died. The roots of this feeling can be seen in his father's behavior. Tony's father talked about how long it took him to recognize that his children had needs, too:

> I was like a couch potato. I would go to work early and work overtime. It kept me very busy, and I made up for the time I lost when my wife was sick. I would come home late and just sit. It took me maybe six months, maybe more, before I realized that my children had lost their mother, too. It wasn't just that my wife died. They had to get to school, eat; I didn't have the vaguest idea how that got done or was getting done for that matter.

Help for this family ideally would involve getting the father to be able to recognize and acknowledge his children's grief as well as his own. The father needed help to develop a role for himself in the family as a single parent. He also needed to see that his complete absorption in his own loss and pain was partly responsible for some of the antisocial behavior his children were displaying. This was not what happened, however. Although this father sought help, it was only for the children's behavior, not for his relationship with them. A year after the death, he was dating a woman who was willing to pay some attention to the children, which he saw as taking care of their needs. However, his dating only angered the children and distanced them further from their father. They needed to hear that this new woman was not a replacement for their mother. With appropriate respect for children's needs, a new relationship can add to the children's lives and make a difference in how they cope. Yet any new relationship has to be negotiated with the children, regardless of their age. This negotiation did not happen in this family, and the children suffered.

NOT ALL HELP IS HELPFUL

It is important to note that not all help is helpful. Sometimes the help people provide does not meet the family's expectations. Other times people volunteer help that is not appropriate. Often people feel disappointed or let down when help is not forthcoming from people they thought would understand. Sometimes friends suggest that the mourner should seek professional counseling when all the person wants is a friendly ear, someone to listen. This behavior is a way of avoiding learning about the pain and how long it can last while still feeling as if they have done something helpful as friends. The suggestion that the bereaved need professional help can leave them feeling hurt and as if something must be wrong with them. One mother recalled her son's teacher's comments and the hurt he experienced:

> My son was devastated. He's only 8 years old and is having a real hard time. His teacher told him that it was time to be over his grief; his sister was already dead three months. She wanted him not to show his tears in the classroom or not to use the death as an excuse for not doing well on a test. I would have thought she would have known better.

Teachers need to be prepared to deal with the continuing grief of their students that can intrude on the class. At a time when they are least able, parents may need to intervene and to educate the teachers. Sometimes, even such intervention is not enough. As you saw in Chapter 6, Ben's mother had to change schools to get him the support he needed.

Physicians may also need to be educated. They often quickly prescribe sedatives or psychotropic drugs to help parents cope with the physical tension and pain that they are experiencing. One mother described her experience with her family doctor:

> After a while I realized that it wasn't drugs I needed. I found out about this parents' group, and I began to learn about other things I could do to help myself. I brought my doctor their literature. At first he was annoyed with me for questioning his medical judgment, but after a while, as he saw me change, he began to listen. Now he keeps the group's literature in his waiting room.

Sometimes counselors and therapists may not understand the need for a different approach than they take with other clients, an issue that is discussed further in the next chapter. As noted earlier, if the help is simply focused on the expression of feelings, it may be insufficient. In addition, many mental health professionals adhere to the idea that letting go of the deceased is an essential step in successful grieving. This view can prevent them from providing the kind of help the bereaved really need. For example, a bereaved mother described her experience:

> I found a psychiatrist about a month after my son's sudden death. I was in such pain. I was overwhelmed and looking for some relief. I had heard of Compassionate Friends, but I didn't think I could deal with a group at this point. My family was upset because I would console myself by watching a family video taken a few days before my son died. This therapist told me that I should not be looking at this video, that I had to start letting go. This only made me feel worse. Finally I stopped going. Then my local librarian saw me taking out all these books on loss, and we started to talk. She suggested I call the local hospice. They would know some therapists who had experience with grief. I found another psychologist, and she could hear me. Later I was willing to consider attending a Compassionate Friends meeting. By that time, I was ready, and it was very helpful.

One of my students provided another example of how pervasive the concept of "letting go" is. He told me about an assignment he was given as a psychology student at another school the year before. When asked to write a paper on an experience that most influenced his life, he wrote about his mother's death five years earlier. His professor did not mark the paper. Instead, he told the student that his description of the death was too vivid, given the time that had passed, and that he should have let it go a long time ago. He suggested that the student see a therapist as soon as possible. My student was stunned and dropped the course.

Working with the bereaved in individual counseling may require the counselor to be more active and ready to educate about bereavement, as well as to listen. After her friend Ethan committed suicide, Sally decided to go to a university counseling service that had advertised its availability to help students deal with a death. She did not find it as helpful as she had hoped:

> The counselor was too passive. She just sat and waited for me to talk. She didn't seem to connect to where I was at. I had no experience in counseling, so I didn't know what to expect. I didn't go back. I'm not sure what was wrong. Part of me said she didn't know enough about bereavement. She needed to direct my thinking with some questions. I wanted more information to help me understand what I was experiencing.

For many people, their relationship to their clergy is important, and they feel especially disappointed when their clergy are not helpful after a death. Clergy are not necessarily exempt from feeling uncomfortable in dealing with a death. Just as neighbors or friends sometimes seem to stay away or avoid conversations about the person who died, so do clergy. When these things happen, families often feel rejected and hurt, as if they have done something wrong because their loved one died. They may also feel stigmatized and angry. This was Leslie's mother's experience:

> We continued to go to church every Sunday. Our minister was always very glad to see us. We told him we wanted to talk. He said he would call and make a time to visit. He never followed up. I finally realized it wasn't us—it was him!

OTHER SOURCES OF HELP

All mourners find their own ways of comforting themselves and dealing with their pain. Older children and parents discover that one of the most important sources of help is their own energy and resourcefulness. Kayla, whose mother and sister both died in the same accident, described the things she found consoling:

> Basically I would just write in my diary and listen to the *Dying Young* soundtrack [a 1991 movie]. Now when I listen, I realize how sad that music was. At that time, it was comforting.

Both adults and adolescents use music, writing, painting, and poetry as sources of comfort. These media give them outlets for expressing their grief and the turmoil of their emotions. One mother, an artist, said:

> I spent most of the first year after my son died in my studio. I painted out all my pain and anger. My art kept me sane.

As was noted in earlier chapters, some people write letters to the deceased (Evans, 1997; Kagan, 1998; Silverman & Silverman, 1979). Maureen's mother kept a journal. Some parents found exercise, yoga, or other physical activities a good way to release their tension. Some learned to meditate as a way of relaxing and renewing themselves. Others found comfort in religion. One parent noted:

> If anything good could have come from my daughter's death, it is that we found Jesus. This has been enormously consoling to us.

Both parents and children referred to their faith as sustaining them. Richard's parents believed in reincarnation; it eased their pain when they thought about his coming back in a healthy body after living his life with muscular dystrophy.

For many parents, having to take care of their children gives them purpose and helps keep them focused in the present. Taking care of others can be an important way of helping themselves.

HELP IN THE LONG TERM

As children grow and mature, they continue to need help from their parents. They will constantly revisit the meaning of the death in their lives and learn anew who died. Their need for care, continuity, and connection changes in content, but is always present. As they move further away in time from the death, most of the help families need is related to remembering and honoring the deceased. Children continue to need their parents' support, in particular, in maintaining a connection to the deceased. Many families create opportunities to help themselves. One way is to celebrate the deceased's birthday, which becomes a family occasion for remembering. Some families go to the cemetery. Three years after her father died, Alice, now 11, talked about this ritual:

> We go to the cemetery and put flowers on the grave. Sometimes I talk to him without saying words out loud to tell him what I have been doing. Then we go for ice cream. He loved ice cream, and he had a favorite place he used to take us to.

How the family maintains a connection will change as the children mature. As Claudia grew older, she found a new way to honor her father that was meaningful. Each year, she and her mother raise money for AIDS by participating in a walkathon. On this occasion, any concern Claudia has about whether her classmates know how her father died is set aside:

> I collected money from my friends in school. Between my cousin, my friends, and people at school, we raised $900. I carry a sign that I am walking in my father's memory. I've done this every year since he died. It's very important that we can help.

Other people can also help by supporting the family as they seek opportunities to remember. Continued involvement in mutual help organizations is one way of doing so. Compassionate Friends has an annual memorial service to which everyone who has ever been a member is invited. This ceremony provides a way of formalizing the families' memories of their children and maintaining a connection to them. One father talked about how important this ceremony was for him:

> This is a very important part of the year for us. We talk about our children. Some parents read poetry they've written, and we release balloons with our children's names on them. Our other children come, too, and it helps us all to remember and to talk about our daughter, their sister.

Some families return to hospice for a similar annual memorial service. If the family is affiliated with a faith community, annual rituals of mourning, such as a memorial mass or reciting the yearly Kaddish, provide a framework in which to remember and revisit the relationship. Often friends participate in these rituals as well.

As children grow, their need for help may be related not directly to the death itself, but to the changing needs of the family. Four years after her father's death, as Jayne approached adolescence, her mother suggested that she go see a counselor:

I told her that since I was her only parent, there may be times when she is not able to tell me what is on her mind. I want her to have someone she could talk to besides me. She went a few times. She liked this woman, and she said it was good to know she was there, but she thought she didn't really need her now.

Getting on with Life: Thinking Differently

As I noted in earlier chapters, for many bereaved people, coping with the death is, in some way, transforming, opening them to new experiences and parts of themselves that they did not know existed. Their growing awareness of these changes and ability to accept the changes as part of who they now are is, in part, what is meant by making an accommodation to the death. It is not clear what brings about this transformation. Parents sometimes attribute it to a sense of empowerment when they realize that they have survived. They can look ahead and see the sun shining again. One mother described how much she changed:

> I was always waiting for someone to give me permission, and here I am very much in charge. Even how I treat my other kids has changed. I've learned to listen better. Sometimes when I see how much I've changed, I almost don't recognize myself.

There is no one type of help that makes it possible for people to reach this point. For parents, it comes from support others provide, from learning in collaboration with their peers, and from the sense of accomplishment they feel for having survived and finding life affirming again. Bruce's mother described her process:

> I joined the Compassionate Friends group for parents whose children committed suicide. I started to learn about what leads to suicide, to deal with my own guilt. We live in a small town. I met someone from the local newspaper, and I started to tell her what I was learning. She wanted to write about it in the local paper. I said if it would help someone else, go ahead. Then a couple of days after the article appeared, I got a call from a minister in town who had a congregant whose daughter had just killed herself. He wanted to know if I would call her. The next thing I knew, I was the town resource, and I was invited to talk at the high school about suicide prevention. It wasn't my intention, but here I am. Me, who could never open her mouth in a group, talking loud and clear. If I can prevent even one death or help one parent, then I feel as if my son's death will have some meaning.

Helping themselves by helping others is an effective way of dealing with the loss and of giving some new meaning to the death. Stephanie's mother finds help in reaching out to mothers whose children have been murdered in her community. She did not let her own helplessness get to her. She described how the experience turned her into a community activist:

> I heard so many families blaming themselves or trying to convince themselves that their children were killed because of the color of their skin. You feel helpless because you could not prevent it. I could have become part of the problem

or part of the solution. I wasn't going to be trapped in helplessness, so I created a way of being part of the solution.

This mother reaches out to newly bereaved families and, if they wish, visits them. She wears a button with her daughter's picture on it. She also organizes a community vigil every Mother's Day in memory of the children who have been murdered in her community.

As their parents are able to function more effectively, children, too, change. These changes are primarily the result of their meeting peers and finding words for their experience in a context in which they feel supported. Sometimes these changes are also manifested in their ability to help others. Kayla discovered this ability when she went away to college:

> I felt that if I needed something, then there must be others, so I put up a notice and five people responded. I started a group similar to the grief group that I was in before. It actually helped me see how far I had come. I realized that now I was dealing with my issues by helping others deal with theirs.

The need for help does not end as people achieve some kind of accommodation. The help is different from the type they needed at the beginning, but help is still required. In many ways, this is part of a lifetime process, not only for the bereaved but for all of us, of helping and being helped. It is something that never ends as long as we are alive.

CHAPTER TWELVE

Finding Help

Services for the Bereaved

> I read about several programs for bereaved children in a national magazine. I saw something on television. I soon realized that if I wanted something in our town, I was going to have to start from scratch and I was going to have to carry the ball.

Part of the dilemma many bereaved families face is finding help outside their families and existing support networks. It is not always easy to make a match between the families' needs and available services. Often services do not exist in their area, so the bereaved themselves, or those close to them, take the initiative to create programs in their communities. This chapter describes existing services that can serve as models for the bereaved and others working with them who wish either to locate or develop such programs in their communities. These are services or approaches to helping that I believe are capable of helping the bereaved cope and adapt. (See Appendix 1 for how to contact organizations described in this chapter.) To these descriptions, I have added comments about how the services facilitate learning and details from my own experience in developing programs.

MUTUAL HELP: BUILDING ON THE EXPERIENCE OF THE BEREAVED

As we saw in the last chapter, help offered by other bereaved people has a special meaning to the bereaved. I call this kind of help a mutual help experience. People learn from their common experience. Participants in mutual help exchanges are provided with opportunities to learn new ways of coping or "the tricks of the trade"—that is, "This worked for me; maybe it would work for you?" Thus, their individual coping repertoires are expanded (Silverman, 1978, 1980). Belenky, Bond, and Weisenstock (1997) stated that the learning that takes place in this context is a result of the collaboration that this setting encourages. Learning is easier when people speak the same language. In this situation, when others say "We understand," they really do. The bereaved no longer see themselves as the only ones with this experience. Participants accept each other's feelings and experiences and provide each other with role models of what is possible. When the newly bereaved meet others who have survived a death, they get a sense of hope that they, too, can survive (Silverman, 1977).

In a mutual help setting, people learn how to live in an affirming manner in their new situation (Goffman, 1963). There is always a mutuality, so the participants move between roles, sometimes recipient and sometimes helper, in an essentially nonhierarchical setting. (Apfel & Telingator, 1995; Borkman 1990; Powell, 1994; Riessman & Carroll, 1995; Silverman, 1978).

Several settings provide opportunities for this kind of learning. In its simplest form, this helping takes place in the informal exchanges of daily life as we share with and learn from others with similar experiences. Often learning is formalized in mutual help groups or organizations (Silverman, 1978, 1980, 1988). Support groups and centers for bereaved children also provide opportunities for the bereaved to learn from each other (Fleming & Adolph, 1986).

Belenky and her colleagues (1997) see collaborative learning and mutual help as experiences to which women are naturally drawn. In my experience with the bereaved, learning in this context is not reserved for women only. Although women are more likely than men to be involved in mutual help groups, I have observed that when bereaved men do get involved, they have similar experiences and similar results (Silverman, 1988).

Mutual Help Organizations

A mutual help organization is usually an incorporated group whose founders joined together to solve a common problem. Many organizations have long histories, but started out as local community groups. Often these groups began when people who had a common loss met, sometimes by accident, and discovered how helpful they were to each other (Powell, 1994; Silverman, 1978, 1980). For example, Compassionate Friends, an organization for bereaved parents, began in the early 1970s in a clergyman's office in a pediatric hospital in England, where a group of parents came together to talk about their grief after the death of their children (Klass, 1988; Stephans, 1973).

In mutual help organizations, people are members, not clients. Members control policy, administration, and the nature of the help offered. These organizations depend on the volunteer energy of their members, who pay dues and donate their time to meet some of the administrative needs of the organizations. Members seek not only support, but to problem-solve together. Each organization develops strategies for coping that are based on the experiences of its members. In this setting, the participants are not constrained by professional roles that put boundaries between the person who is helping and the person being helped. The helpers and beneficiaries are peers, but those who are designated as helpers are usually veteran members who have successfully dealt with their issues. Members learn that they often help themselves by helping others. They frequently stay with the organization, moving between the roles of helper and recipient and into new roles, depending on their needs and the situation.

Many mutual help organizations have a way of identifying and reaching out to newly bereaved people in their communities who may be potential members. These organizations provide many kinds of help: informational meetings, scheduled support groups or regular meetings that provide opportunities to share, a newsletter, and a telephone network or hotline. Most bereavement groups hold an annual nondenominational memorial service for their members' deceased relatives. In addition to group meetings, the members also help each other, as needed, through informal exchanges on the telephone or in other settings. When appropriate, many organizations are involved in political action, such as lobbying their legislatures for laws concerning drinking and driving. Some organizations sponsor advertising campaigns to raise people's awareness about a particular disease and to raise money. They also publish booklets for local distribution and publish newsletters or magazines for their members. Newsletters and magazines provide people who cannot attend meetings with new information and the opportunity to share. This printed material is effective for people who are not ready for a group, are not joiners, or who do not have a group available in their local communities. Many groups now have web pages, through which they provide information and resources to a greater number of people. Mutual help organizations also sponsor educational programs for professionals to help them understand the needs of bereaved families.

Role of Professionals. Professionals can serve as consultants and advisers to mutual help organizations, but they do not set policy or determine what the helping program should be. Some groups hire professionals to facilitate support groups they sponsor. In this case, the professionals work for the organizations. The organizations screen potential facilitators to be sure they appreciate and understand the nature of mutual help (personal communication with M. G. McGovern, Bereaved Families of Ontario, 1997). Some organizations also train their own members to facilitate support groups.

Sometimes professionals serve as collaborators with bereaved people, helping to organize programs and giving potential organizers encouragement and support (Silverman, 1978, 1979). A good collaborator knows how to help people mobilize their own resources and develop their own ideas and knows when to move aside as the members take over (Silverman, 1980). The bereaved often develop expertise from their own experience, so they have a greater understanding and more knowledge about the subject than do trained professionals who have no personal experience with grief. Professionals who work with the bereaved, especially in a mutual help setting, need to recognize that they are the students (McGovern, personal communication, 1997; Silverman, 1978). For example, traditional theories about letting go were challenged by members of mutual help organizations whose experiences had taught them that they remained involved with the deceased. From listening to their stories, professionals learned that grief is a life-cycle event from which people do not recover, but to which they accommodate (Klass, 1988; Silverman, 1978, 1986).

Range of Groups Available. *The Self-Help Sourcebook* (White & Madara, 1998) lists 32 organizations that deal with bereavement. There is an organization for people whose relatives died in airplane accidents; there are organizations for the widowed, for bereaved parents, for survivors of sudden infant death syndrome, for family members and friends of murder victims, for family and friends of victims of drunk driving accidents, and for survivors whose relatives committed suicide. In addition, there are many organizations that focus on particular conditions, such as the Candlelighters Childhood Cancer Foundation, Children's Brain Tumor Foundation, Cystic Fibrosis Association, and Muscular Dystrophy Association.

The groups listed in this directory are national, with local chapters in various parts of the country, and usually have resources for helping interested people organize new chapters. This list does not represent the many local groups that are doing similar work, but are known only to people in their own communities. For example, in the greater Boston area there is an organization called Young Widows and Widowers that has chapters in southern New Hampshire and eastern Massachusetts, but is not listed in any national directory. It is a member-led organization that serves the needs of young widowed persons. It offers groups for the newly widowed and for those who are moving on, as well as occasional children's activities. Members built their own program using ideas from more established and better-known organizations, which they adapted to their situation.

A church basement or a member's living room is the most common meeting place for most local groups or local chapters of national organizations. Most mutual help organizations operate on shoestring budgets. The lifetime of these groups varies, since at the local level, they subsist on the passion of their members. It is this passion that drives their efforts and can make a difference in their communities and in the lives of others like them. It is their energy and commitment that have also informed and driven much of the innovation that is taking place in the field of death and dying.

A Parent's Passion: Starting a New Group. Kids Alive and Loved (KAL) is a good example of how one mother's concern turned into an organization. Bernadette Leite organized the group after her son, Khalil, was killed in a drive-by shooting in Atlanta in 1993. At Khalil's funeral, she saw some of his friends start to fight out of frustration at his meaningless death. They did not know what to do with their grief. She decided to bring these friends together, in her home, where their grief could be recognized and where they could talk about their experience. The acronym KAL is also her son's initials, and this group has become a way of honoring his memory.

The group has now formalized its work. In a brochure on its activities, KAL is described as a bereavement self-help/support group and a violence-prevention program for youth survivors of violence. Membership is open to any survivor of violence and homicide. In its weekly meetings, KAL provides the opportunity for similarly bereaved teenagers and bereaved parents to come together for mutual support, to learn how to cope with their pain and anger, and not to become perpetrators of violence. In addition, members make presentations at schools, do crisis intervention, visit youth survivors in hospitals, accompany families to court, and telephone and visit bereaved families. KAL sponsors an annual memorial service in memory of those who were murdered in Atlanta. Helpers are those who have made changes in their lives or are in the process of change and are willing to use this experience to help others.

This organization is an excellent example of how a grass roots effort can grow into a significant community organization that fights violence and provides young people with a safe place where they can learn to cope with their grief. It is now affiliated with the Institute for Minority Health Research at the Rollins School of Public Health of Emory University, as part of a larger program to prevent violence in the community (Thomas, Leite, & Duncan, 1998).

Support Groups

Support groups are another form of mutual help. A support group is a group of approximately 10 people, with a leader who is typically a mental health professional. The group meets on a regular basis to discuss issues that the group members have in common. Support groups differ from mutual help organizations in that the professionals are in charge, the members are not responsible for convening or continuing the groups, and the members usually pay fees to the leaders. These groups are offered by mental health professionals in private practice or by the staffs of hospitals and hospices. Some funeral homes are now offering aftercare services, including support groups. Faith communities also sponsor groups for their members. The groups that meet in centers for bereaved children, discussed in the next section, can also be seen as support groups.

The role of the facilitator in a support group is to make it possible for people to feel comfortable by creating a supportive and safe environment, to be sure that everyone is heard, and to encourage people to share and learn from each other by asking questions that open up discussions. For a support group to be effective, it needs to be a place where people can not only share their pain, but can learn how to look at their situation differently, how to think differently about themselves, and how to make a shift in the way they meet their own needs. The facilitator needs to understand group dynamics to help the group coalesce and to ensure that everyone participates.

Unlike in mutual help groups, the facilitators of support groups often screen potential participants to ensure that they can benefit from this kind of help. Facilitators look for participants who can use or learn to use the opportunity to talk with each other about their losses and who are not handicapped by major emotional or psychiatric problems. A word of caution is in order: There are limitations in professionals' ability to predict who does well in a group, so facilitators need to be open to opportunities to reevaluate their decisions and make needed changes. Both adults and children have a basic resilience and ability to grow and change as they deal with their grief. Thus, they may change in unexpected ways when involved in a group.

When enough potential participants are available to form separate groups, groups are often organized by type of death (such as violence as opposed to natural causes) and who died. Since the needs of children whose sibling died differ from the needs of children whose parent died, there is value in a group being homogeneous by age and type of death, but this is not always possible. In some ways widowed parents and parents whose children died have similar needs in that they have to learn about how their children grieve and how this way of grieving changes their parenting. On the other hand, their needs are different, in that widowed parents are dealing with being single parents and couples whose children died are renegotiating their relationship to each other.

Support groups can be a meaningful way of helping children and adolescents, as well as adults. When the support group model is used with younger children, discussion is usually accompanied by art activities and play (Bacon, 1996; Fleming & Balmer, 1991; Zambelli & DeRosa, 1992).

Time-Limited versus Open-Ended Groups. One of the main distinctions between types of support groups is that some are time-limited, while others are more open-ended. Bacon (1996) describes the merits of open-ended as opposed to time-limited groups. Open-ended groups allow new members to join as they go along; the groups continue as long as they seem to be meeting the members' needs. These groups seem to work well in the context of a mutual help organization or as part of a program at a child bereavement center. Bereavement services offered by hospice sometimes sponsor open-ended groups whose members join when they are eligible. These groups have the stability of the sponsoring agencies or organizations behind them, which sustains the groups as well.

An open-ended group is well suited to helping people over a long period as they find a way of living with their pain and beyond it. Yet the facilitator has to be sure to help the group members grow and deal with all the changes in their lives and not use the group as a way of staying in the same place. Occasionally, the members can use the group as an opportunity to lick their wounds; they feel supported in their pain but do not move beyond it. One way of keeping the sense of movement in the group is for the leader to develop questions related to a problem that a group member is experiencing. Old members can be helpful in brainstorming with new members to help them find alternative coping strategies. This process can become a regular part of the group. At some point, people may need to graduate or move on to a different sort of group. This is true in mutual help organizations as well. In mutual help organizations, one option is for members to move into the role of helper; in support groups, the option is to form a group that focuses on moving on. Ultimately people may simply move on to other interests and activities.

Time-limited groups meet for a given period, generally between 6 and 10 weeks, and have a predetermined agenda. Establishing an agenda can give the participants a sense of direction and enhance their involvement in the group (Jordan & Ware, 1997). The process of collaborative problem solving can begin here. In parents' groups, the agenda should include sessions on understanding how children express grief and appreciating their developmental differences. It is also important to help families construct a relationship to the deceased. For children, activities that focus on this connection are especially helpful.

Bereaved Families of Ontario. Bereaved Families of Ontario is a mutual help organization with monthly meetings open to all its members. In addition, it sponsors time-limited closed support groups for both parents and children—12-week groups for parents and 8-week groups for children. Usually the groups are homogeneous by type of death; however, if there are not enough participants at any given time, the groups are mixed (for instance, children who lost parents are mixed with those who lost siblings). The content of the children's group is modified according to the ages of the children in a particular group. The group starts with getting acquainted. The first meeting is devoted primarily to the children telling their stories as they understand them. Over time, the children bring in photographs and talk about their relationships with the deceased. They talk about the funeral; their feelings; and changes in themselves, in their families, and in their lives. The final sessions are devoted to the future and to saying good-bye to each other. Art materials and other techniques are used to involve the participants (Fleming & Balmer, 1991; McGovern, personal communication, 1997).

Before a family joins the organization, the parents talk with a volunteer, to tell their story and to decide if they want to join and be part of a support group. The facilitators are volunteers who have coped with grief, either as professionals or laypeople. They are specially trained to lead groups and to understand and appreciate the value of mutual help. Although the leaders initially may set the agenda, in time the participants are encouraged to take over. By the end of the 12 weeks, the parents' group is prepared to continue meeting and supporting each other informally. Many participants become active in other activities in the organization.

Education and Support. Another model that I have used with the widowed combines a support group with an educational session. This model is appropriate for a time-limited group. Each meeting begins with a didactic lecture on a topic of immediate concern to the group, such as an overview of grief, understanding children's reactions to loss, living in a single-parent household, living alone, dating, and managing money. The last session is open and is partly a farewell party. After each lecture, there is a coffee break and then the group breaks up into small groups of no more than 10 each.

The next hour is a support group with a trained facilitator, preferably some-one who has been widowed. If the facilitator is a trained mental health pro-fessional and not widowed, then the group is co-led by a widowed person. In the groups, the participants talk about whatever is on their minds. Ad-dresses are always exchanged, and the group members are encouraged to continue to meet on their own afterward. Members often become perma-nent parts of each other's support network.

Among professionals, there is some discussion about how frequently support groups should meet (Bacon, 1996; Jordan & Ware, 1997). In my ex-perience, it seems to make sense to meet every other week because the par-ticipants need time to process what happens in the group. Since the imme-diate consequences of bereavement clearly extend over a much longer period than was once thought, it may be appropriate to extend the meetings to be available for more of this time. Jordan and Ware (1997) suggested that an-other meeting should be held six months after the group ends, so that peo-ple can touch base, see what has happened, and decide what else may be needed. This meeting may not be as necessary if the group has been meet-ing and doing some of this work on its own.

Centers for Bereaved Children

Centers for bereaved children are agencies designed specifically to meet the needs of bereaved children and their families. They are growing in number throughout the United States and in other parts of the world. Their pro-gramming is designed to facilitate a mutual exchange of support and infor-mation for children and their parents. Centers are housed in various facili-ties in the community. Some groups begin with a simple meeting room that an agency or church has volunteered for this purpose. The toys and art ma-terials for the children are kept in a portable box that is brought to the meet-ing each time (Brabant, 1993).

Many groups continue to meet in church basements. Some have rooms in a hospice; others grow and move into their own facilities. All these pro-grams depend on volunteers—concerned mental health professionals, clergy, teachers, or laypeople, all of whom typically have experienced a loss. As the programs grow, they are able to hire a small staff to do the admin-istrative work, coordinate programs, raise funds, and train volunteers. Most centers have to do some fund-raising, since they do not charge a fee for ser-vice. The participants are invited to make donations when they can. Al-though the activities are focused on children, all the programs provide si-multaneous support groups for the parents.

The Dougy Center. Although there are many variations in the way these centers deliver services, almost all of them are modeled after the Dougy Cen-ter in Portland, Oregon. The Dougy Center is housed in a residential home that was remodeled to meet its needs. Its mission is "to provide support in a safe place so children grieving a death can share their experience as they move through the healing process" (Dougy Center, 1999, p. 7). The center extends supportive services to children, parents, or surrogate caregivers who are responsible for the children. It also actively consults with schools, communities, and parents regarding crisis situations.

The center has two large meeting rooms, one for parents and one for children. The children's meeting room is full of stuffed animals that the children can hold or cuddle as they wish. In addition, playrooms are equipped for various age-specific activities, such as a dress-up room, a room with a dollhouse, a game room, and an art room that can accommodate younger and older children. The backyard is equipped for outdoor games suited to various ages. One of the most interesting rooms, the volcano room, is padded and filled with stuffed animals, pillows, soft balls, and padded bats. In this room, children are allowed, with adult supervision, to hit, bang, and throw things—activities that children of all ages find useful. Some parents have wondered why they, too, cannot use the volcano room to let out some of their tension.

The Dougy Center's formal program consists of biweekly group meetings. There are concurrent groups for both children and their parents or caregivers that are open ended, so members can stay as long as they need to. The children's groups are homogeneous with regard to age and type of death, and as result there is a certain homogeneity in the adult groups as well. There are groups for children whose siblings died, children whose parents died, children whose family members died violent deaths, and those who experienced suicide.

Each group begins with a talking circle. All members wear name tags, which allows new members to learn all the names more easily and to feel included. One member takes what is called the "talking stick," tells the group something he or she wants to share, and then passes the stick on. (The talking stick is adapted from a Native American tradition and, in this instance, is a handsomely carved Native American art piece.) If a member does not want to speak, she or he can pass the stick on. If a member decides later to participate, he or she asks for the stick before the circle closes. The facilitator and volunteers participate in the circle as well, telling who they lost and when or giving other information appropriate to the conversation. Volunteers do not bring their problems to the children, but the children learn that the volunteers are people who have also had losses and that these losses happen to all of us. Afterward, the children disperse to other rooms to pursue their own interests for the evening. Often many older children stay in the meeting room simply to talk about who died, what they think about the death, and what issues the death has created in their current lives. As children move through their grief, there seems to be more fun in their play. The volunteers stay with the children at all times, following their lead on what to talk about and what they want to do. Before and after each meeting, the volunteers meet with the staff member who is coordinating the evening's activities to plan the activities, sort out any of their own issues stimulated by the session, reflect on how things went, and plan the next meeting.

Each meeting consists of one of a variety of activities that are designed to help children learn from each other about their grief and what they do to cope. For example, two of the many activities that the center has developed relate to normalizing grief and to remembering and memorializing the deceased. To normalize grief, a child writes a question on a piece of paper, asking the other children about their grief. Younger children may ask older children to help them write their questions. Framing the questions helps the children learn to think about what is bothering them. Putting something into words makes it easier to examine it and to figure out what to do about it. For example, children have asked such questions as: When are times that you feel sad? What are good memories you have of the person who died? These questions are put in a bowl, and then each child picks and answers one. In the activity to memorialize the deceased, the children write the name of the person who died on pieces of paper, with each letter of the name on a separate line. Next to each letter they write down something that reminds them of the person, using the letters of the name. Then, if they like, they share what they have written with the group.

When a child decides that he or she no longer needs to come to the center, the closing circle that ends each session becomes a ceremony for saying good-bye. A child who is leaving is presented with a small pouch full of polished stones and one unpolished stone. This rough stone is a reminder that there are always difficult moments in life.

The parents' group focuses on helping parents understand their children and learn how to be more responsive to them. It is also a place for parents to talk about bereavement-related issues that concern them. The facilitator's role is to help the parents learn from each other. If the staff and volunteers believe that a family needs more help than the center can offer, they suggest a referral to a mental health clinic. In some instances, the family can continue in the program at the same time. If the staff sees that the family is not getting any help from the program, they may suggest that the family defer participation while they seek other help.

The volunteers participate in an intensive orientation program before they begin to work at the center. In this training, they learn to listen, not to interpret what children are doing, and to give children space to work out for themselves what is on their minds. The volunteers learn to rephrase what the children say; to ask the children what they mean; and, if the children's explanations are not clear, to ask them again in a different way. Phrases, such as "Can you say more?" are used frequently. These are the types of questions that are most helpful in getting people to clarify and then to think differently about their experience.

In addition to its program serving the Portland community, the Dougy Center established the National Center for Grieving Children and Families, which trains people who want to set up programs in their own communities, both in the United States and abroad. The center publishes the *National Directory of Children's Grief Services,* which provides information on the location of programs in various parts of the United States and Canada; a skills-development training manual for volunteers; an activity manual; and handbooks about children whose family members were murdered or committed suicide. It also publishes a series of guides for school administrators and teachers. Fees from training courses and the sale of books help maintain the center.

There are close to 100 similar centers throughout the United States and the number is growing. The New England Center for Loss and Transition now convenes an annual meeting to bring together the staff of children's bereavement centers from around the country to share ideas and learn from each other.

PSYCHOLOGICAL AND FAMILY-CENTERED COUNSELING AND THERAPY

Ideally, in any community, there should be a continuum of help, from informal support, mutual help groups, and support groups, to individual counseling and psychotherapeutic interventions. According to Shapiro (1994), therapy is an additional resource in a pool of community resources. Most bereaved people find that participating in a mutual help organization or a bereavement center's program is sufficient to meet their needs. People who seek individual counseling or family therapy often do so because this is the only help available in their communities. In this sense, they are looking for help that they might otherwise get from a support group or a bereavement center if it was available. Counseling or therapy is typically associated with pathology: what's wrong with me, not what's right with me? Therapists are, after all, trained to deal with deviant or problem behavior. Raphael, Middleton, Martinek, and Misso (1993) suggested that even the best-trained therapist or counselor needs additional training about the nature of the bereavement process. They stated that to avoid pathologizing grief, counselors should focus on enhancing the effectiveness of the family's coping styles and positive problem-solving capacity and flexibility, not on the family's deficits and what family members cannot do. They also recommended that many of the techniques that therapists would use with bereaved clients, even those who have clinical diagnoses, need to be modified.

Some people prefer talking one on one and are not comfortable in a group setting. For others, the death stirs prior problems that can be addressed in therapy. Some mental health professionals distinguish between counseling and therapy (Worden, 1991). Webb (1993) referred to therapy as a process of help conducted by a mental health professional and to counseling as the process of help that is provided by religious leaders and educational personnel. The professional training determines what name is given to the help offered, but the content and the goals of help may be similar.

Support and Learning

Individual therapists, in a one-on-one relationship, can provide grieving families with help that will make adaptation possible in a way that enhances their growth (Shapiro, 1994). Narrative therapy, as described by M. White and Epston (1990), is one technique that encourages change and development. It can be used with both individuals and families. Narrative therapy utilizes people's ability to tell their own stories. By telling and retelling their stories, people are able to gain a new perspective and understanding of what they are experiencing and thus to respond adaptively to what is happening to them (Neimeyer & Stewart, 1996). To help clarify the story being told, the therapist asks a series of questions, building one question on the other. These questions clarify the story for those listening. Simple questions such as, "Can you tell me more about what you mean?" or "How does that work for you?" build on each other to open up the narrative. M. White (1988) developed a set of questions designed specifically to help the bereaved reclaim their connection to the deceased. White is reacting to his observation of the inappropriateness of telling the bereaved "to let go." Typical questions were these: If you were seeing yourself through the eyes of the deceased, what would you be noticing about yourself? How would you let others know what you have discovered? What difference does it make in your next step to know how the deceased saw you? These questions not only expand the narrative, they also help the bereaved recognize the part the deceased plays in their present life. In addition, it helps the bereaved recognize that they provide the deceased with a living legacy, as described in Chapter 2.

Using this approach enables the bereaved to step back from their problems, in a sense to externalize them and see more of their ramifications. As they participate in this process, the bereaved can touch their problems, dissect them, and have conversations with them. As they think differently about their experiences they discover new ways of reframing the meaning of what is happening. They can then "re-story" and "re-author" their lives in a new direction (White & Epston, 1990). This process eases the way to shifting their views of themselves and others with whom they interact.

M. White and Epston (1990) emphasized the importance of externalizing problems with children, so they and their problem are not one. They stated that children should not be defined only by their bereavement and grief. This is true for adults as well. As happens with adults, when issues are externalized in developmentally appropriate ways, children can begin to gain some control over their feelings and behavior and see alternative ways of coping (Freeman, Epston, & Lobontz, 1997).

Externalizing their grief is also a key step in helping parents learn to be more reflective about their reactions to their children and to see the connection between their own and their children's behaviors. Seligman, Reivich, Jaycox, & Gillham, 1995), building on the work of Beck (1979), described a technique for helping parents understand and react more effectively to their children's needs by externalizing or learning to step back from the problem or issues. This technique can be used in individual or group sessions and, as I discuss in Chapter 13, is applicable in the classroom. Seligman et al. (1995) stated that people's explanatory styles (another way of describing meaning making) affect behavior and may need to change. They recommended teaching parents to look initially at what is happening in smaller segments, using what they called an ABC process—adversity, belief, and consequence. By breaking up what is happening, parents can see that the fact that their spouses died is an *adversity* that may or may not lead to their children's lives being ruined. The assumption that their children's lives will be totally spoiled is based on their *beliefs* about what will happen as a result of the death. One choice is for the surviving parents to believe that this death will lead to a catastrophe. By examining their beliefs (for example, "I can't raise my child alone") and the *consequences* of the beliefs (such as "I am helpless; everything is falling apart") they can then test if the consequences would be different with different beliefs.

Another way of looking at the issue might be to think, "This is a serious challenge"; then, the consequences of this belief might be, "I need to learn how to be a single parent." Seligman and his colleagues (1995) presented guidelines for teaching people to argue with themselves about their beliefs and the consequences. Rather than thinking that the event will bring about a catastrophe, parents can look at what is really happening: for example, "My child is doing well in school, and I am getting the bills paid." They can become energized by their recognition of their ability to solve problems. Finding a new direction is easier as they see an event as more specific and less pervasive ("I can do things. We all hurt. I'm not alone; we help each other.") By learning to reason this way, parents find they can examine the consequences of a particular behavior and to see that there are choices to make that did not seem apparent before.

In any given situation, these techniques need to be adapted to meet the individual's or family's needs. They serve only as models for the directions that help can take. O'Donnell (1996) described a family meeting that was convened to deal with custody issues of young children who lost both parents. With careful questions, she was able to help people share and hear each other's fears and concerns about these children, consider new ways of thinking about the problem, and appreciate their different points of view. They could then work together to plan for the care of these children.

Formal educational models can be used to enhance the coping strategies of individual families with children. Two programs developed by hospital social service and psychology departments focus on the need to help parents normalize grief, open communication, and recognize how they must change to meet the new situation. They help parents step back and look at their situation with a new perspective. These models could easily be adapted to other settings, especially as part of a group program.

Siegel, Mesagno, and Christ (1990) developed a series of individual educational sessions at Memorial Sloan-Kettering Hospital in New York for families in which a parent is dying. The purpose of these meetings is to provide the surviving parent with support, thus enabling the parent to be more responsive to their children's needs. The healthy parent meets with a social worker every two to three weeks, eight times before the death and eight afterward. If necessary and appropriate, the ill parent is included in some of the predeath sessions. The children participate in several of the later sessions. In these meetings, the surviving parent is supported as he or she rethinks the parenting role. The parent is given information about typical grieving in children and help in making a realistic appraisal of the children's behavior.

Kempler and Koocher (1994) developed a family-centered program at Children's Hospital in Boston for bereaved parents and surviving siblings. This program was designed to meet families' needs for support after the support of relatives and friends declines after the death of their child (Koocher, 1994). Family sessions, approximately two hours in duration, are held in a facility near the hospital. The meetings are held every two to three weeks for approximately two to three months after the death. In the first family meeting, the goal is for family members to share their personal experience with each other. Young children use drawings to express themselves. This is often the first chance that the family members have to hear how each of them perceives what happened and to clarify their differences. At the second meeting, the family members share their feelings about the event, sometimes using objects as reminders of the deceased, or writing letters to share things they have left unsaid. Another session is held with just the parents, to assess if their differences get in the way of their coping and to help improve communication between them. In the final session, the family makes plans for the future, to commemorate the deceased and provide mutual support.

Serious Behavioral Problems

Thus far, I have been cautious about using words like *pathological* in describing children's or adults' reactions to grief. Yet I cannot ignore the fact that children and their families sometimes experience what Webb (1993) called "disabling grief" or what Rando (1993) called "complicated mourning." Webb identified some of the indicators for seeking individual psychological help for children and their families, which should take place when problems are severe and persistent or interfere with their ability to function on a daily basis. The key issue, for me, in any assessment is the question of timing and degree. The stress and disorder experienced shortly after a death are to be expected. If a family has not moved beyond this stage within a year or so and is part of a supportive network, then other help may be indicated. On the other hand, if a child or adolescent seems severely depressed at any time; talks in a language that may sound suicidal; is not doing well in school; is unable to continue in his or her daily routine; is getting into trouble with peers, the law, or other authority figures; is not sleeping; and/or is withdrawing from friends, then it may be appropriate to seek additional professional help as soon as possible. The same signs and symptoms for identifying children in trouble apply in the bereavement situation as in any other.

In my experience, in families who are severely disabled by their grief, there is little communication among the members and little or no discussion about who died; when asked, children seem unable to articulate much about what has been lost. These are generally families who had previous emotional and social problems that were exacerbated by the death. Help should be family focused, if possible (Shapiro, 1994). Webb (1993) documented how individual play therapy and other therapeutic techniques can help children who continue to be disabled by their grief. Any of the techniques described in this chapter could be useful with troubled families.

PROGRAMS DEALING WITH SUICIDE AND VIOLENCE

When death was self-induced or the result of a violent act by others, families may need many kinds of assistance, ranging from individual counseling to advice about dealing with the judicial system. Again, I want to offer a word of caution about the use of therapy. Because the death was the result of a violent act does not necessarily mean that the survivors need therapy. Rather, they need support and to feel that they are not coping alone. There is a great deal they need to learn, but unless there were other problems in the family, they do not need therapy or help that may label what they are experiencing, even by association, as deviant.

Some children in these situations participate in general programs for bereaved children, as described earlier. However, for the most part, services for victims of violence or for survivors of suicide and general bereavement programs are not sponsored by the same agencies. Under the Victims of Crime Act (1988), the federal government makes funds available to state and local programs to provide psychological counseling to victims of violence. This money supported such programs as the Center for Crime Victims and Survivors in Florida (Redmond, 1989), and supports the Living After Murder Program (LAMP) in Boston. LAMP offers individual counseling, as well as support groups similar to those described earlier. Often people begin in individual counseling and join support groups that involve them in a mutual help experience when they are ready. The Center for Crime Victims provided individual and group therapy and crisis counseling support services, including support when survivors go to court and assistance in obtaining victim compensation.

There are many programs for suicide prevention and for helping after a suicide has taken place. Typically, individual counseling or therapy is involved. One such program is the Samaritans, a nondenominational, nonprofit volunteer organization. In their brochure, they describe the organization as: "Dedicated to reducing the incidence of suicide by befriending individuals in crisis and educating the community about effective preventive strategies." The 12 Samaritan organizations in the United States, all on the East Coast and independent of each other, have the same mission and principles. These organizations were started by Monica Dickens, who founded the Samaritans program in England and developed its first U.S.

program in Boston in the early 1970s, when she immigrated to the United States. All Samaritans groups offer a befriending service, staffed by trained volunteers, that is free, confidential, and available 24 hours a day. This service is designed to provide a caring, sympathetic ear, to listen and understand when someone is contemplating suicide. In addition, in Boston, the program has a help line for teenagers, called the Samariteen program, which is staffed by teenage volunteers who provide peer support to those facing the challenges of adolescence. The Samariteens also offer a support group for survivors, called Safe Place, that is facilitated by trained Samaritan volunteers who are survivors of suicide. The organization provides community education and outreach to identify those at risk of suicide and develop preventive strategies. It also does training in schools and in civic, religious, and social organizations.

Another group that addresses similar issues is the American Association of Suicidology (AAS). Primarily an organization for professionals who are concerned with research and practice related to suicide, AAS also offers programs and provides material for survivors of suicide, based on the principles of mutual help. It holds an annual meeting by and for survivors and publishes a directory of support groups for suicide survivors in the United States and Canada, a bibliography for survivors, and a newsletter by and for survivors.

AIDS

In many ways, the needs of children and parents who are grieving the loss of a parent, sibling, friend, or other relative from AIDS are not that different from those of any mourner. However, many AIDS mourners, both children and adults, are also HIV positive. AIDS survivors are often dealing with multiple losses, and many children are orphaned when both parents die of the disease (Boyd-Franklin, Steiner, & Boland, 1995). Their issues are frequently compounded by poverty and various levels of family dysfunction and stigma. Children, both those who are HIV positive and those who are disease-free, are often placed for adoption or in the care of an extended family member. Their grief is made more difficult by these other factors with which they must also cope.

Many parents who are dying of AIDS are single parents, usually single mothers. One of the key issues they face is planning their children's future. Draimin (1995) described some of the issues involved in making long-term plans for surviving children. Whether children stay with extended family members or are placed in foster care or for adoption, their caregivers need guidance in how to help them with the grief and the changes in their lives. In addition, they need help to remember their parents and find a way to connect to their past, the culture they came from, and the world they knew. They need to find ways of identifying positive experiences in the past that can help them in the present. Some programs are now helping families do this prior to the death. For example, a project called Living Legacy helps single mothers make video recordings for their children in which they talk about their lives, their coming deaths, and what they hope for their children (Taylor-Brown & Wiener, 1993). This program now provides assistance after the death to the children's caregivers, who need help learning how to use this video, as well as other resources that could help give children a sense of continuity between their past and present lives.

Most programs that are devoted to the needs of families who are affected by AIDS end when the ill family members die. Few have follow-up services to help these families deal with survivors' grief. Often relatives are uncomfortable coming to standard bereavement groups because they do not want to disclose the cause of death (O'Donnell, 1996). However, when they do attend most bereavement center programs, children whose siblings or parents died of AIDS are successfully integrated into regular groups. In this setting, there is sufficient trust that this issue, if it comes up, will be quickly addressed so that the participants feel supported and welcome.

When families of people who died of AIDS are reluctant to join groups for the bereaved, they may turn to programs that are designed specifically for AIDS mourners. O'Donnell (1996) described a closed support group, sponsored by the hospice program in which she worked, that was composed entirely of AIDS survivors and met for eight weeks. The first group the hospice convened wrote a step-by-step manual for running an HIV/AIDS-specific bereavement group (O'Donnell, 1989). This manual can serve as a model for what mourners themselves see as relevant. Aronson (1994) described a support group for children of parents with AIDS, many of whom had already died. He suggested that these groups should be run in schools, medical clinics, or adult AIDS service centers, so they are not associated with traditional psychiatric services in which the participants may feel stigmatized as being mentally ill.

HELP IN THE SCHOOLS

In any setting in which children are with their peers, we can assume that elements of mutual help will take place all the time. Peers can share with and support each other, whether it is a family member, classmate, or teacher who died. Although students may be helpful to each other in an informal way, this is often their first encounter with death, and they look to their teachers for guidance and direction. Few teacher training programs prepare teachers to help children when a death occurs.

In a sample of schools in the United States, Wass, Miller, and Thornton (1990) found that 11% had a unit on general death education, 17% offered a grief-education support program, and 25% had suicide prevention or intervention programs. Some schools have developed exemplary programs for crisis intervention in schools after a death has occurred (Stevenson & Stevenson, 1997). Usually, most attention is paid to a sudden and often violent death, such as from an automobile accident in which more than one student was killed or when a student committed suicide. A natural death is rarely followed by the same mobilization of resources.

Given the centrality of schools in children's lives, protocols should be in place in every school to respond to all deaths. Every teacher should be prepared to meet the students' needs in the classroom when their lives are touched by a death, either of a member of their family or of a classmate or teacher (AAS, 1997; O'Toole, 1991; Stevenson & Stevenson, 1997).

Elements of a Good Program

There is no one formula for a program in a given school district or school. Each school has to do its own work in developing an initiative that is suitable to its setting and to the resources in the school and community. The school staff members have to consider if they first need to raise awareness of the value of discussing death in the school or if there is already a readiness to do so.

Hill and Foster (1996) reviewed programs that focus on suicide and its consequences, which are typically called postvention programs, to contrast them with prevention programs. These postvention programs can serve as models for what should be in place in any school, regardless of the cause of death.

Several programs use a clinical orientation, reaching out to the survivors who were closest to the deceased and focusing on the need for individual counseling. Siehl (1990) proposed a program that involves the school and the larger community affected by the death, recognizing the importance of involving not only the family of the deceased, but the families of other students as well. He described a model program that includes crisis centers at key locations in the school that are open to any student who feels the need to talk; at the same time, family members are centrally involved in planning what information is released to the media and special events and memorials.

AAS's (1997) recommendations for school programs are similar. They reinforce the idea that a crisis team should be trained in advance. They add that it is important that details of the death be verified with the family, medical examiner, or police and that the school be sensitive to the family's wishes and always be truthful to the students. Arrangements should be made for students who wish, with their parents' permission, to go to the funeral, and memorial plans should be coordinated by the school. The AAS does not recommend holding a memorial service in the school for a student who committed suicide because it is concerned about stimulating copy-cat suicides. In my view, this may not be as much of a concern if the school has had a program that helps students understand the place of death in their lives prior to this event. Memorial services honor a life. As you saw in Chapter 10, memorial services are important to the deceased's friends and family members and should not automatically be rejected.

Crisis intervention can set the stage for dealing with the issues a death stimulates in students. Yet the long-term need for support and learning must be addressed as well. A program that responds to students' needs should include opportunities for ongoing support groups and other kinds of help, as needed, since the impact of the death is felt over time. These groups may involve community mental health personnel, clergy, and other community caregivers.

HEALS. Many local hospice programs have also developed manuals for working with children in the schools. HEALS (Hospice Expressive Arts Loss Support Program) is a program that uses the expressive arts to help in the school setting after any kind of death, including suicide. HEALS programs in individual schools are run by volunteer facilitators (including counselors and psychologists in the school system) who are trained by HEALS staff (Black & Adams, 1993). In addition, HEALS offers consultation and education to school staff. The program, using the support-group model, is offered in a series of eight sessions. The HEALS agenda is similar to that used by Bereaved Families of Ontario. The focus, maximizing the use of the arts, is on techniques, such as painting, storytelling, and music, that help participants learn about issues related to death and grieving. Bertman (1991) elaborated on the use of the arts for this purpose.

At the end of eight sessions in the HEALS program, although it is clear that the participants' grief has not ended, the participants have learned that they can go on and that the techniques they have learned can be used anytime they need them. This is a good example of what can be offered as a follow-up to crisis intervention for grieving children in a school setting. The HEALS program also provides Death Crisis Intervention Teams that go into the schools in response to a crisis. A team creates a safe room in a school where students or staff can come to use the arts to help deal with their feelings and pain. Items such as flowers, candles, stuffed teddy bears, various art materials, and a memory box, are used to make the room welcoming and comforting.

OTHER RESOURCES

Bibliotherapy

As was noted in the previous chapter, the local library is an important resource for finding books that can help children and their parents deal with a death. Teachers, librarians, and some mental health professionals use books and stories, in what is called bibliotherapy, as a way to aid people. Bibliotherapy has been defined in a number of ways (Rudman, Gagne, & Bernstein, 1993). One way uses specific books and stories as an adjunct to other types of professional therapeutic interventions; others use books with all who are interested in reading about and helping others or themselves with their problems. Essentially, books are a self-help tool, since the readers apply what they are learning to their own situation. Books can be used to help children who are dealing with a death learn to expand their understanding of what is happening and to cope more effectively. Teachers or school librarians can lead discussion groups on a particular book that deals, for example, with an aspect of the bereavement process. The discussion of the book becomes an occasion for sharing and learning from each other. When a group is not available, a child or teenager can read a book alone, or parents and children can do so together.

It is not difficult to put together an appropriate bibliography. Children and young people can review the books to see if they are helpful and consistent with their experience and to decide which books to use in a discussion. Books that focus on letting go of, getting over, or recovering from grief should be eliminated. Many children's librarians already have a list or can easily assemble one from their holdings. Books are constantly being published that deal with the dying and death of various members of the family, different types of illness, and different causes of death. Rudman and her colleagues (1993) reviewed many titles that can be used to build a collection for this purpose. Several mail order companies specialize in books dealing with dying and bereavement, with special emphasis on books for children of all ages (see the Appendix). These can be a resource for the classroom teacher, school librarian, or the librarian at a local public library.

An additional resource for parents is a memory book. Every family should have such a book dedicated to the deceased. It could be a scrapbook or one designed specifically for this purpose. These books can be used by teachers, parents, and/or therapists who help children remember. The focus of memory books should be on helping children develop a sense of who died. As children grow, they need help in developing a more mature sense of the person who died. These books can help them see what they thought shortly after the death and recognize how their thoughts have changed with time. One memory book, prepared by the Child Welfare League of America, is designed to help parents with a terminal illness plan for and with their children for what will happen after they die (Merkel-Holguin, 1994). Although it was written primarily for parents with AIDS, it is equally applicable to parents who are dying from other conditions. Another memory book, by Gaines-Laine (1995), was specifically designed to help children construct a relationship to the deceased.

On-Line Mutual Support

The growth of technology has brought people together in new ways. Most people can access the Internet through their homes, offices, or local public libraries. The Internet offers countless opportunities to make contact with other bereaved people around the world and to obtain information and resources about support groups and programs for the bereaved. On-line networks provide the same kind of help that face-to-face groups offer: social support, practical information for coping, shared experiences, positive role models, helper therapy, empowerment, professional support, and advocacy efforts. Madara and White (1997) reported that 62% of the self-help groups known to the American Self Help Clearinghouse are available on the Internet. Of these groups, 46% have web pages and another 16% have at least an E-mail address. The wealth of information and resources available on-line can be overwhelming. There are discussion (or chat) groups, on-line mutual help and support groups, bulletin boards for exchanging information and posting questions, organizational resources, and databases, as well as personal web pages of bereaved individuals and professionals. For example, the Self Help Clearinghouse has a web site (http://www.mentalhelp.net/ selfhelp) with links to hundreds of on-line and "real-life" self-help groups and grief-related sites. This web site also provides information about starting a group. This is just one starting point. Web searches through any search engine will lead to hundreds of other resources.

CHAPTER THIRTEEN

Teachable Moments
Preparing Children to Understand Death

> I remember when I was about 8 years old. I think my friend's grand-
> mother had just died. I couldn't fall asleep, and suddenly I realized I
> could die, too. I was terrified. I think the worst part was that I felt so
> alone. I knew I couldn't ask my parents. They would just tell me not
> to worry.
>
> > —A graduate student remembering her
> > first awareness of her own mortality.

Children of all ages, alert to the world around them, know much more than
we realize about death and dying. They respond to and understand their
knowledge in their own unique ways. Building on the perspective provided
in this book, this chapter describes ways in which children's ability to cope
with this fact of life can be enhanced. I look at how to expand the role of
parents, faith communities, and schools in helping children understand
death and grieving at times when there is no crisis in their lives.

I began this book with a discussion of the difficulty we have in integrating into our lives and the lives of our children the fact that people die.
I told the story of how my son learned about the Holocaust, one of the most
violent events in our history. It seems fitting that this chapter, which ends
the book, should end with a discussion of efforts that are being made to prevent inner-city violence. The programs described at the end of the chapter
provide hope that children can learn new ways of dealing with each other
that will prevent unnecessary deaths from violence and help them deal better with those deaths that occur in the normal course of living.

REDEFINING HOW WE RESPOND

All parents need to consider how they will educate their children to understand death and to be more open and accepting of the fact that people die
and we grieve the loss. In the Introduction, I described my own awkward-
ness in my conversations with my son Aaron. As I learned, we do not simply sit our children down to tell them the "facts of life." However, we can
create an atmosphere in which they feel free to ask. We can be responsive
to their developing sense of self and their changing relationships to themselves and others. Our openness will affect the questions they ask, the kinds

of answers they can accept, and the very nature of the dialogue. In creating this atmosphere we try to provide our children with tools that promote their ability to cope and adapt positively to the vicissitudes of life.

Garmazy, Masten, and Tellegen (1984) observed that children have the competence or resilience that enables them to cope in spite of exposure to stress. It is this resilience and competence that we need to enhance and support. Haggerty, Sherrod, Garmazy, and Rutter (1994) identified protective factors, in children and in their environment, that can support their resilience and thus reduce the likelihood of their behaving in a maladaptive fashion. These factors are not protective in the classic sense of insulating children from negative forces in their world. They are protective because they provide children with resources to support their ability to be resilient, so that they can solve problems within the context of the world they live in and feel more effectual and good about themselves. Some of these factors are qualities that children are endowed with, such as their dispositions and personalities. Others come from available affirming social support, as well as attitudes and values in their families and communities that help children develop a positive sense of themselves as active problem solvers. This sense of self includes the ability to be reflective about a situation, that is, to be able to consider what is going on. The school system and faith community, as well as the neighborhood, can contribute to helping children be more responsive to each other, which is an important protective factor. For example, in a community where children are on the defensive, where people feel endangered by violence, it is difficult to teach children that they can affect what happens to them and that they can cooperate with each other and be open and involved. Again we see that the process of educating our children is an interactive one. We cannot leave it to the children to educate themselves. We need to create environments in which we can learn from each other.

One way of helping children learn to cope with life and living and death and dying is to take advantage of events that occur around them, which have been called "teachable moments" (Carson, 1984). Opportunities that occur in the course of living can be used to teach children to distinguish between fact and fancy—to teach them that death does happen. During these teachable moments, we can help them to develop a vocabulary for what they feel and experience, to learn what are appropriate behaviors given the circumstances, and to appreciate their need for others at such times. We can help them learn how our attitudes, values, and beliefs guide our thinking as they try to make sense out of the fact that people die. We can influence the community in which we live to change attitudes and practices. Many parents may feel totally unprepared for this task. It can be seen as a burden, yet another subject or a "should" that parents think is required of them so as not to feel guilty about how they are raising their children. Perhaps there are some "shoulds" that parents need to put at the head of their list. Creating an environment in which it is possible to deal with death may be one of them.

One of the major impediments to creating such an environment, as I noted in the Introduction, is our own anxiety and fear about death. We need to be conscious of our own reactions to death and the grief that follows, to look at our own experience of how death has affected us. If we ignore a piece of our life experience, we perhaps ignore our own personhood. To some extent, we then ignore the personhoods of our children, so that they are unprepared for the inevitable life-cycle issues that they will face. Only when we accept that death is very much a part of the human experience will we be able to learn how to comfort, console, and support each other at this time in our lives. This is true of parents, as well as teachers and others who have responsibility for educating our children.

We do not need to be thinking about death all the time, but we should not be afraid of it when the subject comes up. As Weisman (1972) wisely observed, we cannot live with a constant awareness of death in our lives. We need to find a middle ground where there is a place for the fact that people die while our energies remain devoted to ongoing life. There needs to be a place in how we make meaning, in our value and belief systems, for dealing with end-of-life issues and for recognizing the pain of a loss and how it changes our lives. This place will change as we mature and as our life circumstances change. This conversation with our children and with ourselves will continue throughout their and our lives.

To prepare ourselves, that is, to have some idea about how to take advantage of teachable moments, parents need support from each other, the faith community to which they belong, the schools, parent educators, health care professionals with whom they come in contact, and from agencies with which they may be involved. There is almost no caregiver who is involved with children who should not be prepared to help children accept death as part of the life cycle.

TEACHABLE MOMENTS: THE ROLE OF PARENTS

When opening a dialogue with children about death, we cannot always choose our moments. Children raise questions as they think of them and when they are ready. They raise questions when they think that there is someone who will answer them or someone who is receptive to the idea of a conversation on the topic. They ask questions about things for which we may have no answers, such as what is death. They can ask the same question over the years as their perceptions change and previous answers no longer satisfy them. Sometimes opportunities for educating our children come when we least expect it—like a ride on a bus or an incident published in a newspaper or broadcast on a television program. Sometimes it is an actual death, usually one removed enough from them so they can learn about it in manageable segments. In such situations, their immediate family is intact. If these moments are utilized well, children learn to be respected as mourners and that they have a legitimate role as part of their community.

They can touch the experience, feel its importance in their lives, and develop a vocabulary that allows them to give words to what they are experiencing.

An example from my own family is a case in point. Two years ago, my daughter Nancy's family dog Teepee was diagnosed with incurable cancer. The veterinarian asked if the family wanted to "put the dog down" after he told them this news. He also said that Teepee could live several more months before the disease would make his life intolerable. Nancy and her husband Ariel both agreed that when someone we love is sick and dying, we give him or her care and attention. This was a lesson they wanted their children to learn. They explained to the children, 6-year-old Maya and 10-year-old Zohar, what was going on and set up a sick room in the house. The doctor was understanding and supportive of their decision. They faced some difficult moments as Teepee got sicker. It reached a point when this wonderful dog who "ran with the wind," in Zohar's words, could not move, could not eat, and was in continuous pain. The family fed him, comforted him, and watched his agony with an agony of their own. Finally, my daughter and her husband realized that they had to let him go. They made an appointment with the doctor, but Teepee died at home before they could keep the appointment. The family dug his grave and buried him in their backyard. My daughter called the school to help her decide if the children should stay home. Both children's teachers said to send them, so their friends could comfort them. The children were encouraged to talk about Teepee's death in class, which made it possible for Maya and Zohar to share their pain with their classmates and to hear from their friends about their experiences when their pets died.

The family mourned Teepee, and we all remember and miss him. As the children get older, they revisit the meaning of his death; they talk about him and remember things they did together, including his illness and how they cared for him. They did not try to replace Teepee immediately with another dog. Only about six months later did they find another dog who is a "character" in his own right.

Some people say they could have lessened the pain for the children by putting Teepee "down" as soon as they knew there was no hope and replacing him as quickly as possible. Yet, how would it have benefited the children not to be allowed to care for their friend and not to mourn him after he died? Their grief would have been no less real; it would just not have been honored and thereby not legitimated. Both their parents and teachers were able to help these children learn and grow with the experience by comfortably taking advantage of several teachable moments. Doing so was not easy. Looking back, Nancy says that she would not do it differently. She told me: "You get through it, like caring for a screaming baby when you haven't slept all night. You just do it because that's what you have to do." As I wrote this book, my daughter and her family felt comfortable talking with me about the loss. Zohar and Maya recognize that they have something to teach their grandmother and are pleased that they can do so.

Another example of a teachable moment grew out of a parent's attempt to protect her children, just as my mother tried to protect me years ago. A mother of three children, ages 7, 10, and 12, told me of a fight she had with her sister. The mother wanted to take her children to say good-bye to their great-grandmother who was dying in a nearby nursing home. She also expected to take her children to the funeral. Her niece and nephew, her sister's children, wanted to go with her. Their mother was adamantly opposed. She did not want her children to visit the nursing home or to go to the funeral. She thought both events would be too upsetting for them. She agreed reluctantly only when her children persisted in wanting to join their cousins at the nursing home. When they returned from the nursing home, she was surprised at how pleased the children were that the last thing their great-grandmother heard was the song they sang for her. She reexamined her fear and recognized that her children could cope with their great-grandmother's death, perhaps better than she could. Both the older woman's life and her death had new meaning for the children as, at the funeral and afterward, they learned more about her place in the family and its life cycle. As we have seen throughout this book, when children are involved, they cope better and can sometimes help their parents do the same.

In Chapter 6 you met Dale, who died of leukemia. Dale's parents told me about the way his cousins have kept him a part of their lives. They are creating opportunities to teach their own children, who never knew Dale, how to accept that people die and how to talk about death with others. Dale's parents told the story:

> One of the nicest things that has happened to us is how our niece and nephew have reacted. They are now adults with children of their own. They talk to their children about this kid Dale. When one of their children was 5, he told us "Daddy told me all about cousin Dale and how he died; I am very sorry, that is very sad." Their parents obviously had said something about what he should say to us. But then this 5-year-old went on to ask: "Tell me what kind of kid he was . . . what did he like to do?" So we sat there and talked about how he liked soccer and animals and then the 5-year-old got to be 6 and got into Batman. Dale had a Batman costume, so I photocopied pictures of him in his Batman stage and enclosed a present about Batman. This family keeps him alive for us. It means a good deal to us. They did this without our saying anything. Their message to their children is that he was a great kid, he was part of our family, and you should know about him.

These cousins have found a way of continuing a connection to their cousin, who was like a brother to them. In the process of doing so for themselves, they are also teaching their children about death and its place in their lives and that they, too, have something to offer the bereaved parents.

THE ROLE OF EDUCATIONAL INSTITUTIONS

As we talk about teaching and learning, our attention has to turn to those institutions whose mission is formal learning. The primary setting is the school. School is the one place in which all children in this society are actively engaged. The school can have a great influence on how children see life and death. It can do so on two levels: by teachers taking advantage of the informal teachable moments in the classroom and by including this subject in the formal curriculum. Both public and religious schools have a responsibility to extend what they teach to include death and dying. They do, however, have different missions.

Role of Faith Communities and Their Schools

It is almost impossible to talk about death and dying without touching on questions of faith and religious practice and their relationship to how children make meaning about death. Faith communities have a responsibility that goes beyond teaching how their particular religion views death and the rituals and practices that guide people when a death occurs. They also need to help children understand grief and how death affects their daily lives. Children need to learn to look at other aspects of this experience, so they can express their concerns, fears, and feelings about what they understand and know. Clergy and teachers in religious schools can provide an important perspective when children are learning about these issues. In so doing, religious communities can also provide parents with support and help in talking to their children and relating to their evolving understanding of death, as well as the place of religion in how they make sense of it all. Davis and Sandoval (1991) also suggested that religious schools should educate their students about suicide prevention and learn to respond appropriately when there is a threat of suicide.

In many ways the curriculum described below for the public school classroom is applicable to religious schools as well. In public schools, children may learn about the diverse views of death in different religions. These programs are not teaching religion, but recognizing with their students that a range of customs, rituals, and beliefs informs people's behavior. Faith communities can teach directly about the belief system of their particular community.

Role of Public Schools

As noted in the previous chapter, in the vast majority of schools, education about death is not a part of the curriculum. Stevenson and Stevenson (1997) described the positive value for children when death is dealt with openly in the classroom. In this setting, children can learn the language and practice talking about what they may already know. Bertman (1979–80) pointed out that the term *death education* may be a misnomer, since there is little that teachers can tell children about death itself. Death education really means giving children permission to share attitudes, fears, and concerns. In many ways, the goal of education about death is to help students learn to think differently about their life experiences and what they can do about what happens to them. Death education can support children's developmental processes as they grow from grade to grade. It also provides opportunities for teachers to change as they examine the issues and consider the impact and meaning of the issues for their own lives. When educating about death, it is almost impossible for teachers to separate the content of the lesson from their personal experiences, attitudes, and feelings. These experiences, attitudes and feelings have to be named and understood because they influence the classroom atmosphere and teaching opportunities. Only then can teachers help children do so for themselves.

Teachable Moments in the Schools: Opportunities Lost and Found. Most classroom teaching depends on following established curricula. However, in every teaching segment, there are opportunities for teachers to extend what students are learning. For example, the issue of death often comes up in books that children are reading. Teachers can then bring these issues into the discussion as an integral part of the stories (Garvin, 1996).

An example of such a classroom opportunity that was lost occurred when Claudia, whom we met in Chapter 5 and whose father died of AIDS, was in the fourth grade. Claudia was in a new school, and her classmates and teachers did not know her father. Her class made Christmas angels as classroom decorations for the holiday and dedicated them to someone they cared about. Claudia made her angel in her father's memory and wrote on it that he had died of AIDS. Her teacher suggested privately to her that perhaps Claudia would be happier putting the angel on her tree at home, rather than in school. The teacher later told Claudia's mother that she did not want her to be stigmatized by classmates who would learn the cause of her father's death for the first time. Claudia's mother was angry, but more with herself than with the teacher, for not insisting and helping the teacher use this incident as an opportunity to teach her class about AIDS and about stigma. This was a lost teachable moment. Claudia herself was less upset than her mother and, at the end of the semester, without much discussion, raised money in the classroom for the AIDS walkathon, as I described in Chapter 11. Through this act and her own acceptance of her father's illness, she taught the class how to be open.

In contrast, Johanna Katz, a kindergarten teacher in the Lexington, Massachusetts school system, described how she used an opportunity that arose in her classroom:

> In my first year of teaching in Lexington we hatched ducks in the classroom. Each night a different child took the ducks home to care for them and one night one of the ducks died. The family was upset but understanding. Beyond the reassurance they gave their child, they agreed that I should deal with it in the classroom. We had a phone chain and called the parents to tell them what happened. One parent called to say her daughter was very distraught and she was planning on keeping her home. I encouraged her to send her daughter and told her that we would try to be supportive and helpful. She let her daughter come to school. When the children got to school I explained what happened. I encouraged them to ask questions, some of which I couldn't answer. We talked

about the duck's brief life, and I explained that we should have a funeral for the duck. We wrote a burial song, and made a grave marker with a good-bye poem on it. We walked to a spot near the school where we could bury the duck, singing our burial song, carrying the duck in a shoe box. I dug a hole and the duck was placed in it. Each child threw on a handful of dirt, several offering memories. We waved good-bye and returned singing back to school for our previously planned birthday party for the remaining ducks. Without realizing it at the time, this was my introduction to death education and healthy grieving. Birth, life and death—the full cycle—celebration and remembrance all in the matter of two hours. The ultimate teachable moment. (Katz, 1997, p. 1)

Following this experience, Katz wrote a curriculum on death education for grades K–2. She designed five classroom sessions using children's books, the arts, and discussion as part of each lesson (Katz, 1997).

Death Education Programs. There are many ways that teachers can help students become aware of issues of life and death, of different styles of coping with loss, and of the grieving process. Death education programs in schools should include opportunities for teachers to share their hesitations about bringing up this subject and provide them with guidance about how to proceed in the classroom. They can learn from each other, as well as from any formal curriculum.

In Chapter 12 I described crisis programs in the schools for after a death occurs. These programs should be part of an ongoing death education program in the schools. Such programs can help both children and their teachers develop a vocabulary for discussing death and an understanding of their feelings and how they can help each other cope. Any given curriculum needs to be modified to meet the needs of a particular teacher and his or her class. In all cases, parents should be involved, to some extent, in what is happening in the classroom. Discussion groups for parents can help them become aware of what is being taught so that children can continue the conversation at home if they wish. Bertman (1979–80) described how to use the arts as part of a classroom program in death education. Most programs follow her lead in using the arts in the classroom to help children learn (Black & Adams, 1993; Katz, 1997; Moore, 1989; O'Toole, 1991).

O'Toole (1991) designed a series of curricula for various age groups to bring death into the classroom and to help children understand death as part of life. The objectives in any given segment relate to children's cognitive capacities at various ages. In grades K–3 the objectives are to help children identify situations and events that bring about changes in life and nature. Children learn how some changes can constitute losses and that feeling sad, alone, and confused are natural responses to loss. Children in grades 4–8 look at death in greater depth and discuss the various reactions people can have to it. There is a progression in the curriculum so that gradually death is introduced as a natural part of the life cycle. Different beliefs and mourning rituals are examined. With high school students, the curriculum is more personal, focusing on their own reactions to death and loss and how it affects their lives.

Another curriculum, designed by Moore (1989), is a four-week unit for ninth-grade students as part of a broad home economics/family life education course that she teaches. Moore includes information about the perspectives of different cultures and religions and the need to develop personal and interpersonal skills for coping with loss and death. In public schools, teaching children about different belief systems and religious practices can help them see how people make meaning in a variety of ways at this time in their lives (Stevenson, 1993). This information broadens students' perspectives and helps them clarify their own values.

Many curricula rely on additional readings to develop a topic on which they want to focus. As teachers choose books to use in death education initiatives, they should evaluate them for the message they give children about a death. As noted in Chapter 12, a book should emphasize ritual at the time of the death and afterward. It should not talk about recovery or getting over it, but should allow children to find ways to remember and to keep a connection to the deceased. Children should be able to get a realistic sense of the range of feelings and changes that are associated with a death and how these feelings and changes are expressed over time. In an age-appropriate manner, the book should show them ways in which they can cope (C. Berns, school consultant, Miami, FL. Personal communication, 1998). No one book will do all these things. Teachers may have to pick and choose among what is available. They should remember that the books are designed to stimulate discussion, not to provide all the answers.

Suicide Prevention

Programs for suicide prevention are often separated from death education in the schools (Leenaars & Wenckstern, 1990; Ryerson, 1990). Most preventive programs, as noted in Chapter 12, focus on identifying people at risk. They train teachers and other school personnel to be aware of early warning signs, such as depression, giving away all of one's possessions, or withdrawing. They also put in place buffers for students, so if a student threatens suicide, there are ways of getting him or her help as soon as possible. This line of defense does not have an impact on the curriculum or reach most students. It can prevent some students from hurting themselves, but it does little to promote more effective ways of responding to stress so that suicide does not become an option.

Davis and Sandoval (1991) wrote about the need to help students learn new methods of problem solving and to create more supportive and caring school environments as a way of preventing suicide and promoting students' ability to cope. They focused on the peer community in a school, suggesting that the faculty and administration need to foster the development of friendships and contact among students to decrease feelings of isolation and loneliness, and to reduce the need for students to deal with the stress they are experiencing alone. They recommended programs that improve communication among students and between students and faculty and thus lead to better problem-solving techniques.

Isolation and feeling alone can be contributing factors when young people consider suicide. Any community that wants to support students who are isolated and prevent suicidal behavior needs to improve communication and provide opportunities for sharing. To do so, Davis and Sandoval (1991) recommended starting active peer counseling programs, especially in high schools. In peer counseling programs, trained students are available to other students to talk and to be resources in times of trouble. Another intervention that helps develop supportive feelings in the school is that of conflict managers—peers or faculty who help resolve differences in a peaceful manner. Some high schools offer programs that make students aware of the danger signs of someone contemplating suicide. These programs help students understand suicide and its causes, appreciate that depression is sometimes natural and a transitory part of life and recognize when it is not, see the relationship between suicide and stress, develop skills for assisting friends who are suicidal and recognizing their own limitations in this situation, and increase students' knowledge of school and community resources for suicidal individuals and how to get them help (Davis & Sandoval, 1991). In my mind, such a curriculum should not focus only on suicide, but should emphasize how to create caring communities and how to develop good problem-solving methods as part of an ongoing relationship that students have with their teachers. These types of programs can also be helpful to young bereaved people who may feel alone with their grief.

To teach a course on suicide or death, teachers need training and support, which have to be part of an ongoing relationship that teachers have with each other and with the school administration. The most important thing is to create environments in which children are encouraged to become active thinkers and problem solvers. The emphasis should be on peers teaching each other using the methods of mutual help or collaborative learning. An excellent example of this process is a program to prevent violence in the Boston schools that is described in the next section.

VIOLENCE IN CHILDREN'S LIVES: THE ROLE OF THE SCHOOL

One of the most serious issues that children face today is the amount of violence in their lives. As I was writing this book, there were several occasions when children killed their classmates in school. These incidents have been widely covered in newspapers and on television so that almost every schoolchild in the country is aware of what happened. Inner-city children experience this violence on a regular basis. In some communities, it is difficult to find a child who does not know someone who was murdered. This is one kind of death that can surely be prevented. We cannot tell children not to be afraid; we cannot make light of the grief they are feeling, nor can we point to a simple cause-and-effect relationship that will reassure them that this behavior can be stopped.

One response is to provide teachers with lists of warning signs that may indicate when a child is troubled and could be dangerous to himself or others. Yet teachers need to do more than watch. Watching children does not help children learn to cope differently, nor does it help teachers learn to take advantage of what could be teachable moments. Teachers need to create opportunities to help children find other ways of reacting to the violence around them. Teachers can help children learn how to solve problems, how to think, and how to use reason and their own resources to do things differently. The Louis D. Brown Peace Curriculum is a good example of how this can be done as part of the regular school curriculum.

A Program to Prevent Violence in High School Students

In this book I have tried to capture some of the creative energy that a death can stimulate in the mourners. Louis Brown was murdered at age 15 on the streets of Boston. He was caught in the crossfire of a gang war on his way to the subway station in December 1993 (Bolick, 1996). As a way of honoring his memory and trying to find a better way of responding to the violence in the community, his parents set up the Louis D. Brown Social Development Corporation, which raises money from cake sales and from returning deposit bottles, as well as from foundations. This money supports the Louis D. Brown Peace Curriculum. This curriculum, developed by a committee of teachers from the Boston School Department, is available to teachers who teach the tenth grade. It is designed to help children understand that there are alternatives to the use of violence in solving problems. The teaching objective is to increase knowledge and understanding of peaceful behavior and to improve students' reading, writing, and critical-thinking abilities. Teachers find it easy to implement this program because the curriculum is so detailed that they can readily apply it in the classroom without additional training.

The Louis D. Brown Peace Curriculum uses literature to teach the value of peace and the constant practice of peaceful ways as an alternative to violence. It is a learning experience that is designed to bring together teachers, students, and adults in the community. The consequences of violent behavior are openly discussed in the classroom. The core of the curriculum is a set of books that mirror the violent reality confronting urban students and embody the peaceful values to be fostered in the students. A teaching guide for each book provides the teachers, chapter by chapter, with a set of activities to help the students better explore the concept of peacemaking. Teacher's guides provide detailed instructions for how to involve the students and teach them new ways of thinking about problems and problem solving.

Teachers are given direction to guide students in learning critical thinking skills. They use an ABCDE process that is similar to Seligman and his colleagues' (1995) approach to problem solving, described in Chapter 12. Spivak and Shure (1977) used a similar approach with younger children. Students are taught to *assess* the problem or identify it and to look at it from different points of view. The students are encouraged to *brainstorm* possible choices they may have to solve the problem; they examine the *consequences* of each proposed choice, *decide* on the best choice, and *evaluate* the outcome.

Journal keeping, acting out part of the story, and community service are also used as part of the experience. When they finish a book, the students are asked to write an essay about the meaning of the experience. The better essays are published annually in a small book that is distributed widely in the community and sold in a local bookstore. The students learn the value of thinking before they act, of reflecting on their own behavior and its consequences. This new ability takes them to a new developmental place. In the words of one student:

> I learned that in order to make peace you need to stay away from trouble and be your own person. I deal with my conflicts by ignoring insults, walking away from fights and not letting people take advantage of me. . . . The support and help I needed were the voices inside my head. They would tell me not to fight and to do the right things. (Green, 1997, pp. 45–46)

Another student described what he learned about the choices that are his to make:

> Life is a terrible thing to waste. Make something of yourself, stay focused, and if you slip occasionally dust yourself off and get back in the game. You can do it . . . but you must believe you can. Trust me, it has been working for me. (Cortes, 1997, pp. 62–63)

This type of program could be adapted to other kinds of self-destructive violence, such as suicide, and would enhance any prevention program in a school setting. Although it is not called by this name, the program is essentially one of mutual help or collaborative learning. It provides students with opportunities to problem solve together, to understand each other better, and to be able to help each other as appropriate. When they see alternatives that they can make happen, students do not feel as helpless. By studying what happened to Louis Brown, they begin to realize that changing themselves may not be enough. They have to work toward changing the community as well. Nonetheless, when some of these students are close to using violence against others as a way of dealing with their experience, they begin to see that they have some control over their behavior and that they can make a difference. As one student wrote:

> You cannot make peace unless you made peace within yourself first (Massie, 1997, pp. 47–49)

Afterword

A book like this cannot really have an ending. Dealing with death is an on-going process that has no end. We continue to grow and change and grieve throughout our lives. How we cope with death and grief may change as conditions in our society change, as our understanding of bereavement and human behavior changes, and as we continue to experience life.

We cannot protect children from knowing death and from mourning by diverting their attention. Protection in this case involves giving them the tools to cope by educating and involving them. As a result, children learn that life does go on. They continue to grow and find pleasure in life. While children's lives always have a continuing, compelling momentum, they learn to respect and acknowledge that the death has diverted this momentum into new directions. As you saw throughout this book, the greatest wisdom comes from children themselves. When we learn to listen to them, we can find ways of helping them to, in the words of one bereaved child: "Learn to remember and learn how to carry on with your life."

Intuitively children feel and appreciate their relationship to the deceased. They also understand that, with help from family and friends, life continues.

Healing is a word that is often used to describe this accommodation to a death. This word has many meanings. One woman who lost a sibling as a young child told me she is "healed" because she is more able to integrate the loss into her life, to let the feelings come up, as they do from time to time, and to understand that the death has affected her life in many ways. Kathleen, whose mother died when she was a teenager, also used the word *healed*. Her words say best what that means and provide a fitting ending to this book:

> Healing is a good word, even though I know now that there will be no point at which it is over. I looked as if my heart was broken, and slowly I wanted my heart to heal. I do feel whole again. But no matter how old I am, I will always miss my mom . . . and there will never be a stage in my life when I will wake up and say I am all better now . . . wash away everything. That will never be because at each stage I will miss her: at graduation, when I have my first child, and when I reach her age when she died. My mother's death resulted in many positives. . . . I'm stronger, I'm more confident. I always believe there is a reason for whatever happens. Even when my mother died, I believe there was a reason. My reason is because I am a stronger woman. It would never have happened if she had lived. My relationship to God, to life, is stronger. I've learned to accept things better . . . and that is part of grieving, healing, and living.

References

Aarons, L. (1995). *Prayers for Bobby: A mother's coming to terms with the suicide of her gay son*. New York: HarperCollins.

Altschul, S. (1988). *Childhood bereavement and its aftermath* (Emotions and Behavior Monograph No. 8). Madison, CT: International Universities Press.

American Association of Suicidology. (1997). *Suicide postvention guidelines: Suggestions for dealing with the aftermath of suicide in the schools*. Washington, DC: Author.

Antonovsky, A. (1979). *Health, stress, and coping*. San Francisco: Jossey-Bass.

Antonovsky, A. (1987). *Unraveling the mystery of health: How people manage stress and stay well*. San Francisco: Jossey-Bass.

Apfel, R., & Telingator, C. (1995). What can we learn from children of war? In S. Geballe, J. Gruendel, & W. Andiman (Eds.), *Forgotten children of the AIDS epidemic* (pp. 107–121). New Haven, CT: Yale University Press.

Aries, P. (1981). *The hour of our death*. New York: Alfred A. Knopf.

Aronson, S. (1994). Group interventions with children of parents with AIDS. *Group, 18*, 133–139.

Attig, T. (1996). *How we grieve: Relearning the world*. New York: Oxford University Press.

Bacon, J. B. (1996). Support groups for bereaved children. In C. A. Corr & D. M. Corr (Eds.), *Handbook of childhood death and bereavement* (pp. 285–304). New York: Springer.

Bakan, D. (1966). *The duality of human existence: Isolation and community in western man*. Boston: Beacon Press.

Baker, J. E., & Sedney, M. A. (1996). How bereaved children cope with loss: An overview. In C. A. Corr & D. M. Corr (Eds.), *Handbook of childhood death and bereavement* (pp. 109–129). New York: Springer.

Balk, D. E., & Hogan, N. S. (1995). Religion, spirituality and bereaved adolescents. In D. W. Adams & E. J. Deveau (Eds.), *Beyond the innocence of childhood: Helping children and adolescents cope with death and bereavement* (Vol. 3, pp. 61–88). Amityville, NY: Baywood.

Bank, S. (1992). Remembering and reinterpreting sibling bonds. In F. Boer & J. Dunn (Eds.), *Children's sibling relationships: Developmental and clinical issues* (pp. 139–151). Hillsdale, NJ: Lawrence Erlbaum Associates.

Bank, S., & Kahn, M. D. (1982). *The sibling bond*. New York: Basic Books.

Bartholome, W. G. (1995). Care of the dying child: The demands of ethics. In A. Strickland & L. DeSpelder (Eds.), *Path ahead: Readings in death and dying* (pp. 133–143). Mountain View, CA: Mayfield.

Basch, M. F. (1983). The concept of "self": An operational definition. In B. Lee &

G. G. Noam (Eds.), *Developmental approaches to the self* (pp. 7–58). New York: Plenum Press.

Bearison, D. J. (1991). *They never want to tell you: Children talk about cancer.* Cambridge, MA: Harvard University Press.

Beck, A. T. (1979). *Cognitive therapy and emotional disorders.* New York: International Universities Press.

Belenky, M. F. (1996). Public homeplaces: Nurturing the development of people, families and communities. In N. T. Goldberger, J. M. Tarule, B. Clinchy, & M. Belenky (Eds.), *Knowledge, difference and power* (pp. 393–430). New York: Basic Books.

Belenky, M. F., Bond, L. A., & Weisenstock, J. S. (1997). *A tradition that has no name: Nurturing the development of people, families and communities.* New York: Basic Books.

Belenky, M. F., Clinchy, B., Goldberger, N., & Tarule, J. (1996). *Women's ways of knowing.* New York: Basic Books.

Bell, R. Q., & Harper, L. (1977). *Child effects on adults.* Hillsdale, NJ: Lawrence Erlbaum Associates.

Belle, D. (1989) (ed.). *Children's social networks and social supports.* New York: Wiley.

Berman, A. L., & Jobes, D. A. (1991). *Adolescent suicide: Assessment and intervention.* Washington, DC: American Psychological Association.

Bertman, S. L. (1974). Death education in the face of a taboo. In E. A. Grollman (Ed.), *Concerning death: A practical guide for the living* (pp. 333–361). Boston: Beacon Press.

Bertman, S. L. (1979–80). The arts: A source of comfort and insight for children who are learning about death. *Omega, 10,* 147–162.

Bertman, S. L. (1991). *Facing death: Images, insights and interventions.* New York: Hemisphere.

Bianchi Dickinson, M., & Leete, A. L. (Eds.) (1932). *The poems of Emily Dickinson.* Boston: Little, Brown & Company.

Black, A., & Adams, P. S. (1993). *The art of healing childhood grief: A school-based expressive arts program.* Brattleboro, VT: Center for Creative Healing.

Bluebond-Langner, M. (1978). *The private worlds of dying children.* Princeton: Princeton University Press.

Bluebond-Langner, M. (1996). *In the shadow of illness: Parents and siblings of the chronically ill child.* Princeton, NJ: Princeton University Press.

Boer, F., & Dunn, J. (1992). *Children's sibling relationships: Developmental and clinical issues.* Hillsdale, NJ: Lawrence Erlbaum Associates.

Bolick, N. O. (1996) *Louis D. Brown.* Dorchester, MA: Louis D. Brown Social Development Corporation.

Borkman, T. (1990). Experiential, professional and lay frames of reference. In T. Powell (Ed.), *Working with self-help.* Silver Spring, MD: National Association of Social Workers.

Bouman, J. (1993). Jimmy died, call the church. In K. J. Doka & J. Morgan (Eds.), *Death and spirituality* (pp. 363–378). Amityville, NY: Baywood.

Bowlby, J. (1961). Childhood mourning and its implications for psychiatry. *American Journal of Psychiatry, 118,* 481–498.

Bowlby, J. (1980). *Attachment and loss: Vol. 3. Loss: sadness and depression.* New York: Basic Books.

Boyd-Franklin, N., Steiner, G. L., & Boland, M. G. (1995). *Children, families and HIV/AIDS: Psychosocial and therapeutic issues.* New York: Guilford Press.

Brabant, S. (1993). Successful facilitation of a children's support group when conditions are less than optimal. *Clinical Sociology Review, 2,* 49–60.

Brown, L. M., & Gilligan, C. (1992). *Meeting at the crossroads: Women's psychology and girl's development*. Cambridge, MA: Harvard University Press.

Bruner, J. (1990). *Acts of meaning*. Cambridge, MA: Harvard University Press.

Bruner, J. (1989). On interaction. In M. H. Bornstein & J. S. Bruner (Eds.), *Interaction in human development* (pp. 1–14). Hillsdale, NJ: Lawrence Erlbaum Associates.

Bryant, B. K. (1982). Sibling relationships in middle childhood. In M. E. Lamb & B. Sutton-Smith (Eds.), *Sibling relationships: Their nature and significance across the lifespan* (pp. 87–121). Hillsdale, NJ: Lawrence Erlbaum Associates.

Byock, I. (1997). *Dying well: The prospect for growth at the end of life*. New York: Riverhead Press.

Campbell, S. & Silverman, P. R. (1996). *Widowers: When men are left alone* (Death, Value and Meaning Series). Amityville, NY: Baywood.

Caplan, G. (1974). *Support systems and community mental health: Lectures on concept development*. New York: Behavioral Publications.

Carson, U. (1984). Teachable moments occasioned by "Small Deaths." In H. Wass & C. Corr (Eds.), *Childhood and Death* (pp. 315–343). Washington, DC: Hemisphere.

Charmaz, K. (1994). Conceptual approaches to the study of death. In R. Fulton & R. Bendickson (Eds.), *Death and identity* (3rd ed., pp. 28–79). Philadelphia: Charles Press.

Clinchy, B. (1996). Connected and separate knowing: Toward a marriage of two minds. In N. Goldberger, J. M. Tarule, B. Clinchy, & M. Belenky (Eds.) *Knowledge, difference, and power* (pp. 205–247). New York: Basic Books.

Cobb, S. (1976). Social support as a moderator of life stress. *Psychosomatic Medicine, 38*, 300–314.

Coles, J. E. (1996). *Enduring bonds: Sibling loss in early adulthood*. Unpublished D. Psych dissertation, Massachusetts School of Professional Psychology.

Conant, R. D. (1996). Memories of the death and life of a spouse: The role of images and sense of presence in grief. In D. Klass, P. R. Silverman, & S. L. Nickman (Eds.), *Continuing bonds: New understandings of grief* (pp. 179–196). Bristol, PA: Taylor & Francis.

Cook, J. A. (1988). Dads' double binds: Rethinking fathers' bereavement from a men's studies perspective. *Journal of Ethnography, 17*, 308–385.

Cook, J. A., & Wimberly, D. W. (1983). If I should die before I wake: Religious commitment and adjustment to the death of a child. *Journal for the Scientific Study of Religion, 22*, 222–238.

Corless, I. B. (1985). The hospice movement in North America. In C. Corr & D. Corr (Eds.), *Hospice care: Principles and practice* (pp. 335–351). New York: Springer.

Cortes, A. (1997). Peace. In J. W. Chery & B. Shackleton (Eds.), *Boston's book of peace* Vol. 3, pp. 62–63). Dorchester, MA: Louis D. Brown Social Development Corporation.

Davies, B. (1988). Shared life space and sibling bereavement responses. *Cancer Nursing, 11*, 339–347.

Davies, B. (1996). Long term effects of sibling death in childhood. In D. W. Adams & E. J. Deveau (Eds.), *Beyond the innocence of childhood* (pp. 89–98). Amityville, NY: Baywood.

Davies, B., Reimer, J. C., Brown, P., & Martens, N. (1995). *Fading away: The experience of transition in families with terminal illness*. Amityville, NY: Baywood.

Davis, J. M. & Sandoval, J. (1991). *Suicidal youth: School-based intervention and prevention*. San Francisco: Jossey-Bass.

Debold, E., Tolamn, D., & Brown, L. M. (1996). Embodying knowledge, knowing desire: Authority and split subjectivities in girls' epistemological development. In N. Goldberger, J. M. Tarule, B. Clinchy, & M. Belenky (Eds.), *Knowledge, difference and power* (pp. 85–125). New York: Basic Books.

DeSpelder, L., & Strickland, A. L. (1996). *The last dance: Encountering death and dying* (4th ed.). Mountainview, CA: Mayfield.

Doka, K. (Ed.). (1989). *Disenfranchised grief: Recognizing hidden sorrow*. Lexington, MA: Lexington Books.

Doka, K., & Morgan, J. (1993). *Death and spirituality*. Amityville, NY: Baywood.

Dougy Center (1999). *Program Development Manual*. Portland, OR: Dougy Center.

Draimin, B. (1995). A second family? Placement and custody decision. In S. Geballe, J. Gruendel, & W. Andiman (Eds.), *Forgotten children of the AIDS epidemic* (pp. 125–129). New Haven, CT: Yale University Press.

Dunn, J. (1992). Sisters and brothers: Current issues in developmental research. In F. Boer & J. Dunn (Eds.), *Children's sibling relationships: Developmental and clinical issues* (pp. 1–17). Hillsdale, NJ: Lawrence Erlbaum Associates.

Dunn, J., & Plomin, R. (1990). *Separate lives: Why siblings are so different*. New York: Basic Books.

Edelman, H. (1994). *Motherless daughters*. Reading, MA: Addison-Wesley.

Edmonds, M. E. (1847–1899). *Diary* (unpublished).

Elbow, P. (1973). Appendix essay: The doubting game and the believing game—An analysis of the intellectual enterprise. In *Writing without teachers* (pp. 197–91). London: Oxford University Press.

Elkind, D. (1994). *Ties that stress: The new family imbalance*. Cambridge, MA: Harvard University Press.

Elliot, G. R., & Eisdorfer, C. (1982). *Stress and human health: Analysis and implications of research: A study by the Institute of Medicine, National Academy of Science*. New York: Springer.

Erikson, E. H. (1950). *Childhood and society*. New York: Norton.

Evans, S. (1997). *Later Courtney: A mother says goodbye*. Omaha, NE: Centering Corporation.

Feifel, H. (Ed.). (1959). *The meaning of death*. New York: McGraw-Hill.

Feifel, H. (1986). Foreword. In F. Wald (Ed.), *In the quest of the spiritual component of care for the terminally ill: Proceedings of a colloquium* (pp. 15–22). New Haven, CT: Yale School of Nursing.

Figley, C. R., Bride, B., & Mazza, N. (Eds.) (1997). *Death and trauma: The traumatology of grieving*. Washington, DC: Taylor & Francis.

Finkbeiner, A. K. (1996). *After the death of a child: Living with the loss through the years*. New York: Free Press.

Fleming, S. J., & Adolph, R. (1986). Helping bereaved adolescents: Needs and responses. In C. A. Corr & J. N. McNeil (Eds.), *Adolescence and death* (pp. 97–118). New York: Springer.

Fleming, S., & Balmer, L. (1991). Group intervention with bereaved children. In D. Papadatou & C. Papadatos (Eds.), *Children and death* (pp. 105–124). Washington, DC: Taylor & Francis.

Fowler, J. W. (1996). *Faithful change: The personal and public challenges of postmodern life*. Nashville, TN: Abingdon Press.

Frankl, V. (1972). *The doctor and the soul: From psychotherapy to logotherapy*. New York: Alfred A. Knopf.

Frankl, V. (1978). *The unheard cry for meaning: Psychotherapy and humanism*. New York: Simon & Schuster.

Freeman, J., Epston, D., & Lobovits, D. (1997). *Playful approaches to serious problems: Narrative therapy with children and their families.* New York: W. W. Norton & Co.

French, V. (1977). History of the child's influence: Ancient Mediterranean civilizations. In R. Q. Bell & L. V. Harper (Eds.), *Child effects on adults* (pp. 3–49). Hillsdale, NJ: Lawrence Erlbaum Associates.

Freud, S. (1961). Mourning and melancholia. In J. Strachey (Ed. and Trans.), *The standard edition of the complete psychological works of Sigmund Freud* (Vol. 14, pp. 243–258). New York: Basic Books.

Friedan, B. (1963). *The feminine mystique.* New York: Dell.

Fry, V. L. (1995). *Part of me died, too.* New York: E. P. Dutton.

Fulton, R. (1965). *Death and identity.* New York: Wiley.

Fulton, R., & Owen, G. (1994). Death in contemporary American society. In R. Fulton & R. Bendickson (Eds.), *Death and identity* (3rd ed., pp. 12–27). Philadelphia: Charles Press.

Furman, E. (1974). *A child's parent dies: Studies in childhood bereavement.* New Haven, CT: Yale University Press.

Gaines-Laine, G. (1995). *My memory book.* Gaithersburg, MD: Chi Rho Press.

Gaines-Laine, G. (1997). *Play therapy with grieving children.* Paper presented at the Annual Meeting of the Association for Death Education and Counseling, Washington, DC.

Garmazy, N., Masten, A. S., & Tellegen, A. (1984). The study of stress and competence in children: A building block for developmental psychopathology. *Child Development, 55,* 97–111.

Garvin, J. (1996). Death themes in literature: Uses in the high school classroom. In R. G. Stevenson & E. P. Stevenson (Eds.), *Teaching students about death: A comprehensive resource for educators and parents* (pp. 169–181). Philadelphia: Charles Press.

Geballe, S., Gruendel, J., & Andiman, W. (Eds.). (1995). *Forgotten children of the AIDS epidemic.* New Haven, CT: Yale University Press.

Gilligan, C. (1990). Teaching Shakespeare's sister: Notes from the underground of female adolescence. In C. Gilligan, N. Lyons, & T. Hanmer (Eds.), *Making connections: The relational world of adolescent girls at Emma Willard School* (pp. 6–29). Cambridge, MA: Harvard University Press.

Gilligan, C. (1993). *In a different voice: Psychological theory and women's development* (2nd ed.). Cambridge, MA: Harvard University Press.

Glaser, B., & Strauss, A. (1965). *Awareness of dying.* Chicago: Aldine.

Goffman, E. (1963). *Stigma: Notes on the management of spoiled identities.* Englewood Cliffs, NJ: Prentice Hall.

Gorer, G. (1965). *Death, grief and mourning in contemporary Britain.* London: Cresset Press.

Green, S. (1997). My life . . . My mission. In J. W. Chery & B. Shackleton (Eds.). *Boston's book of peace* (Vol. 3, pp. 45–46). Dorchester, MA: Louis D. Brown Social Development Corporation.

Grollman, E. A. (1967). *Explaining death to children.* Boston: Beacon Press.

Haggerty, R. J., Sherrod, L., Garmazy, N., & Rutter, M. (Eds.) (1994). *Stress, risk and resilience in children and adolescents: Processes, mechanisms and interventions.* Cambridge, England: Cambridge University Press.

Harris, M. (1995). *The loss that is forever: The lifelong impact of the early death of a mother or father.* New York: A Plume Book, Penguin Books.

Harter, S. (1993). Self and identity development. In S. S. Feldman & G. R. Elliott

(Eds.), *At the threshold: The developing adolescent* (pp. 352–387). Cambridge, MA: Harvard University Press.

Hause, E. T. (1989). *The silent ones speak: The experience of sibling death*. Unpublished Ph.D. dissertation, Union Institute.

Hauser, S., & Bowlds, M. K. (1993). Stress, coping and adaptation. In S. S. Feldman & G. R. Elliott (Eds.), *At the threshold: The developing adolescent* (pp. 388–413). Cambridge, MA: Harvard University Press.

Hetherington, E. M., & Baltes, P. B. (1988). Child psychology and life-span development. In E. M. Hetherington, R. M. Lerner, & M. Perlmutter (Eds.). *Child development in life-span perspective* (pp. 1–19). Hillsdale, NJ: Lawrence Erlbaum Associates.

Hetherington, E. M., & Parke, R. D. (1993). *Child psychology: A contemporary viewpoint*. New York: McGraw-Hill.

Hill, D. C., & Foster, Y. M. (1996). Postventions with early and middle adolescents. In C. A. Corr & D. E. Balk (Eds.), *Handbook of adolescent death and bereavement* (pp. 250–272). New York: Springer.

Hoff, B. J. (1991). *Thorns and roses*. Anderson, IN: Warner Press.

Hogan, N., & DeSantis, L. (1992). Adolescent sibling bereavement: Ongoing attachment. *Qualitative Health Research, 2*, 159–177.

Jordan, J. R., & Ware, E. S. (1997). Feeling like a motherless child: A support group model for adults grieving the death of a parent. *Omega, 35,*

Kagan, H. (1998). *Gili's book: A journey into bereavement for parents and families*. New York: Teachers College Press.

Kantor, D., & Lehr, W. (1975). *Inside the Family*. New York: Harper & Row.

Kastenbaum, R., & Kastenbaum, B. (1989). *Encyclopedia of death*. New York: Avon Books.

Katz, J. (1997). *Learning about loss: Bringing death into the life cycle, A K–2 curriculum*. Lexington, MA: Lexington Public Schools.

Kegan, R. (1982). *The evolving self*. Cambridge, MA: Harvard University Press.

Kegan, R. (1994). *In over our heads: The mental demands of modern life*. Cambridge, MA: Harvard University Press.

Kelly, J. D. (1995). Grief: Re-forming life's story. In A. Strickland & L. DeSpelder (Eds.), *Path ahead: Readings in death and dying* (pp. 242–245). Mountain View, CA: Mayfield.

Kempler, B., & Koocher, G. (1994). *Program manual for bereaved families*. Boston: Children's Hospital Medical Center.

Klass, D. (1988). *Parental grief: Solace and resolution*. New York: Springer.

Klass, D. (1996). Grief in an Eastern culture: Japanese ancestor worship. In D. Klass, P. R. Silverman, & S. L. Nickman (Eds.), *Continuing bonds: New understandings of grief* (pp. 59–70). Bristol, PA: Taylor & Francis.

Klass, D., Silverman, P. R., & Nickman, S. L. (Eds.) (1996). *Continuing bonds: New understandings of grief*. Bristol, PA: Taylor & Francis.

Kohlberg, L.(1984). *The psychology of moral development*. San Francisco: Harper & Row.

Koocher, G. (1994). Preventive intervention following a child's death. *Psychotherapy, 31*, 377–382.

Krause, H. (1977). *Family law in a nutshell*. St. Paul, MN: West.

Krulik, T., Holaday, B., & Martinson, I. M. (Eds.) (1987). *The child and family facing life-threatening illness: A tribute to Eugenia Waechter*. Philadelphia: Lippincott.

Kübler-Ross, E. (1969). *On death and dying*. New York: Macmillan.

Kushner, H. S. (1989). *When bad things happen to good people* (2nd ed.). New York: Schocken Books.

Lattanzi-Licht, M., Mahoney, J. J., & Miller, G. W. (1998). *The hospice choice: In pursuit of a peaceful death.* New York: Fireside.

Lazarus, R. S., & Folkman, S. (1984). *Stress, appraisal, and coping.* New York: Springer.

Leenaars, A. A., & Wenckstern, S. (1990). Suicide prevention in schools: An introduction. *Death Studies, 14*, 297–302.

Lerner, R. M. (1989). Developmental contextualism and the life-span view of person-context interaction. In M. H. Bornstein & J. S. Bruner (Eds.), *Interaction in human development* (pp. 217–239). Hillsdale, NJ: Lawrence Erlbaum Associates.

Levine, S. (1984). *Meeting at the edge.* New York: Anchor Books.

Lifton, R. (1983). *The broken connection: On death and the continuity of life.* New York: Basic Books.

Lindemann, E. (1944). Symptomatology and management of acute grief. *American Journal of Psychiatry, 101*, 141–148.

Lofland, L. (1978). *The craft of dying: The modern face of death.* Beverly Hills, CA: Sage.

Lord, J. H. (1997). American's number one killer: Vehicular crashes. In K. Doka (Ed.), *Living with grief after sudden loss: Suicide, homicide, accident, heart attack, stroke* (pp. 25–39). Washington, DC: Taylor & Francis.

Lyons, N. (1990). Listening to voices we have not heard. In C. Gilligan, N. Lyons, & T. Hanmer (Eds.), *Making connections: The relational world of adolescent girls at Emma Willard School* (pp. 30–72). Cambridge, MA: Harvard University Press.

Madara, E., & White, B. T. (1997). On-line mutual support: The experience of a self-help clearinghouse. *Information and Referral: The Journal of the Alliance of Information and Referral Systems, 19*, 91–107.

Malone, M. L. (1987). Consciousness of dying and projective fantasy of young children with malignant disease. In T. Krulik, B. Holaday, & I. M. Martinson (Eds.), *The child and family facing life-threatening illness: A tribute to Eugenia Waechter* (pp. 165–174). Philadelphia: Lippincott.

Marris, P. (1974). *Loss and change.* London: Routledge & Kegan Paul.

Martin, J. R. (1985). *Reclaiming a conversation: The ideal of the educated woman.* New Haven, CT: Yale University Press.

Martinson, I. M. (Ed.) (1976). *Home care for the dying child.* New York: Appleton-Century-Crofts.

Martinson, I. M. (1987). The feasibility of home care for the dying child with cancer. In T. Krulik, B. Holaday, & I. M. Martinson (Eds.), *The child and family facing life-threatening illness: A tribute to Eugenia Waechter* (pp. 313–326). Philadelphia: Lippincott.

Martinson, I. M., & Campos, R. G. (1991). Long-term responses to a sibling's death from cancer. Journal of Adolescent Research, *6*, 54–69.

Massie, M. (1997). A true peacemaker. In J. W. Chery & B. Shackleton (Eds.), *Boston's book of peace* (Vol. 3, pp. 47–49). Dorchester, MA: Louis D. Brown Social Development Corporation.

McClowry, S. G., Davies, E. B., May, K. A., Kulenkamp, E. J., & Martinson, I. M. (1987). The empty space phenomenon: The process of grief in the bereaved family. *Death Studies, 11*, 361–374.

Mead, G. H. (1930). *Mind, self, and society.* Chicago: Chicago University Press.

Merkel-Holguin, L. A. (1994). *Because you love them: A parent's planning guide.* Washington, DC: Child Welfare League of America.

Meyer, J. W. (1988). The social construction of the psychology of childhood: Some contemporary processes. In E. M. Hetherington, R. M. Lerner, & M. Perlmutter (Eds.), *Child development in a life-span perspective* (pp. 47–65). Hillsdale, NJ: Lawrence Erlbaum Associates.

Miller, J. B. (1986). *New psychology of women*. Boston: Beacon Press.

Morgan, J. D. (1993). The existential quest for meaning. In K. Doka & J. Morgan (Eds.), *Death and spirituality* (pp. 3–9). Amityville, NY: Baywood.

Morgan, J. D. (1995). Living our dying and our grieving: Historical and cultural attitudes. In H. Wass & R. A. Neimeyer (Eds.), *Dying: Facing the facts* (pp. 25–46). Washington, DC: Taylor & Francis.

Moore, C. M. (1989). Teaching about loss and death to junior high school students. *Family Relations, 38*, 3–7.

Nagy, M. (1948). The child's theories concerning death. *Journal of Genetic Psychology, 73*, 3–27.

Neimeyer, R. (Ed.). (1994). *Death anxiety handbook: Research, instrumentation and application*. Washington, DC: Taylor & Francis.

Neimeyer, R. (1997). Meaning reconstruction and the experience of chronic loss. In K. J. Doka & J. Davidson (Eds.), *Living with grief when illness is prolonged* (pp. 159–176). Washington, DC: Taylor & Francis.

Neimeyer, R., & Stewart, A. E. (1996). Trauma, healing, and the narrative emplotment of loss. *Family in Society, 77*, 360–375.

Neuberger, J. (1987). *Caring for dying people of different faiths*. London: Austen Cornish.

Newberger, C. M., & White, K. M. (1989). Cognitive foundations for parental care. In D. Cicchetti & V. Carlson (Eds.), *Child maltreatment* (pp. 302–316). New York: Cambridge University Press.

Nickman, S. L., Silverman, P. R., & Normand, C. L. (1998). Children's construction of a deceased parent: The surviving parent's contribution. *Journal of Orthopsychiatry, 68*, 126–134.

Normand, C. L. (1994). *A longitudinal analysis of bereaved children's continuing relationships to their deceased parents*. Unpublished doctoral dissertation, Waterloo University, Waterloo, Canada.

Normand, C. L., Silverman, P. R., & Nickman, S. L. (1996). Bereaved children's changing relationships with the deceased. In D. Klass, P. R. Silverman, & S. L. Nickman (eds.), *Continuing Bonds: New Understandings of Grief* (pp. 87–111). Bristol, PA: Taylor & Francis.

Nuland, S. B. (1995). *The way we die: Reflections on life's final chapter*. New York: Vintage Books.

O'Donnell, M. C. (Ed.) (1989). *The sheltered heart*. Fort Lauderdale, FL: Hospice Care of Broward County.

O'Donnell, M. C. (1996). *HIV/AIDS: Loss, grief, challenge and hope*. Washington, DC: Taylor & Francis.

Olson, D. H., McCubbin, H. I., Barnes, H. L., Larsen, A., & Wilson, M. (1989). *Families, what makes them work*. Newbury Park, CA: Sage Publications.

Orbach, I. (1988). *Children who don't want to live: Understanding and treating the suicidal child*. San Francisco: Jossey-Bass.

O'Toole, D. (1991). *Growing through grief: A K–12 curriculum to help young people through all kinds of losses*. Burnville, NC: Compassion Books.

Parkes, C. M. (1996). Bereavement. In T. Kendrick, A. Tylee, & P. Freeling (Eds.), *The prevention of illness in primary care* (pp. 74–87). Cambridge, England: Cambridge University Press.

Parkin, R., & Dunne-Maxim, K. (1995). *Child survivors of suicide: A guidebook for those who care for them*. New York: American Foundation for Suicide Prevention.

Parsons, T. (1994). Death in the western world. In R. Fulton & R. Bendickson (Eds.), *Death and identity* (pp. 60–79). Philadelphia: Charles Press.

Pattison, E. M. (1977). *The experience of dying*. Englewood Cliffs, NJ: Prentice Hall.

Pazola, K., & Pugsley, S. (1992). *The journey home: A guide for parents*. Boston: Pediatric Nursing Service Massachusetts General Hospital.

Piaget, J. (1954). *The construction of reality in the child*. New York: Basic Books.

Pincus, L. (1974). *Death and the family: The importance of mourning*. New York: Pantheon.

Powell, T. (Ed.). (1994). *Understanding the self-help organization*. Oak Hills, CA: Sage.

Prothrow-Stith, D. (1990). The epidemic of violence and its impact on the health care system. *Henry Ford Hospital Medical Journal, 38*, 175–177.

Quint Benoliel, J., & Degner, L. F. (1995). Institutional dying: A convergence of cultural values, technology, and social organization. In H. Wass & R. A. Neimeyer (Eds.), *Dying: Facing the facts* (pp. 117–141). Washington, DC: Taylor & Francis.

Rando, T. A. (1993). *Treatment of complicated mourning*. Champaign, IL: Research Press.

Raphael, B., Middleton, W., Martinek, N., & Misso, V. (1993). Counseling and therapy for the bereaved. In M. Stroebe, W. Stroebe, & R. O. Hansson (Eds.), *Handbook of bereavement: Theory, research and intervention* (pp. 427–435). New York: Cambridge University Press.

Redmond, L. (1989). *Surviving when someone you love was murdered: A professional guide*. Clearwater, FL: Psychological Consult.

Reiss, D. (1981). *The family's construction of reality*. Cambridge, MA: Harvard University Press.

Rhodes, S. (1981). *Surviving family life: The seven crises of living together*. New York: G. P. Putnam's Sons.

Riessman, F., & Carroll, D. (1995). *Redefining self-help: Policy and practice*. San Francisco: Jossey-Bass.

Robert Wood Johnson Foundation. (1995). *On dying in America: Annual Report*. Princeton, NJ: Author.

Rogoff, B. (1994). Cross-cultural perspectives on children's development. In P. K. Bock (Ed.), *Psychological anthropology* (pp. 231–242). Westport, CT: Praeger.

Rosen, E. J. (1988). Family therapy in cases of interminable grief for the loss of a child. *Omega, 19*, 187–202.

Rosenblatt, P. C., Walsh, R. P., & Jackson, D. A. (1976). *Grief and mourning in cross cultural perspective*. New Haven, CT: HRAF Press.

Ross, H. G., & Milgram, J. I. (1982). Important variables in adult sibling relationships: A qualitative study. In M. E. Lamb & B. Sutton-Smith (eds.), *Sibling relationships: Their nature and significance across the lifespan*. Hillsdale, NJ: Lawrence Erlbaum Associates.

Rubin, L. (1985). *Just friends: The role of friendship in our lives*. New York: Harper & Row.

Rubin, S. S. (1992). Adult child loss and the two-track model of bereavement, *Omega, 24*, 183–202.

Rudman, M. K., Gagne, K. D., & Bernstein, J. E. (1993). *Books to help children cope with separation and loss*. New Providence, NJ: R. R. Bowker.

Rutter, M. (1983). Stress, coping and development: Some issues and questions. In N. Garmazy & M. Rutter (Eds.). *Stress, coping and development in children* (pp. 1–41). New York: McGraw-Hill.

Ryerson, D. (1990). Suicide awareness education in schools: The development of a core program and subsequent modifications for special populations or institutions. *Death Studies, 14,* 371–390.

Sandlar, E., Miller, P., Short, J., & Wolchik, S. (1989). Social support as a protective factor for children in stress. In D. Belle (Ed.), *Children's social networks and social support* (pp. 277–307). New York: Wiley.

Saunders, C. (1994). Foreword. In I. B. Corless, B. B. Germino, & M. A. Pittman (Eds.), *A challenge for living* (pp. xi–xiv). Boston: Jones & Bartlett.

Savin-Williams, R., & Bernd, T. J. (1993). Friendship and peer relations. In S. S. Feldman & G. R. Elliott (Eds.). *At the threshold: The developing adolescent* (pp. 277–307). Cambridge, MA: Harvard University Press.

Scarr, S. (1982). Development is internally guided, not determined. *Contemporary Psychology, 27,* 852–853.

Scarr, S., & Ricciuti, A. (1991). What effects do parents have on their children? In L. Okagaki & R. J. Sternberg (Eds.), *Directors of development: Influences on the development of children's thinking* (pp. 1–25). Hillsdale, NJ: Lawrence Erlbaum Associates.

Schiff, H. (1986). *Living through mourning: Finding comfort and hope when a loved one has died.* New York: Viking Penguin.

Seligman, M. (1990). *Learned optimism.* New York: Pocket Books.

Seligman, M., Reivich, K., Jaycox, L., & Gillham, J. (1995). *The optimistic child.* Boston: Houghton Mifflin.

Selman, R. L., & Schultz, L. H. (1990). *Making a friend in youth: Developmental theory and pair therapy.* Chicago: University of Chicago Press.

Shapiro, E. R. (1994). *Grief as a family process: A developmental approach to clinical practice.* New York: Guilford Press.

Shneidman, E. (1996). *The suicidal mind.* New York: Oxford University Press.

Shneidman, E., & Mandelkorn, P. (1994). Some facts and fables of suicide. In E. Shneidman, N. L. Farberow, & R. Litman (Eds.), *The psychology of suicide: A clinician's guide to evaluation and treatment* (pp. 87–95). Northvale, NJ: Jason Aaronson.

Siehl, P. M. (1990). Suicide postvention. A new disaster plan: What a school should do when faced with a suicide. *School Counselor, 38,* 52–57.

Siegel, K., Mesagno, F. P., & Christ, G. (1990). A prevention program for bereaved children. *American Journal of Orthopsychiatry, 60,* 168–175.

Silverman, P. R. (1966). Services for the widowed during the period of bereavement. In *Social Work Practice.* New York: Columbia University Press.

Silverman, P. R. (1969). The widow-to-widow program: An experiment in preventive intervention. *Mental Hygiene, 54,* 540–547.

Silverman, P. R. (1977). *If you will lift the load: A guide to the creation of widowed-to-widowed services.* New York: Jewish Funeral Directors of America.

Silverman, P. R. (1978). *Mutual help groups: A guide for mental health workers* (DHEW Publication No. (ADM) 78-646). Washington, DC: U.S. Government Printing Office.

Silverman, P. R. (1980). *Mutual help groups: Organization and development.* Beverly Hills, CA: Sage.

Silverman, P. R. (1981). *Helping women cope with grief.* Beverly Hills, CA: Sage.

Silverman, P. R. (1982). Transitions and models of intervention. *Annals of the American Academy of Political and Social Science, 464,* 174–187.

Silverman, P. R. (1986). *Widow to widow.* New York: Springer.

Silverman, P. R. (1987). Impact of parental death on college-age women. *Psychiatric Clinics of North America, 10,* 387–404.

Silverman, P. R. (1988). In search of new selves: Accommodating to widowhood. In L. A. Bond & B. Wagner (Eds.), *Families in transition: Primary programs that work* (pp. 200–219). Newbury Park, CA: Sage.

Silverman, P. R. (1993). Spoiled identities. In I. Corless, B. Germino, & M. Pittman-Lindeman (Eds.), *Death, dying, and bereavement* (pp. 239–251). Boston: Jones and Bartlett.

Silverman, P. R. (1994). Helping the bereaved through social support and mutual help. In I. B. Corless, B. B. Germino, & M. A. Pittman (Eds.), *A challenge for living* (pp. 241–257). Boston: Jones & Bartlett.

Silverman, P. R., & Englander, S. (1975). A widow's view of her dependent children. *Omega, 6*, 3–20.

Silverman, P. R., & Klass, D. (1996). Introduction: What's the Problem? In D. Klass, P. R. Silverman, & S. L. Nickman (Eds.), *Continuing bonds: New understandings of grief* (pp. 3–27). Bristol, PA: Taylor & Francis.

Silverman, P. R., & Nickman, S. L. (1996). Children's construction of their dead parent. In D. Klass, P. R. Silverman, & S. L. Nickman (Eds.), *Continuing bonds: New understandings of grief* (pp. 73–86). Washington, DC: Taylor & Francis.

Silverman, P. R., Weiner, A., & El Ad, N. (1995). Parent-child communication in bereaved Israeli families. *Omega, 31*, 275–293.

Silverman, P. R., & Worden, J. W. (1992). Children's reactions to the death of a parent in the early months after the death. *American Journal of Orthopsychiatry, 62*, 93–104.

Silverman, P. R., & Worden, J. W. (1993). Children's reactions to the death of a parent. In M. Stroebe, W. Stroebe, & R. O. Hansson (Eds.), *Handbook of bereavement* (pp. 300–316). Cambridge, England: Cambridge University Press.

Silverman, S. M. (1997). Justice Joseph Story and death in the early 19th century America. *Death Studies, 21*, 397–416.

Silverman S. M., & Silverman, P. R. (1979). Parent-child communication in widowed families. *American Journal of Psychotherapy, 33*, 428–441.

Smith, H. I. (1996). *Grieving the death of a friend*. Minneapolis, MN: Augsburg Fortress.

Speece, M. W. (1984). Children's understanding of death: A review of three components of a death concept. *Child Development, 55*, 1671–1686.

Speece, M. W., & Brent, S. B. (1996). The development of the concept of death among Chinese and U.S. children 3–17 Years of age: From binary to fuzzy concepts? *Omega, 33*, 67–83.

Spivak, G., & Shure, M. B. (1977). Preventively oriented cognitive education of preschoolers. In D. C. Klein & S. E. Goldston (Eds.), *Primary prevention: An idea whose time has come*. DHEW Publication No. 77-447 (ADM), pp. 79–82. Washington, DC: U.S. Government Printing Office.

Stephans, S. (1973). *When death comes home*. New York: Morehouse-Barlow.

Stevenson, R. G. (1993). Religious values in death education. In K. Doka & J. Morgan (Eds.), *Death and spirituality* (pp. 281–290). Amityville, NY: Baywood.

Stevenson, R. G., & Stevenson, E. P. (1997). *Teaching students about death*. Philadelphia: Charles Press.

Stillion, J. M., & McDowell, E. E. (1996). *Suicide across the life span*. Washington DC: Taylor & Francis.

Story, W. W. (Ed.). (1951). *Life and letters of Joseph Story* (Vol. 1). Boston: Little, Brown & Company.

Stroebe, M., Gergen, M., Gergen, K., & Stroebe, W. (1996). Broken hearts or broken bonds. In D. Klass, P. R. Silverman, & S. L. Nickman (Eds.), *Continuing bonds: New understandings of grief* (pp. 73–86). Washington, DC: Taylor & Francis.

Stroebe, M., & Schut, H. (1999). The dual process model of coping with bereavement: Rationale and description. *Death Studies 23.*

Sullivan, H. S. (1972). *Personal psychopathology, Early formulations.* New York: Norton.

Taylor-Brown, J., Acheson, A., & Farber, J. M. (1993). Kids can cope: A group intervention for children whose parents have cancer. *Journal of Psychosocial Oncology, 11,* 41–53.

Taylor-Brown, S., & Wiener, L. (1993). Making videos of HIV-infected women for their children. *Families in Society: The Journal of Contemporary Human Services. 74,* pp. 468–480.

Teplow, D. R. (1995). *Sibling loss: The death of a brother or sister in childhood.* Unpublished doctoral dissertation, Massachusetts School of Professional Psychology.

Thomas, S. B., Leite, B., & Duncan, T. (1998). Breaking the cycle of violence among youth living in metropolitan Atlanta: A case history of kids alive and loved. *Health Education and Health Behavior, 25,* 158–172

Toray, T., & Oltjenbruns, K. A. (1996). Children's friendships and the death of a friend. In C. A. Corr & D. M. Corr (Eds.), *Handbook of childhood death and bereavement* (pp. 165–178). New York: Springer.

Vachon, M. L., & Stylianos, S. K. (1993). The role of social support in bereavement. In M. Stroebe, W. Stroebe, & R. O Hansson (Eds.), *Handbook of bereavement: Theory, research and intervention* (pp. 397–410). New York: Cambridge University Press.

Van der Kolk, B., McFarlane, A., & Weisaeth, L. (Eds.). (1996). *Traumatic stress: The effects of overwhelming experience on mind, body, and society.* New York: Guilford Press.

VanGennep, A. (1960). *The rites of passage.* Chicago: University of Chicago Press.

Vigotsky, L. S. (1978). *Mind in society.* Cambridge, MA: Harvard University Press.

Volkan, V. D. (1981). *Linking objects and linking phenomena.* New York: International Universities Press.

Waechter, E. H. (1987). Children's awareness of fatal illness. In T. Krulik, B. Holaday, I. M. Martinson (Eds.), *The child and family facing life-threatening illness: A tribute to Eugenia Waechter* (pp. 101–107). Philadelphia: Lippincott.

Wald, F. (1995). Finding a way to give hospice care. In I. B. Corless, B. G. Germino, & M. Pittman (Eds.), *Dying, death, and bereavement: Theoretical perspectives and other ways of knowing* (pp. 31–47). Boston: Jones & Bartlett.

Wampler, K. S., Halverson, C. F., & Deal, J. (1996). Risk and resiliency in nonclinical young children: The Georgia Longitudinal Study. In E. M. Hetherington & E. A. Blechman (Eds.), *Stress, coping, and resiliency in children and families* (pp. 135–153). Mahwah, NJ: Lawrence Erlbaum Associates.

Wass, H. (1984). Concepts of death: A developmental perspective. In H. Wass, & C. Corr, C. (Eds.) *Childhood and death* (pp. 3–24). Washington, DC: Hemisphere.

Wass, H., Miller, D., & Thorton, G. (1990). Death education and grief/suicide intervention in the public schools. *Death Studies, 14,* 253–268.

Webb, N. B. (Ed.) (1993). *Helping bereaved children: A casebook for practitioners.* New York: Guilford Press.

Webster's Third International Dictionary. (1968). Springfield, MA: C. & C. Merriam Co.

Weisman, A. (1972). *On dying and denying: A psychiatric study of terminality.* New York: Behavioral Publications.

Wertlieb, D., Weigel, C., & Feldstein, M. (1987). Measuring children's coping. *American Journal of Orthopsychiatry, 57,* 548–560.

White, B. T., & Madara, E. T. (1998) (Eds.). *The self-help sourcebook* (6th ed.). Denville, NJ: Northwest Covenant Medical Center.

White, M. (1988). Saying hello again: The incorporation of the lost relationship in the resolution of grief. *Dulwidge Centre Newsletter.* Adelaide, Australia: Dulwidge Centre.

White, M., & Epston, D. (1990). *Narrative means of therapeutic ends.* New York: Norton.

White, R. W. (1959). Motivation reconsidered: The concept of competence. *Psychological Review.*

Worden, J. W. (1991). *Grief counseling and grief therapy: A handbook for the mental health practitioner.* New York: Springer.

Youniss, J. (1980). *Parents and peers in social development: A Sullivan-Piaget perspective.* Chicago: University of Chicago Press.

Youniss, J. (1994). Rearing children for society. *New Directions for Child Development,* (Vol. 66, pp. 37–50). San Francisco: Jossey-Bass.

Youniss, J., & Smollar, J. (1985). *Adolescent relations with mothers, fathers and friends.* Chicago: University of Chicago Press.

Zambelli, G. C., & DeRosa, A. P. (1992). Bereavement support groups for school-age children: Theory, intervention, and case examples. *American Journal of Orthopsychiatry, 62,* 484–493.

Appendix
Resources for the Bereaved

Mutual Help Organizations

American Self-Help Clearing House
St. Clare's Hospital
Denville, NJ 07834-2995
Telephone: (973) 625-3037
Web site:
http://www.mentalhelp.net/selfhelp

Bereaved Families of Ontario
562 Eglinston Ave. East, Suite 401
Toronto, Ontario M4P 1P1 Canada
Telephone: (416) 440-0290
Fax: (416) 440-0304
E-mail: BFO@inforamp.net
Web site: http://www.inforamp.
net/~BFO

Candlelighters Childhood Cancer Foundation
7910 Woodmont Avenue, Suite 460
Bethesda, MD 20814-3015
Telephone: (800) 366-2223 or
(301) 657-8401
E-mail: info@candlelighters.org
Web site: http://www.
candlelighters.org

Compassionate Friends
PO Box 3696
Oak Brook, IL 60522-3696
Telephone: (630) 990-0010
Fax: (630) 990-0246
E-mail: TCF_national@prodigy.com
Web site: http://www.
compassionatefriends.org

Cystic Fibrosis Foundation
6931 Arlington Road
Bethesda, MD 20814-5200
Telephone: (800) 344-4823
E-mail: info@cff.org
Web site: http://www.cff.org

Mothers Against Drunk Driving (MADD)
511 East John Carpenter Freeway,
Suite 700
Irving, TX 75062
Telephone: (214) 744-6233
Victim hot line: (800) GET-MADD
Fax:(972) 869-2206
Web site: http://www.madd.org

Muscular Dystrophy Association
3300 East Sunrise Drive
Tucson, AZ 85718-3208
Telephone: (520) 529-2000
Fax: (520) 529-5300
E-mail: MDA@mdausa.org
Web site: http://www.mdausa.org

Parents of Murdered Children
100 East 8th Street, B-41
Cincinnati, OH 45202
Telephone: (513) 721-5683
Toll free: (888) 818-POMC
Fax: (513) 345-4489
E-mail: NatlPOMC@aol.com
Web site: http://www.pomc.com

Sudden Infant Death Syndrome (SIDS) Alliance
1314 Bedford Avenue, Suite 210
Baltimore, MD 21208

Telephone: (410) 653-8226 or
(800) 221-7437
Fax: (410) 653-8709
Web site: http://www.sidsalliance.org

Young Widows and Widowers
PO Box 4091 BV
Andover, MA 01810-0812
Telephone: (888) 999-5838
(YWW-LTD8)

Centers for Bereaved Children and Families

Dougy Center for Grieving Children
3909 S.E. 52nd Avenue
PO Box 86852
Portland, OR 97286
Telephone: (503) 775-5683
Fax: (503) 777-3097
Web site: http://www.dougy.org
E-mail: help@dougy.org

New England Center for Loss and Transition
PO Box 292
Guilford, CT 06437
Telephone: (203) 458-1734

Kids Can Cope, Too!
A Program of the American Cancer
Society
For local chapters and program
sites, call (800) ACS-2345

Hospice Programs

Children's Hospice International
Referral and Education
2202 Mount Vernon Avenue,
Suite 3C
Alexandria, VA 22301
Telephone: (800) 24Child or
(703) 684-0330
E-mail: chiorg@aol.com
Web site: http://WWW.Chionline.org

National Hospice Organization
1901 North Moore Street, Suite 901

Arlington, VA 22209
Telephone: (703) 243-5900
Fax: (703) 525-5762
Web site: http://www.nho.org
Information and Referral
Hospice Help Line: (800) 658-8898
Pediatric Professional Interest
Network (PIN) for help in
starting a program: telephone
(703) 243-5900

Violence Prevention Programs

Kids Alive and Loved (KAL)
Institute for Minority Health
Research
Rollins School of Public Health of
Emory University
1518 Clifton Road
Atlanta, GA 30322
Telephone: (404) 727-4437 or
(800) 401-7050
Fax: (404) 727-1369

Living After Murder Program (LAMP)
Roxbury Comprehensive
Community Health Center
Behavorial Health Collaborative
330 Martin Luther King Boulevard
Roxbury, MA 02119
Telephone: (617) 541-3790
Fax: (617) 541-3797
E-mail: vovu@gis.net

Louis D. Brown Peace Curriculum
5 Louis D. Brown Way
Dorchester, MA 02124-1011
Telephone: (617) 825-1917
Fax: (617) 265-2278
E-mail: peace@thecia.net
Web site: http://www2.thecia.net/users/
peace

National Organization for Victim Assistance
1757 Park Road N.W.
Washington, DC 20010
Telephone: (202) 232-6682
Fax: (202) 462-2255

E-mail: nova@digex.net
Web site: http://www.try-nova.org

Violence Prevention Program
Harvard School of Public Health
718 Huntington Avenue, 1st floor
Boston, MA 02115
Telephone: (617) 432-0814
Fax: (617) 432-0068

Suicide Prevention Programs

**American Association of
  Suicidology**
4201 Connecticut Ave, N.W.,
  Suite 408
Washington, DC 20008
Telephone: (202) 237-2280
Fax: (202) 237-2282
Web site: http://www.suicidology.org

Samaritans of Boston
500 Commonwealth Avenue
Boston, MA 02215
Telephone: (617) 536-2460
Hotline: (617) 247-0220
Samarateen Hotline: (617) 247-8050

AIDS Related Program

The Living Legacy Program II
Boston Pediatric and Family AIDS
  Project
Dimock Community Health Center
55 Dimock Street
Roxbury, MA 02119
Telephone: (617) 442-8800, ext. 1331

Curricula

**Family Program for Bereaved
  Siblings**
Manual available from:
B. Kempler or G. Koocher
Department of Psychiatry
Children's Hospital Medical Center
300 Longwood Avenue
Boston, MA 02115
Telephone: (617) 355-6000

**Growing Through Grief: a K–12
  Curriculum to Help Young
  People Through All Kinds
  of Losses**
Available through Compassion
  Books (see Mail-Order Resources)

**Hospice Expressive Arts Loss
  Support Program (HEALS)**
Training manual published by
  The Center for Creative Healing
PO Box 1576
Brattleboro, VT 05302
Telephone/Fax: (802) 257-1600

**Learning About Loss: Bringing
  Death into the Life Cycle: K–2
  Curriculum**
Available from J. Katz
Lexington Educational Foundation
1557 Massachusetts Avenue
Lexington, MA 02420

Mail-Order Resources

Compassion Books
477 Hannah Branch Road
Burnsville, NC 28714
Telephone: (704) 675-5909
Fax: (704) 675-9687
E-mail: Heal2grow@aol.com
Web site: http://www.compassion
  books.com

Centering Corporation
1531 North Saddle Creek Road
Omaha, NE 68104
Telephone: (402) 553-1200
Fax: (402) 553-0507
E-mail: j1200@aol.com

Child Welfare League of America
to order *Because You Love Them:
  A Parent's Planning Guide*:
440 First Street, NW, Suite 310
Washington, DC 20001-2085
or
CDC National AIDS Clearinghouse
  Telephone: (800) 458-523

Index

The Social Work Interview

Kadushin   to 5-5

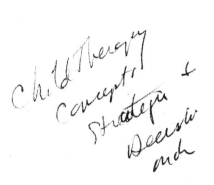
Child Therapy
Concepts &
Strategies
Decision
making